MYLES MUNROE on RELATIONSHIPS

A 365-Day Devotional

MYLES MUNROE on RELATIONSHIPS

A 365-Day Devotional

Publisher's note: All ***emphasis*** in the Scripture quotations is the author's.

MYLES MUNROE ON RELATIONSHIPS:
A 365-Day Devotional

Dr. Myles Munroe
Bahamas Faith Ministries International
P.O. Box N9583
Nassau, Bahamas
e-mail: bfmadmin@bfmmm.com
websites: www.bfmmm.com; www.bfmi.tv; www.mylesmunroe.tv

ISBN: 978-1-60374-070-8
Printed in the United States of America

Whitaker House
1030 Hunt Valley Circle
New Kensington, PA 15068
www.whitakerhouse.com

Library of Congress Cataloging-in-Publication Data

Munroe, Myles.
Myles Munroe on relationships : a 365-day devotional / Myles Munroe.
p. cm.
Summary: "A year-long daily devotional focusing on a biblical understanding of the nature and dynamics of human relationships; includes a program for reading through the Bible in a year"—Provided by publisher.
ISBN 978-1-60374-070-8 (trade hardcover : alk. paper) 1. Interpersonal relations—Religious aspects—Christianity. 2. Interpersonal relations—Biblical teaching. 3. Devotional calendars. I. Title.
BV4597.52.M86 2008
242'.2—dc22
2008029611

1 2 3 4 5 6 7 8 9 10 11 12 ꟺ 16 15 14 13 12 11 10 09 08

MYLES MUNROE ON RELATIONSHIPS: *A 365-Day Devotional* is based on Dr. Munroe's groundbreaking books *Understanding the Purpose and Power of Men*, *Understanding the Purpose and Power of Woman*, and *The Fatherhood Principle.*

Introduction

Everything in creation was created to relate to something in its environment. The Creator designed things to serve and benefit from their relationships with other components within their environments. The plant needs the sun, the fish needs the water, the bird needs the air, and the tree needs the soil.

Human being were created to be social creatures and can survive and thrive only within the context of relationships with other humans. The successful and effective development and adaptation of our kind cannot succeed without healthy and meaningful relationships.

However, the unique needs of the human species cannot be met effectively by elements in the lower strata of creation, such as animals, plants, birds, insects, and inanimate objects in nature, but can only be served by those of the same kind. It is interesting to note that the first created man, Adam, was in the company of all the species of animals, plants, birds, and sea creatures and yet the conclusion of the Mastermind behind this massive creation project was that the man was still *"alone"* (Genesis 2:18). In essence we were not created or designed to exist without an effective relationship with another of our kind. Relationship is to humanity what oxygen is to the lungs and what blood is to the entire body.

This daily devotional is, therefore, about the most important aspect of your life on earth. The principles in this book apply to your relationships with your spouse, other family members, friends, coworkers, and people you encounter in society at large. You will discover biblical truths that explain why we experience both joy and conflict as we interact with others and why many of us have difficulty establishing and maintaining good relationships.

When we think about improving our relationships, we usually start by asking questions, such as "What do I want?" "How can I get my needs met?" "Why can't I get other people to treat me with respect?" "How can I have a lasting relationship with someone who will bring me fulfillment?" and "How do I deal with people who aren't like me?" This book answers all these questions, though not from the usual approach. Instead of focusing on ourselves and how we can get what we want from other people, we will look at our relationships through the eyes of our Creator and His original purposes for men and women. As you follow this approach, you will discover it to be greatly effective and satisfying for building strong, lasting, and loving relationships with others.

For thirty years, I have studied, counseled, and guided thousands of individuals to live lives of personal fulfillment and social and spiritual well-being. The knowledge and experience I have gained has led me to the conclusion that the central principle of life is *purpose.* Exploring the implications of purpose leads us to an understanding of all realms of life, especially our relationships. It reveals God's wonderfully complementary designs for males and females as they join together in His purposes for humanity.

The quality of our relationships affects every other aspect of our lives. If we do not really understand the basis for relationships and how they are meant to work, we can never be truly fulfilled. Purpose is inherent in our desire for meaningful lives and intimacy and fellowship with others.

As you progress through this full year of devotionals, you will discover more about your reason for existence and how men and women were created to live harmonious, productive, and purposeful lives. You will understand biblical truths and principles of purpose that explain the design and relationship of males and females, and be given practical application for implementing what you have learned in your daily life.

Also featured are convenient daily Scripture readings to guide you through the Bible in one year, with one Old Testament passage and one New Testament passage for each day. Since we find our purpose only in the mind of our Maker, it is essential to read His Manual for ourselves in order to clearly see how the revelation of His purposes for humanity runs from Genesis through Revelation. We must allow God's Word to dwell richly in our hearts so that, as we meditate on it and absorb it, it truly becomes a part of our lives. Whenever we study the Word of God, we should also pray and ask God for wisdom. The Holy Spirit is our teacher, and we need to ask Him to illuminate the Word and to give us insight.

The fulfillment of God's purposes on earth requires two genders working together in cooperation. Let us discover how to live according to His plan. In this way, we can become all we were created to be as men and women made in His image. We are God's fellow workers who have been given the shared responsibility of exercising dominion over the earth through our complementary strengths and gifts, to His glory.

May God bless you in your relationship with Him and with the people He has placed in your life.

–Dr. Myles Munroe

Why Did God Create Us?

The ultimate purpose behind the creation of man—both male and female—was love. The Scripture tells us that *"God is love"* (1 John 4:8, 16). What I especially like about this statement is that God doesn't just give love, He doesn't just show love, He *is* love. He desires to share His love with us because love is His essential quality.

God has many other qualities besides love that we could list. He is righteous, holy, omnipotent, and almighty. He is all of these wonderful things and so many more. Yet God could be all of these other attributes and still exist by Himself in isolation. He doesn't need anyone else in order to be holy. He doesn't need anyone else to be righteous. He doesn't need anyone to be almighty. He can be omnipotent, omnipresent, and all the rest of His qualities by Himself. However, it is the nature of love to give of itself, and it cannot give in isolation. In order for love to be fulfilled, it has to have someone to love, and it has to give to its beloved.

"I am the Lord, and there is no other; apart from me there is no God" (Isaiah 45:5). There is no other God besides the Lord, yet He is a God of relationship, not isolation. He desires someone of His nature and likeness whom He can love. Therefore, God's primary motivation in the creation of man was love. He created men and women because He wanted to share His love with beings like Himself, beings created in His image. This truth is amazing to me!

Thought for the Day

God desires to share His love with us because love is His essential quality.

January 2

Created and Redeemed for Love

The book of Genesis tells us that God created the heavens and the earth. He created all the plants and animals. He made the sun, the stars, and the galaxies. He looked at all these remarkable things that He had created, and He said that they were good. However, He couldn't truly love these things because they were not like Him. Yes, they reflected His power, glory, and creativity; they revealed His nature and qualities, but they were not made in His essential likeness. It was mankind that God created in His image to love.

In the New Testament, Jesus both affirmed and exemplified God's love for us. He said, *"For God so loved the world that He gave His only begotten Son"* (John 3:16 NKJV). *"He gave."* He gave because He loved. You cannot love without giving. When you love, you give. It's automatic. Yet in order to give love in a way that is truly fulfilling, the receiver has to be like the giver in nature; otherwise, the love would not be complete. You cannot give in a meaningful way to something that is not like you, because it cannot receive your gift in a way that will satisfy your giving. Giving is only complete when the receiver and the giver are alike. God desired a shared and mutual love, not a one-sided love.

God looked at what He had created, and here was this man, this beautiful duplicate of Himself. Here was someone to fulfill His love. This relationship of love was the primary purpose that God created man. This is not an abstract concept. This means that the entire human race—including you and me—was created by God to be loved by Him.

Thought for the Day

It was mankind that God created in His image to love.

Reading: Genesis 1–3; Matthew 1

January 3

Created in His Image

So God created man in his own image, in the image of God he created him; male and female he created them.

—Genesis 1:27

Man was made in the image of God. When God made man, He essentially drew man out of Himself, so that the essence of man would be just like Him. Since "*God is spirit*" (John 4:24), He created man as spirit. Spirit is eternal. Man was created as an eternal being, because God is eternal. It is important to recognize that we are not yet talking about male and female. It was *mankind* that God created in His image. Man is spirit, and spirits have no gender. The Bible never talks about a male or female spirit.

What was the reason God created mankind in His image? He didn't create any of the animals or plants in His image. He didn't even make angels in His image. Man is the only being of God's creation that is like Him.

God created mankind for relationship with Himself—to be His family, His offspring, spiritual children of God. The nature of God is to love and to give. Since "*God is love*" (1 John 4:8, 16), He wanted a being who could be the object of His love and grace. He wanted man to be the recipient of all that He is and all that He has.

The fact that man was created in God's image is an awesome revelation about our relationship to Him. God desired children who would be like Himself. Yet He didn't just desire it and then walk away without doing anything about it. He conceived His desire and made it a reality.

Thought for the Day

When God made man, He essentially drew man out of Himself, so that the essence of man would be just like Him.

Reading: Genesis 4–6; Matthew 2

January 4

THE CREATION OF MAN

Then God said, "Let us make man in our image, in our likeness, and let them rule ["have dominion" NKJV] over the fish of the sea and the birds of the air, over the livestock, over all the earth, and over all the creatures that move along the ground." So God created man in his own image, in the image of God he created him; male and female he created them. God blessed them and said to them, "Be fruitful and increase in number; fill the earth and subdue it."

—Genesis 1:26–28

Men and women can know the true meaning of their existence only by understanding who they are in relation to God's creation of mankind as a whole. They need to see how they fit into God's great picture of humanity, which He designed and then constructed when the world began.

The first thing we must realize is that there is a distinction between being *man* and being *male*, and that each has unique purposes for being. What do I mean by this? The account of creation in the first two chapters of Genesis reveals the essential difference. Genesis 1 is a declaration chapter. It declares what God did in creation. Genesis 2 is an explanation chapter. It explains how God accomplished His act of creation and shows how the creation of man relates to the creation of man's two physical manifestations: male and female. These two manifestations reflect God's various purposes for man's rule or dominion on earth.

Thought for the Day

Men and women can know the true meaning of their existence only by understanding who they are in relation to God's creation of mankind as a whole.

Reading: Genesis 7–9; Matthew 3

January 5

Two Physical Houses

So God created man in his own image, in the image of God he created him; male and female he created them.

—Genesis 1:27

After God created man, He placed him in two physical "houses": male and female. This means that man the spirit exists within every male and every female. All of us—males and females alike—are man. The essence of both male and female is the resident spirit within them, called "man." Genesis 5:1–2 says, "*When God created man, he made him in the likeness of God. He created them male and female and blessed them. And when they were created, he called them* [together] *'man.'*"

Why did God take man, who is spirit, and put him in two separate physical entities rather than just one? It was because He wanted man to fulfill two distinct purposes. We'll explore the significance of this fact in more detail in coming months. For now, we need to remember that the spirit-man has no gender and that, in order to fulfill His eternal purposes, God used two physical forms to express the spiritual being made in His image.

Therefore, whether you are male or female, the person who lives inside you—the essential you—is the spirit-man. Although males and females have differences, they are of the same essence. Since human beings fellowship with God and worship Him through their spirits, this means that men and women both have direct spiritual access to God and are individually responsible to Him.

Thought for the Day

God used two physical forms to express the spiritual being made in His image.

Reading: Genesis 10–12; Matthew 4

January 6

Of the Same Substance

The Lord *God caused the man to fall into a deep sleep; and while he was sleeping, he took one of the man's ribs and closed up the place with flesh. Then the* Lord *God made a woman from the rib he had taken out of the man, and he brought her to the man.*

—Genesis 2:21–22

There was beautiful structuring in the creation of woman, as well as profound meaning. When God had finished making her, she was just like the man in substance. She was so much in likeness to him that, when God presented her to him, his first words were, "*This is now bone of my bones and flesh of my flesh; she shall be called 'woman,' for she was taken out of man*" (v. 23). And she became his wife. The man's words are both beautiful and instructive. Something that is built has the same components as the material from which it is made. Therefore, God built the female out of the part that He took from the male so that they would be made of exactly the same substance.

The word "*rib*" in Genesis 2:22 is the Hebrew word *tsela.* It does not necessarily mean a rib as we understand the word. It could mean "side" or "chamber." The Scripture is telling us that God drew the woman from a part of the man. Why? It is because the receiver has to be exactly like the giver. Just as man needed to be spirit in order to receive love from God and be in relationship with Him, the female needed to be of the same essence as the male in order to receive love from him and be in relationship with him.

Thought for the Day

Male and female are of the same substance.

Reading: Genesis 13–15; Matthew 5:1–26

God's Design for Men and Women

For we are God's workmanship, created in Christ Jesus to do good works, which God prepared in advance for us to do.
—Ephesians 2:10

Something has been happening in our society: people have been trying to change their designs. There are women who want to be like men, and there are men who want to be like women. God is saying to them, "You don't have the circuits for it." We are God's workmanship, His creation. To pursue these desires is the equivalent of short-circuiting. People are living static lives in which they don't know their purpose. They can't appreciate why people are different.

Imagine a car battery saying, "I want to be a carburetor," and trying to function as a carburetor. The car won't work. Batteries and carburetors are different because they have different functions. Although their differences make them valuable, a carburetor isn't anything without a battery. They need each other, because they are both integral parts of something larger—the car. We must understand that males and females are all part of something larger called man. Yet they are different, because they have different purposes.

God is so wonderful. He set things up so that the relationship between God and man is intended to be expressed through the relationship between male and female. The Bible refers to Jesus as the Bridegroom and the church as His bride. God is giving us an earthly and physical illustration to communicate the spiritual truth of our relationship and unity with Him. Therefore, we need to appreciate our creation as males and females, designed specifically for God's love and His purposes in this world.

Thought for the Day

We must understand that males and females are all part of something larger called man.

Reading: Genesis 16–17; Matthew 5:27–48

January 8

Principles of Creation

Today, review these principles of God's creation of man, thinking about their implications for your God-given purpose on earth:

1. Men and women can know the true meaning of their existence only by understanding who they are in relation to God's creation of mankind as a whole.
2. Mankind was created in the image of God.
3. God created man to be spirit, as He is Spirit.
4. After God created man, He placed him in two physical "houses": male and female.
5. Man—the spirit-man—resides within both male and female.
6. God made male and female because He wanted man to fulfill two distinct purposes on the physical earth.

> *You are worthy, our Lord and God, to receive glory and honor and power, for you created all things, and by your will they were created and have their being.* (Revelation 4:11)

Dear Father,
You are the Creator, the Maker of all things—including me. You have a purpose for my creation beyond anything I can easily understand. Help me to keep my eyes upon You and Your Word as You reveal my purpose on this earth. In Jesus' name, amen.

Reading: Genesis 18–19; Matthew 6:1–18

January 9

Eden Was a Delight

Now the Lord God had planted a garden in the east, in Eden; and there he put the man he had formed.

—Genesis 2:8

The male's priority in creation means that he was the first to be positioned on earth according to God's purposes. He was the first to have a relationship with God, to experience God's creation, and to receive God's instructions.

The male was placed in the environment in which he was meant to carry out his purpose. This point is crucial. God put the man in the place where he was supposed to remain in order to fulfill his reason for being. What was this environment like?

"*Eden*" comes from a Hebrew word meaning "delicate," "delight," or "pleasure." The word for "*garden*" means "an enclosure" or something "fenced in." This was more than an ordinary garden. All that was influencing heaven influenced that particular location on earth. God did not start by placing man over the entire earth or by placing him just anywhere on the earth. He placed man at the specific spot called Eden, where there was a glory connection between the seen and the unseen. There was glory flowing back and forth from this particular place on earth. The garden can be considered God's "incubator" for His new offspring. It was a controlled environment, a little spot of heaven on earth. God began the relationship by giving man the absolute best.

Thought for the Day

Eden was a little spot of heaven on earth.

Reading: Genesis 20–22; Matthew 6:19–34

January 10

A Place of God's Continual Presence

God chose a special place on the planet and put His anointing on it for the sake of man, whom He had created. First Adam, and then Eve, as well, was placed in a delightful environment—a little spot of heaven on earth.

A central reason that God placed Adam and Eve in the garden was so that they could be in His presence all the time. They could walk and talk with the Lord in the cool of the day. They could hear God's voice. This was a place where communion, fellowship, and oneness with God was always intact.

A manufacturer will always position a part in the location where it can best carry out its purpose. God, as our Maker, chose the best possible location and plan for mankind. We can conclude from what we've learned about the environment of the garden that the primary purpose of man is to be in God's presence. Man is not wired to function outside the presence of the Lord.

Here's the significance: God never intended for Adam and Eve to move from the garden. He intended for the *garden to move over the earth.* God wanted them to take the presence of the garden and spread it throughout the world. This is what He meant when He told Adam and Eve to have dominion over the earth. This is still God's purpose. As it says in Isaiah 11:9, "*The earth will be full of the knowledge of the* L*ORD*, *as the waters cover the sea.*" They could fulfill this purpose only if they were in constant communion with the God of the garden.

Thought for the Day

God didn't intend for Adam and Eve to move from the garden.
He intended for the garden to move over the earth.

Reading: Genesis 23–25; Matthew 7

The Source of Conflict

If Adam and Eve were created to be in fellowship with God and one another, what happened? Genesis 3 explains the initial source of the conflict between women and men. The devil, in the form of a serpent, tempted the first woman, Eve, to eat what God had forbidden her to eat. (See Genesis 2:16–17.) Personally, I don't think this was the first time the serpent had approached her. First, she didn't seem surprised to see him or to hear him speaking. Second, I believe they had talked earlier about God's instructions because of the way the devil phrased his crafty question: "*Did God really say, 'You must not eat from any tree in the garden'?*" (Genesis 3:1). He wanted to cast doubt on Eve's understanding of what God had said.

Eve replied, "*We may eat fruit from the trees in the garden, but God did say, 'You must not eat fruit from the tree that is in the middle of the garden, and you must not touch it, or you will die'*" (vv. 2–3). She had most of her information correct, so the devil's next ploy was to try to undermine God's integrity in her eyes. "*'You will not surely die,' the serpent said to the woman. 'For God knows that when you eat of it your eyes will be opened, and you will be like God, knowing good and evil'*" (vv. 4–5). Eve succumbed to the temptation, Adam joined her of his own free will, and they both ate of the fruit of the tree. (See verse 6.) This decision to reject God's purposes resulted in the spiritual deaths of the man and the woman. It was the beginning of the conflict between man and God and men and women that we are still dealing with today.

Thought for the Day

The devil's first tactic was to cast doubt on what God had said.

Reading: Genesis 26–27; Matthew 8:1–17

January 12

Whose Fault Was It?

And [God] *said, "Who told you that you were naked? Have you eaten from the tree that I commanded you not to eat from?"*
—Genesis 3:11

Adam and Eve went against God's commandment. It was the spirit-man—the responsible spiritual being—within both the male and female that made the fateful choice to eat the fruit in disobedience to God's command. This is why mankind's ultimate dilemma is a spiritual one.

When Adam and Eve rebelled, they immediately died a spiritual death—just as God had warned—and eventually the physical houses God had given them to live in on the earth also died. However, the spiritual death was the worse predicament of the two because it separated them from their former perfect fellowship with God. God still loved them, but they no longer had the same open channel to Him with which to receive His love. While they still retained elements of their creation in God's image, they no longer perfectly reflected the nature and character of their Creator.

The devil had presented Adam and Eve with a big lie, and they had fallen for it, to their own sorrow. However, there was an underlying reason that mankind fell. To understand it, we need to look to two foundational principles of purpose: (1) To discover the purpose of something, never ask the creation; ask the creator. (2) We find our purpose only in the mind of our Maker. Adam and Eve stopped looking to their Creator for their purpose and instead looked to themselves. In doing so, they lost their ability to fulfill their true purpose.

Thought for the Day

We find our purpose only in the mind of our Maker.

Reading: Genesis 28–29; Matthew 8:18–34

Losing the Garden

When Adam and Eve sinned, not only did they lose their perfectly balanced relationship with one another, but they also lost their harmonious relationship with the earth. Now they had to live under harsh conditions. God told Adam, "*Cursed is the ground because of you; through painful toil you will eat of it all the days of your life. It will produce thorns and thistles for you, and you will eat the plants of the field*" (Genesis 3:17–18). He was saying, "It is the earth that is really going to feel the impact of your disobedience. Because of this, you will have to struggle to survive in it."

In these consequences of sin—the broken relationship between Adam and Eve and the cursed ground—we see Satan's scheme to undermine God's purposes of dominion. Satan was afraid of the power that would be released through a man and woman united in God's purposes. Therefore, he sought to distort the relationship between males and females and limit the garden of Eden by bringing an atmosphere of thorns and thistles to the rest of the earth.

Yet, even though Adam and Eve fell, God's purpose for humanity has never changed. At the very hour of humanity's rejection of His purpose, God promised a Redeemer who would save men and woman from their fallen state and all its ramifications. (See Genesis 3:15.) The Redeemer would restore the relationship and partnership of males and females. Jesus Christ is that Redeemer and, because of Him, men and women can return to God's original design for them. We can fulfill His purposes once again. We can have true dominion over the earth—but only through Christ.

Thought for the Day

Satan is afraid of the power of a man and woman united in God's purposes.

Reading: Genesis 30–32; Matthew 9:1–17

January 14

God Is Purposeful

God is purposeful, and He always carries out His purposes. Let's read Scripture passages from Isaiah and Hebrews that illustrate a vital aspect of God's purposeful nature. *"The Lord Almighty has sworn, 'Surely, as I have planned, so it will be, and as I have purposed, so it will stand'"* (Isaiah 14:24). The first part of this verse states that God has sworn an oath. Now, when people swear an oath, they have to find something higher than themselves by which to swear. As we read in Hebrews 6:16, *"Men swear by someone greater than themselves, and the oath confirms what is said and puts an end to all argument."* We usually swear by the Bible or by some great institution. There is only one problem with God's swearing an oath: there is no one above Him. So God has to swear by Himself.

If you were called to be a witness in court, you would be asked to swear on the Bible, "I swear to tell the truth, the whole truth, and nothing but the truth, so help me, God." If you were to lie, it would be the same as desecrating the integrity of the Bible, and you would destroy your own integrity as well.

When God swears an oath regarding something, He has to fulfill what He swore to do, because He is totally faithful to Himself. God doesn't want us to have any doubt about this aspect of His nature. *"Because God wanted to make the unchanging nature of his purpose very clear to the heirs of what was promised, he confirmed it with an oath"* (Hebrews 6:17). We can be assured that God will fulfill His purposes for us as we allow Christ the Redeemer to restore us to Him and to restore the relationship and partnership of men and women.

Thought for the Day

God is purposeful and He always carries out His purposes.

Reading: Genesis 33–35; Matthew 9:18–38

January 15

Everything Is Created with a Purpose

I cry out to God Most High, to God, who fulfills his purpose for me.
—Psalm 57:2

God created everything with a purpose in mind, and He also created it with the ability to fulfill its purpose. Everything God has made is the way it is because of why it was created. The *why* dictates its makeup. The purpose of a thing determines its nature, its design, and its features.

You don't make something until you know what you want and why you want it. You'll never find a manufacturer starting a project in a plant, hoping it will turn out to be something useful. Its purpose and design are complete before production starts.

Since God created everything with a purpose, both males and females need to go to Him if they want to know their true reason for being. If they try to change His plans or fight against them, they are in essence fighting against themselves, because they're working against their own nature, their own makeup, and the way they function best based on the Creator's design. Moreover, because God is love, His plans embody what is best for us, so they would also be working against their own highest good.

God's purpose requires two genders working together in cooperation to accomplish a mutual vision. Accordingly, males and females have complementary designs that enable them to fulfill God's purpose together.

Thought for the Day

The purpose of something determines its nature, its design, and its features.

Reading: Genesis 36–38; Matthew 10:1–20

January 16

Created for Fellowship

For men and women to fulfill their purposes, they must understand their essential reasons for being. Mankind was created primarily to have fellowship with God, like a close family relationship. The only reason man can have this fellowship with God is that God made man to be spirit, just as He is Spirit. That is why the apostle John tells us that "*God is spirit, and his worshipers must worship in spirit and in truth*" (John 4:24).

Although God is the Creator, He has always emphasized that He is man's Father. It wasn't His desire to be primarily thought of by man as an awesome God or a "*consuming fire*" (Deuteronomy 4:24). Although at times it is difficult for our religious minds to grasp this concept, God wants us to approach Him as a child would a loving father. "*Let us then approach the throne of grace with confidence, so that we may receive mercy and find grace to help us in our time of need*" (Hebrews 4:16).

God created man so that He could have someone to love, someone who would walk with Him and work with Him in His purposes for the earth. That is why, no matter how many relationships you have or how many gifts you buy for others, in the end, you aren't going to be satisfied until you love God. God must have the primary place in your life. Your love was designed to be fulfilled in Him.

Thought for the Day

You aren't going to be satisfied until you love God.

Reading: Genesis 39–40; Matthew 10:21–42

Created to Reflect God's Nature

The spirit of man is the candle of the LORD.
—Proverbs 20:27 (KJV)

A second essential reason God created man is so that man could reflect His character and personality. When God created man, heaven and earth stood in awe of this amazing being who manifested the Creator's very nature and reflected His glory. As children of the Most High God, we have His nature and share His purposes. Physically, we are children of men, but spiritually, we are children of God.

Two foundational aspects of God's character are *love* and *light*, and man is meant to exhibit these qualities. However, just because man was made in God's image does not mean that man can reveal God's qualities apart from Him. Man was always meant to reveal God's nature in the context of being continually connected to Him in fellowship.

Jesus spoke of that connection when He referred to Himself as the Vine and we as the branches: "*I am the vine; you are the branches. If a man remains in me and I in him, he will bear much fruit; apart from me you can do nothing*" (John 15:5). First John 4:16 says, "*Whoever lives in love lives in God, and God in him,*" and Proverbs 20:27 says, "*The spirit of man is the candle of the* LORD" (KJV). This means that when you have fellowship with God, you reflect His light. You show the nature of God, for "*God is light; in him there is no darkness at all*" (1 John 1:5).

Thought for the Day

Physically, we are children of men, but spiritually, we are children of God.

Reading: Genesis 41–42; Matthew 11

January 18

Created to Rule

Let us make man in our image,...and let them rule [*"have dominion"* NKJV].
—Genesis 1:26

A third reason for the creation of humanity was so that men and women could share God's authority. God never wanted to rule by Himself. Love doesn't think in those terms. You can always tell a person who is full of love. He doesn't want to do anything for his purposes alone. A selfish person wants all the glory, all the credit, all the recognition, all the attention, all the power, all the authority, all the rights, and all the privileges. But a person of love wants others to share in what he has.

The word *"man"* in Genesis 1:26 refers to the spirit-being created in God's image. The purpose of dominion was given to man *the spirit*. This was before the creation of male and female. Therefore, spiritually, both male and female have the same responsibility toward the earth because rule was given to the spirit-man, which resides in both of them.

Man has been given the freedom to exhibit creativity while governing the physical earth and all the other living things that dwell in it. The earth is to be ruled over, taken care of, fashioned, and molded by beings made in the image of their Creator. In this way, man is meant to reflect the loving and creative Spirit of God.

God also created man to demonstrate His wisdom and the goodness of His precepts. This purpose is part of God's eternal plans: *"His intent was that now, through the church, the manifold wisdom of God should be made known to the rulers and authorities in the heavenly realms, according to his eternal purpose which he accomplished in Christ Jesus our Lord"* (Ephesians 3:10–11).

Thought for the Day

Spiritually, both male and female have the same responsibility toward the earth.

Reading: Genesis 43–45; Matthew 12:1–23

January 19

CREATED TO BE GOD'S CHILDREN

When God created men and women to share His authority, it was in the context of their relationship to Him as His offspring. God didn't create us to be servants but to be children who are involved in running the family business. This was His plan for mankind from the beginning. He has always wanted His children to help Him fulfill His purposes.

This means that God doesn't want us to work *for* Him; He wants us to work *with* Him. The Bible says that we are "*God's fellow workers*" (2 Corinthians 6:1) or "*workers together with him*" (KJV). In the original Greek, "*fellow workers*" means those who "cooperate," who "help with," who "work together."

It's common to hear people say, "I'm working for Jesus." If you are working *for* Jesus, you are still a hired hand. When you understand the family business, then you become a worker alongside Christ.

What are some of the implications of our being God's children, working in His business? First, we don't have to worry about our day-to-day living expenses. If your father and mother owned a prosperous business, and they put you in charge of it, should you wonder where you will get food to eat? Should you wonder where you will get water to drink? Should you wonder where you're going to get clothes to wear? No, you are family, and you are going to be provided for.

In God's company, there's always plenty of provision to go around, and you can rely on that with confidence.

Thought for the Day

God didn't create us to be servants but to be children who are involved in running the family business.

Reading: Genesis 46–48; Matthew 12:24–50

January 20

Consequences of Lost Purpose

Although they claimed to be wise, they became fools.
—Romans 1:22

Despite all of God's good purposes for humanity, man and woman thought *they* knew what was best for them. Therefore, they rejected their true reason for being and suffered the loss of many of the blessings God had given them. They also began to abuse each other's purposes. Men and women cannot function in true harmony and effectiveness outside God's plan. Adam and Eve's tragic choice led to the fulfillment of this principle of purpose: Where purpose is not known, abuse is inevitable.

Adam and Eve lost their perfectly balanced relationship. Immediately following their rejection of God's purposes, we see conflict between them. When God asked Adam, "*Have you eaten from the tree that I commanded you not to eat from?*" Adam accused Eve, saying, "*The woman you put here with me—she gave me some fruit from the tree, and I ate it*" (Genesis 3:11–12). Feeling trapped, Eve tried to put the blame on the devil. (See verse 13.) Yet God held each of them accountable because they were spiritual beings responsible to Him.

We see how Adam and Eve's decision to disobey God altered their relationship. One of the consequences of their sin was that they would strive with one another. "*Your desire will be for your husband, and he will rule over you*" (Genesis 3:16). The male and female were originally created to rule together. They were designed to function together equally. God had said to them, "*Fill the earth and subdue it*" (Genesis 1:28). Both of them were supposed to be rulers—and that is still His plan.

Thought for the Day

Men and women cannot function in true harmony and effectiveness outside God's plan.

Reading: Genesis 49–50; Matthew 13:1–30

January 21

Restoring Right Relationships

Can a mortal be more righteous than God? Can a man be more pure than his Maker?
—Job 4:17

Nobody knows how something is supposed to function better than its maker. I suggest to you that the best way for us to make progress in the relationship between men and women is to go back to the beginning and see what was in the mind and heart of the Creator when He made humanity. Knowing our original design and inherent makeup is the only way to bring about lasting, positive change in the way men and women interact with one another in all the realms of life.

Proverbs 19:21 summarizes this idea well: "*Many are the plans in a man's heart, but it is the Lord's purpose that prevails.*" God is a God of purpose, and everything that He made in this life, including men and women, has a purpose. We can fight against His purpose, but if we do, we will be unfulfilled and frustrated. He made us the way we are for His purposes and for our benefit.

Throughout the months of this devotional, we will continually come back to these two essential principles:

1. The purpose of something determines its nature or design.
2. The nature or design of something determines its needs.

Our Creator purposed and designed male and female, and He has provided a way to restore us to His original purposes for both.

Thought for the Day

Understanding and living in God's original purpose is crucial to restoring right relationships between men and women.

Reading: Exodus 1–3; Matthew 14:1–21

January 22

God's Original Intent

Purpose is defined as the "original intent and reason" for the creation of a thing. Here are seven principles of purpose to keep in mind as you understand and return to God's original design for men and women:

1. God is a God of purpose.
2. God created everything with a purpose.
3. Not every purpose is known to us because we have lost our understanding of God's original intent for us.
4. Where purpose is not known, abuse is inevitable.
5. To discover the purpose of something, never ask the creation; ask the creator.
6. We find our purpose only in the mind of our Maker.
7. God's purpose is the key to our fulfillment.

Many of the problems males and females face today come from a lack of understanding of their own purpose in life. Principles one and two assure you that you do have a purpose on this earth. Without an understanding of God's purpose for you, however, you will abuse your life and, most likely, the lives of those around you. The solution is not to try to conjure up a purpose for yourself but to discover your Maker's original intent for you, because your purpose is found in the mind of your Maker.

The great news is that discovering and living out that purpose is the key to your fulfillment as a male or female, a son or daughter, a sibling, a spouse, a parent, a member of your church, a citizen in your community and nation, and a human being in the world. *"For in him we live and move and have our being"* (Acts 17:28).

Thought for the Day

You have a God-given purpose on this earth.

Reading: Exodus 4–6; Matthew 14:22–36

A Crisis of Roles

People used to acquire their ideas of manhood and womanhood from observing their fathers and mothers or from longstanding cultural traditions. Yet hundreds, even thousands, of years of tradition have been set aside in just one or two generations. My life is completely different from my father's life. I can't use the way my father did things as a model for myself, and my sisters can't use the environment in which my mother functioned as an example for themselves. Our parents lived not only in a different generation, but also with different concepts of maleness and femaleness. Historically speaking, until recently, the man had certain accepted roles and the woman had certain accepted roles, and they didn't usually overlap.

What makes our current cultural situation unsettling for men, in particular, is that males have traditionally defined their manhood by their roles: the functions they perform for their families and in society. However, there's been a major shift in the roles of both males and females. The rules of society are changing. This has happened just in the last forty years or so. We're in the middle of a cultural transition, and competing ideas of masculinity are causing perplexing problems for men. They are being pulled in several directions at once while they try to figure out what it means to be a real man in today's world.

Men's basic conceptions of manhood are therefore being disrupted. They feel displaced. They are either frustrated or struggling to adapt to a new but vague concept of who they are, or they're angry and trying to reverse the flow of change.

Are cultural roles to be totally abandoned? If so, what will replace them? *"The plans of the LORD stand firm forever, the purposes of his heart through all generations"* (Psalm 33:11).

Thought for the Day

There's been a major shift in the roles of males and females.

Reading: Exodus 7–8; Matthew 15:1–20

January 24

WHAT IS A REAL MAN?

Imagine that you are watching a television show similar to *To Tell the Truth.* Several contestants try to convince you that they are the Real Man. Which one is authentic and which ones are the imposters?

Contestant #1 tells you he is the Real Man because he fills the traditional male role: he supports his family financially while his wife cares for the children and the home. As long as he provides a roof over their heads and food for them to eat, he's fulfilling his duty as a husband and father. This man doesn't consider his wife to be his true equal.

Contestant #2 says he is the Real Man because he has a culturally progressive role: he shares household and child-rearing responsibilities with his wife while they both pursue careers. He thinks of his wife as his equal.

Contestant #3 explains that he is the Real Man because he has been freed from male stereotypes and has decided to take on the nurturer role of caring for the children and home while his wife goes to work. He considers his wife equal to himself—or maybe even better, since she has a more compassionate, sensitive nature than he does.

These are some of the images of manhood that are competing for men's acceptance today. There seems to be no clear-cut winner. In addition, society keeps mixing and matching these images until men don't know what's expected of them anymore. Confusion over purpose undermines people's lives. Do you know yours?

Thought for the Day

To what extent does your image of a "real man" correspond with what the Bible teaches about men of God?

Reading: Exodus 9–11; Matthew 15:21–39

January 25

THE NUMBER ONE CHALLENGE

We have lost our understanding of God's intent for human beings. This is why the number one challenge to the male in today's society is an identity crisis. The average man is confused about his manhood, his masculinity, and his sexuality. He doesn't have a clear definition of what a man is supposed to be. Some men have confused their cultural, social, and traditional roles with the definition of manhood. However, this has proven to be one of the major causes of the problem because, as the roles change, so does a man's image of himself. Males are at a crucial crossroads, and where they go from here will have a serious effect on the course of society.

How do we measure a man? What is true manhood? How do you define masculinity? What is true male sexuality? What is the true purpose of the male in relation to the female? Is there a universal definition of manhood? Can it be attained? Where do we go to get this definition? These are difficult questions, but we can discover the answers to them.

The male is the key to building strong, enduring social infrastructures, stable families, sane societies, and secure nations. It is critical that the subject of the male's crisis be a priority for men, women, and national governments, so that we can secure positive social developments within the countries of the world. As we progress through this year, we will take a journey through the land of cultural confusion and beyond to rediscover the purpose and power of the true male and female as God, our Creator, intended them to be. *"He who gets wisdom loves his own soul; he who cherishes understanding prospers"* (Proverbs 19:8).

Thought for the Day

The male is the key to building stable families, sane societies, and secure nations.

Reading: Exodus 12–13; Matthew 16

January 26

Roles versus Purpose

For the Lord *Almighty has purposed, and who can thwart him?*
—Isaiah 14:27

Today, what do males use as a basis for their self-worth and identity? Men have linked their identity to their roles, and now that the roles have changed, they have left themselves no basis for manhood. Whatever they replace their old idea of masculinity with may or may not be a true or fulfilling role for them. What is more troubling, when men don't understand their place in the world, they will often either withdraw from it or use their influence in harmful ways, such as committing crimes.

What can men do to regain their footing and identity? First, they must adopt an entirely new way of thinking. They need to think in terms of *purpose* rather than *roles*. As we have discovered, the reason they are having problems today is that they have been basing their worth on the wrong thing all along. Roles have never been the true basis of a male's identity and purpose. Roles can be helpful or harmful, but ultimately they merely reflect culture and tradition.

What men really need to discover is their underlying purpose, which transcends culture and tradition. The Lord Almighty has a purpose in everything. A man's position and actions must flow out of his purpose, not the other way around. That is why the answer to the male's dilemma is not just to adjust to changing times—although some of this will be needed—but to discover the inherent purpose of the male. Men therefore need a God-given identity if they are to fulfill their true purpose. Tomorrow we will begin to look in detail at the Creator's original plan for both men and women and its implications for their relationships.

Thought for the Day

Men must think in terms of purpose rather than roles.

Reading: Exodus 14–15; Matthew 17

January 27

The Purpose of the Male

Many are the plans in a man's heart, but it is the Lord's purpose that prevails.
—Proverbs 19:21

Not only do we have many plans in our hearts, but we also have many opinions about what a man should be! Yet the Lord's purpose is the only one that counts—and this purpose is the key to our fulfillment. What we want to consider today is the male's *ideal* purpose. This is not where we are right now. Yet God's ideal is what we should be moving toward; and by His grace, we will.

We should always remember that God creates according to the requirements of His purposes. God desires to dominate and influence the earth through mankind. Remember that the purpose of something determines its nature, its design, and its features. This means that the nature, design, and qualities of males were decided upon by God according to what He determined was best for the sake of His purposes.

I believe that the purpose of the male may be summed up as *his priority, his position,* and *his assignment.*

Priority refers to the man's order in creation and what this means in regard to his reason for being.

Position refers to the environment and place in which the man is to carry out his purpose.

Assignment means the functions or tasks that the man has been given by God.

Thought for the Day

God creates according to the requirements of His purposes.

Reading: Exodus 16–18; Matthew 18:1–20

January 28

The Male's Priority

The Lord *God formed the man from the dust of the ground and breathed into his nostrils the breath of life, and the man became a living being.*
—Genesis 2:7

Why did God make the male first? It was not because the male was better, but because of his purpose. The order in which the male was created gives us the first indication of his reason for being.

When you think about it, God really made only one human being. When He created the female, He didn't go back to the soil, but He fashioned her from the side of the man. (See Genesis 2:21–23.) Only the male came directly from the earth. This was because the male was designed by God to be the foundation of the human family. The woman came out of the man rather than the earth because she was designed to rest on the man—to have the male as her support.

God planned everything before He created it, and He started with the foundation. Have you ever seen a contractor build a house starting with the roof? No. Likewise, you don't start with the windows. You don't start with the gutters or the rafters. God starts like any other builder. The priority in building is always what you need to do first. You start with the foundation.

I believe that the foundation of society, the infrastructure God intended for this world, has been misunderstood. We often say that the family is the foundation of society. It is very true that the family is the adhesive that holds it together. Yet God did not start to build earthly society with a family. He began it with one person. He began it with the male.

Thought for the Day

The male is the foundation of the human family.

Reading: Exodus 19–20; Matthew 18:21–35

January 29

Jesus Christ, the Ultimate Foundation

God's communications to man in the Bible indicate the importance He places on building from the foundation up. What did Jesus describe as our foremost priority? What we're building on—our foundation. (See Matthew 7:24–27.) The apostle Paul wrote, "*No one can lay any* [spiritual] *foundation other than the one already laid*" (1 Corinthians 3:11). What—or rather, *who*—is that foundation? "*Jesus Christ*" (v. 11).

God does not think of foundations in terms of only concrete and water, but also in terms of people. That is why, when God began to build the human race, He began by laying the foundation of the male. He placed males at the bottom of the entire building of humanity. This means that society is only as strong as its males. And for the males to be truly strong, they must build their own foundation on Jesus Christ.

If the males don't learn what it means to be a strong foundation in God, then society is sunk. That goes for America, Canada, Russia, China—all the nations of the world. If the male leaves the home, or if he neglects his responsibility, you have a house built on sand. The rafters rock when the pressures come because the man isn't there.

When the male has cracks and faults in the substructure of his life, then the whole building is on shaky ground. Men, let's talk. This is the year you must decide to get on solid ground, for as the man goes, so goes the family, society, and the world. Take a look at the condition of our societies and nations. How do you think the men are doing?

Thought for the Day

Society is only as strong as its males.

Reading: Exodus 21–22; Matthew 19

January 30

The Foundation's Responsibility

Everyone who hears these words of mine and puts them into practice is like a wise man who built his house on the rock.

—Matthew 7:24

How can you build a human race on a foundation that is made up of sand mixed with straw? A foundation is always measured by how much weight can be placed on it. Our societies are in a mess because, as the foundation, men have become "sandy"—uncertain and unstable.

When God made the male first, He wasn't saying that the male is more important than the female. He was saying that the male has a *specific responsibility*. He has a purpose to fulfill that is just like the foundation. Even though the foundation is important, it's not more important than the other parts of the building. The foundation can't perform all the functions itself. It cannot protect the occupants from the weather. When the rain comes, the foundation can't keep you dry; only the roof can. It's the same way with the human family. The foundation is crucial, but the rest of the family is essential as well.

Remember that the foundation is often hidden. I don't see the foundation of my house anymore, even though I was involved in discussions about it and watched it being dug and poured. Today, I walk on the foundation all the time, but I never see it. The foundation is meant to be solid and dependable, but not necessarily seen.

Thought for the Day

A foundation is measured by how much weight can be placed on it.

Reading: Exodus 23–24; Matthew 20:1–16

January 31

Becoming a Strong Foundation

The rain came down, the streams rose, and the winds blew and beat against that house; yet it did not fall, because it had its foundation on the rock.
—Matthew 7:25

Many of you men need to live like the foundation you were created to be. Just be there and keep the home steady so that your wife and children can always lean on you and know that you aren't going to crack. Many young boys with absentee fathers—men who are missing either physically or emotionally—are walking in mud instead of on concrete. These young boys are trying to find a foundation for their lives, but there's mud all over them, because there's just no place where they can stand on solid ground. Their foundations are missing. When they grow up, they will go out and try to become foundations themselves, yet they never will have been shown what a true foundation is.

I once heard the statement, "A young boy becomes a man when his father tells him he's a man." Many young boys have never had a father to tell them who they are. The purpose of the male is to give foundation to the structure of life.

I'm praying that God will raise up some strong foundational men—men who will stand by their wives and stand with their children; men who will be stabilizers so that their families will feel secure in their strength. It doesn't matter what your father was—you can be a strong foundation by becoming the man God created you to be.

Thought for the Day

The purpose of the male is to give foundation to the structure of life.

Reading: Exodus 25–26; Matthew 20:17–34

Is It Only a Man's World?

In the mid-1960s, renowned musical artist James Brown came out with a song that exposed the spirit of the age, entitled "It's a Man's World." The song sold a million copies. (I wonder who bought it?) James Brown was singing about an attitude that pervades the nations and cultures of the world. That attitude is, in effect, "Even though women are here, this world was made for men. It's designed for males. Women are just filling in where needed. You women stay in your place; this is a man's world."

Does the world belong to men? What place do women hold in it?

One of the most controversial issues of our modern times—a topic that has been debated with much discussion and dissension—is the role, position, and rights of women. Historically, in nearly every nation and culture, women have been regarded as holding a secondary place in the world. The following are traditional perceptions of women that still persist today: Women are considered inferior to men, second-class citizens, objects for sensual gratification alone, incapable of real strength, lacking in intelligence and therefore having nothing to contribute to society, the personal property of men, personal servants whose only purpose is to meet the needs of their masters, and deserving of abuse. Women are misunderstood and degraded around the world, and it is causing them emotional, physical, and spiritual distress.

These attitudes differ strikingly from the way God sees the woman's place in His creation. It is all about His plan! "*God created man in his own image, in the image of God he created him; male and female he created them*" (Genesis 1:27).

Thought for the Day

What place do women hold in the world?

Reading: Exodus 27–28; Matthew 21:1–22

February 2

Woman's True Nature

What is the woman's true nature and purpose? Do we really know? If we don't know, how can we address the abuse woman have experienced for centuries?

Women and men alike must come to know the woman's true nature and purpose if we are to address the plight that has affected women throughout history and still affects them in the twenty-first century. Women, as well as men, must gain new perspectives of themselves, since women have largely developed their self-concepts from cultural traditions shaped by men who did not understand females.

The basic problem can be summarized in this way: There are fundamental truths about the inherent makeup of women and men that have been lost to the cultures of the world as well as to the hearts and minds of individual men and women. They have been replaced with distorted views of women and of male-female relationships, and these distortions have been promoted through culture and tradition. Because of these lost truths, women and men alike do not understand a woman's nature, potential, role, and unique contribution to the world. The result is that women are misunderstood, held back from fulfilling their potential, and abused. The hurt, loss, trauma, and physical peril this has placed on women are tragic. There has been a terrible waste of life and potential over hundreds and thousands of years; this waste has been catastrophic not only for women, but also for men and human society as a whole.

We must look beyond the cultures of the world and rediscover intrinsic truths about the nature of women and men. We must transcend tradition and recapture biblical principles that can free women to be fulfilled and valued, regardless of their nationality or geographic location.

Thought for the Day

We must transcend tradition and recapture biblical principles that can free women to be fulfilled and valued.

Reading: Exodus 29–30; Matthew 21:23–46

What Is a Woman's Place?

"A woman's place is in the home."
"A woman's place is in the world—in business, education, and government."

Over the years, the controversy over the role, position, and rights of the woman has often centered on these apparently competing views of what a woman's place is. Both of these views fail to capture the essence of a woman's purpose and design.

Where, ultimately, is a woman's place? *A woman's place, before anything else, is in God.* (The same is true for a man.) It is in the way He created her, in the tremendous value He gives her, and in the purposes He has for her. Only when we grasp the implications of this truth will we resolve the controversy and conflict surrounding the role of the woman in the world.

The nature of the woman must be understood in light of her purpose, and her needs must be understood in light of her nature. Otherwise, she will be unable to fulfill the purpose for which she was created. A woman's position and rights are God-given and inherent.

The most important thing we can find out about ourselves and others is the purpose of our existence. In coming days, we will learn the female's design and needs, while also making reference to how her makeup complements the makeup of the male.

Lord, you have been our dwelling place throughout all generations.
(Psalm 90:1)

Thought for the Day

Before anything else, a woman's place is in God.

Reading: Exodus 31–33; Matthew 22:1–22

February 4

One in Christ

You are all sons of God through faith in Christ Jesus....There is neither Jew nor Greek, slave nor free, male nor female, for you are all one in Christ Jesus.

—Galatians 3:26, 28

What is the ultimate cause of the universal devaluing of women in societies around the globe? Culture cannot take the full blame, because the problem spans ages and cultures and seems to point to a deep-seated discord or adversarial relationship between men and women. Women as well as men need to understand the *inherent* nature of the woman, because most women have developed their identity from men, and they do not see themselves as God does. Women have essentially become the products of the societies in which they were born and raised.

Men and women were created equal. Men and women are equal. That's not for a senate or a congress or a cabinet or a parliament of any nation to decide. God already made this decision in creation! Then He reaffirmed it with the redemption of mankind in Jesus Christ. Male and female are one in Christ. Don't ever give anybody the right to say what kind of human value you have. Don't let anybody else tell you how much of a person you are. When you understand that equality is inherent in creation and discover how it is to be manifested in your life, then you can begin to live in the full realm of that equality, regardless of what others tell you about yourself.

Thought for the Day

Male and female are one in Christ.

Reading: Exodus 34–35; Matthew 22:23–46

February 5

Different, Not Superior or Inferior

Today those who advocate equal rights say that there is no difference at all between women and men. Yet while women and men were created equal, they were also created different. This is part of their unique design. This statement may confuse some and anger others, because somehow we have come to believe that *different* means *inferior* or *superior*. Don't confuse being different with being either lesser or greater. Different does not imply superiority or inferiority; different simply means different. This is especially true in regard to men and women; their differences are necessary because of their purposes.

In many spheres of life, we don't consider differences to be weaknesses but rather mutual strengths. In music, who is more important to a full symphony orchestra, a violin player or an oboe player? Both work together in harmony. In sports, who is more important to a medley relay, the swimmer who swims the breaststroke or the swimmer who swims the backstroke? Both have to be strong swimmers in their particular specialties, for a medley race cannot be swum with only one type of swimmer. When they win, they share the honor together.

The answer to the historical devaluing of women does not lie in declaring that there are no differences between females and males, but in recognizing and affirming their complementary differences. We must understand and accept these differences so they can be used in harmony like a finely tuned orchestra.

Thought for the Day

Different does not imply superiority or inferiority;
different simply means different.

Reading: Exodus 36–38; Matthew 23:1–22

February 6

Competition or Cooperation?

Two are better than one, because they have a good return for their work: if one falls down, his friend can help him up. But pity the man who falls and has no one to help him up!
—Ecclesiastes 4:9–10

If males and females were created with perfectly complementary designs, why do men and women experience conflict and competition rather than cooperation? Why does the purpose of dominion over the earth seem more like a quest for domination of one sex over the other? God created men and women to dominate the earth, not one another!

Males and females were created in God's image. The basis of their equality before God is that man, the spirit, resides within both of them. As physical beings they were created of the same essence, but differently—because each has been designed with specific purposes to fulfill. The different ways in which their dominion assignment is carried out does not affect their equality; it only reflects their distinct purposes, designs, and needs.

The male was created to exercise dominion over the earth through his priority, position, and assignment. The female was created to help the male fulfill God's dominion purposes for mankind in both the earthly and spiritual realms. It is God's intention that, together, their individual strengths would combine to produce exponential results (as the Scripture says in Ecclesiastes, "*They have a good return for their work*")—outcomes much greater than either could accomplish alone. The woman adds to the man's power in living and working, so that the sum is far greater than its parts.

Thought for the Day

God created men and women to dominate the earth, not one another!

Reading: Exodus 39–40; Matthew 23:23–29

February 7

Do Men Honor Women?

Treat [wives] *with respect as the weaker partner and as heirs with you of the gracious gift of life.*
—1 Peter 3:7

One of the reasons the plight of women has been such a difficult issue to remedy is that it is not easy to change a man's mind about a woman's place in the world. The idea that this is a man's world is very deeply entrenched. Even though legislation might be passed or public policy might change, you can't easily change a man's mind-set.

God's intent that women be equal heirs with men in creation and redemption remains largely an ignored truth. Men's internal devaluing of women is the reason they generally continue to be discounted and exploited in almost every society in the world, regardless of recent social and political advances. In industrial nations as well as developing nations, the plight of the female is still very real. It is tragic to have to admit this is true in our modern society.

Many women are involved in opportunities and activities that were formerly reserved for males, such as leadership, management, and sports. However, although we can say that there has been some improvement, in most societies, women are still suffering the prejudice of the male against the female. Men's hearts cannot be changed by legislation. Even though the law now says, "Women are equal to men," this doesn't mean that men think so. The persistent devaluing of women continues to hold back progress, and women are being treated in every way *except* in the way God originally intended: *"Heirs with you of the gracious gift of life."*

Thought for the Day

God's intent that women be equal heirs with men in creation and redemption remains largely an ignored truth.

Reading: Leviticus 1–3; Matthew 24:1–28

A Change of Perspective

John 4 tells us about Jesus' encounter with the Samaritan woman at the well. When Jesus first began to speak with her, she was wary of Him. It was unheard of for a Jewish man to speak to a Samaritan, especially a woman. She spoke to Him only in the context of the prejudices between the Samaritans and the Jews that prevailed at that time. "*You are a Jew and I am a Samaritan woman. How can you ask me for a drink?*" (John 4:9). Jesus answered her, "*If you knew the gift of God and who it is that asks you for a drink, you would have asked him and he would have given you living water*" (v. 10).

The woman had a problem, and it was not that she was being rude. She thought that since Jesus was a Jew and she was a Samaritan woman, He wouldn't speak with her. She didn't know who He really was. He was saying, in effect, "If you only knew who was talking to you, everything would be all right. However, I know you don't know, so go ahead and talk foolishly for a few minutes." He allowed her to be foolish. Then He said, "Let Me tell you who I am," and He began to reveal to her the deep secrets of her heart. After that, she changed the way she thought about Him. She said, "*You are a prophet*" (v. 19).

Next, she went into the town and said, "*Come, see a man who told me everything I ever did*" (v. 29). She didn't say, "Come, see a Jew" but "*Come, see a man.*" People will change their perspective toward you when they know why you're here, when they begin to understand your purpose.

Thought for the Day

The Samaritan woman didn't know who Jesus really was.

Reading: Leviticus 4–5; Matthew 24:29–51

February 9

God Transforms Us

Therefore, I urge you, brothers, in view of God's mercy, to offer your bodies as living sacrifices, holy and pleasing to God–this is your spiritual act of worship. Do not conform any longer to the pattern of this world, but be transformed by the renewing of your mind. Then you will be able to test and approve what God's will is–his good, pleasing and perfect will.

–Romans 12:1–2

God's ways will transform your spirit, your mind, and your outlook. When you present yourself to God and learn from Him, you will begin to understand His purpose. "*The law of the LORD is perfect, reviving the soul. The statutes of the LORD are trustworthy, making wise the simple*" (Psalm 19:7).

The greatest way for you to find purpose is to yield your life to the Manufacturer. You shouldn't come to God because it's the religious thing to do. You shouldn't come to God because "everybody" is doing it. You shouldn't come to God because it's good to be a part of the church. You should come to God because you want to find out how not to waste your life. No one knows you like the One who made you. That's the bottom line.

We are so special to God that He sent His only Son to die for us. There must be something unique about each one of us for God to want us to receive salvation so that we can fulfill the purpose for which He gave us life. We need to seek Him earnestly in order to discover that purpose. "*You will seek me and find me when you seek me with all your heart*" (Jeremiah 29:13).

Thought for the Day

The greatest way for you to find purpose is to yield your life to the Manufacturer.

Reading: Leviticus 6–7; Matthew 25:1–30

February 10

Woman as Enhancer

Males were not meant to live in isolation or fulfill their calling on their own. Although the male was created first and was given the role of foundation and responsible spiritual leader, the female is an enhancer, a coleader. She shares his vision and works with him to accomplish what they were both created to do. The woman takes who the man is and what the man has and enlarges and extends it. In this way, his leadership is effective and their shared vision becomes reality.

God always tells you why He makes something before He makes it. *"The Lord God said, 'It is not good for the man to be alone. I will make a helper suitable for him'"* (Genesis 2:18). Therefore, the first purpose of the female as enhancer is to be a companion for the male, so that he won't be alone. The word *alone* is made up of two words, "all" and "one." When you put these words together, you see that *alone* basically means "all in one."

God said, "It is not good for this male to be all in one, having everything in himself." God made the female so that the male would have someone to give to, someone to share his vision with, someone to be a part of his life. Isn't it sad that many men don't see women in this way? The female was created so that the male would not have to be alone. She is his life companion. "To companion" means to accompany, to attend, and even to guide someone. It is in this sense that a woman is a man's companion.

Thought for the Day

The woman shares the man's vision and works with him to accomplish what they were both created to do.

Reading: Leviticus 8–10; Matthew 25:31–46

February 11

For Man's Good

God saw all that he had made, and it was very good.
—Genesis 1:31

Before the creation of Eve, God said, "It is not good for this male to be alone." It is clear that, when God made this statement, He meant that what He was about to create for Adam would be good for him. Therefore, God's Word affirms, "Women are good. Females are good." The woman was created for the man's good.

I want to say to my female readers that God knew what men needed, and it was *you*! When something is made for something else, it has within it that which the other thing needs. When something is made to be good for something else, it has that which is good for the other thing. Therefore, everything God created the female to be is good for the male.

A female is very good for a male, but where purpose is not known, abuse is inevitable. A woman can abuse her nature and purpose if she doesn't understand why she is the way she is. In addition, a woman who does not understand her purpose can be a detriment to a man, and a man who doesn't understand the woman's purpose can be a detriment to a woman.

Yet God said that the highest good for a man, besides Himself, is a woman. So, in some mysterious way, in spite of what your past experiences in relationships might have been, a woman is, by her very nature, good for a man.

Thought for the Day

Women, God knew what men needed, and it was *you*!

Reading: Leviticus 11–12; Matthew 26:1–25

Created to Be a Helpmate

I will make a helper suitable for him.
—Genesis 2:18

A woman is a helpful agent for a man. In God's wisdom, if a woman is *meant* to be a helper, she has been designed with many qualities and abilities that *equip her to help*. Remember that the Creator always has a plan for His creations.

The woman's purpose is to assist the man in fulfilling God's plan for his life. The implications of this are profound. First, it means the male has to have a plan; otherwise, the female is in trouble. Second, it means that the female must understand that her fulfillment is related to the male's vision. In other words, she can never really be complete if she does not help him fulfill his vision.

When a wife decides she wants a completely different vision for her life than her husband's vision, they will experience a division. *Di* means two or double. The word *division* could be thought of as "double vision." Whenever you have a couple who has double vision, they are in danger of divorce, because *"a house divided against itself will fall"* (Luke 11:17). You can't have two visions in the same household, or the man and the woman will be going in different directions. That is why God created the woman to be in a helping position. Helpers don't take over; rather, they assist. This certainly does not mean that a woman should not have her own interests and develop her own abilities. It means that, as a couple, they need to share the same vision for their lives.

Thought for the Day

You can't have two visions in the same household, or the man and the woman will be going in different directions.

Reading: Leviticus 13; Matthew 26:26–50

Woman as Reflector

Several times in Ephesians 5, Paul exhorted men to love their wives: *"Husbands, love your wives, just as Christ loved the church and gave himself up for her....Husbands ought to love their wives as their own bodies. He who loves his wife loves himself....Each one of you also must love his wife as he loves himself"* (Ephesians 5:25, 28, 33).

The single most important reason that the female was created was so that she could receive love. Therefore, the first purpose of the female as reflector is that she was made to be the receiver of the male's love and to reflect the love that he gives her.

When God made woman, He drew her out of man so that the man would have someone to love who was of his own nature. In this way, the man was created to be a giver of love and the woman to be a receiver of love. Remember that man, the spirit, was created out of the essence of God and in the image of God in order to receive God's love. The female was created in the same pattern. She was made out of the essence of the male and in the physical image of the male in order to receive the male's love.

What this means is that God has designed the woman to function on love. Love is the fuel of a female. When you don't give a car fuel, it can't run. The same thing happens for humans. In the woman's case, if you don't give her the love God meant for her to receive, she can't fully function in the way God created her to function. In order to be fulfilled, the woman needs love.

Thought for the Day

The primary purpose of the female's receiving nature is to receive love.

Reading: Leviticus 14; Matthew 26:51–75

February 14

The Attributes of Love

Why are men to love women? The man should love the woman because she was drawn from him and is a part of him. If he doesn't love her, it is the equivalent of the man hating himself. (See Ephesians 5:29.) A husband treats himself well when he treats his wife well. The man's role, then, is to love his wife as himself, with all the attributes of love that are found in the Love Chapter:

> *Love is patient, love is kind. It does not envy, it does not boast, it is not proud. It is not rude, it is not self-seeking, it is not easily angered, it keeps no record of wrongs. Love does not delight in evil but rejoices with the truth. It always protects, always trusts, always hopes, always perseveres. Love never fails.* (1 Corinthians 13:4–8)

When you give a woman love, she comes alive. Yet when she receives anything less than genuine love, it is as if she short-circuits. When you don't love a woman, you are abusing her very nature. A woman will reflect the love or lack of love that she receives.

It is interesting to note that nowhere in the Bible does God tell the woman to love the man. A wife is instructed to respect her husband, to honor him, and to submit to him. Yet God commands the husband over and over again to love his wife. You would be wise, men, to obey the Lord's counsel; it is meant for your best!

Thought for the Day

The man's role is to love his wife with all the attributes of love found in 1 Corinthians 13.

Reading: Leviticus 15–16; Matthew 27:1–26

February 15

Love Expressed through Affection

What is affection? One definition is "tender attachment." Women need to have love continually expressed to them through affection, including tender words and gestures.

Men are basically logical and unemotional in their outlook on life, and they have a tendency to treat women in the same manner. Yet because of the way women are designed, they interpret a man's logical approach as coldness. Men need to learn how to love their wives in such a way that they can understand and receive their love. It isn't enough for a man to *think* that he is giving a woman love; he needs to learn the ways in which she receives love. He needs to learn how women in general recognize love, and he needs to learn how his wife *in particular* recognizes love.

Again, a woman functions on love; she needs to hear it expressed often. Many women say that receiving gestures of kindness and tenderness on a regular basis from their husbands, such as physical affection, notes, and flowers, is what communicates love to them. It is not the expense of the gifts as much as the true thoughtfulness behind them and the consistency of receiving them that makes the difference.

Many men believe that they are expressing proper love to their wives by providing them with the essentials in life, such as shelter, food, and clothing, or by giving them expensive items, such as major appliances, cars, and even diamond jewelry. Certainly, many men give these things out of a motivation of love; however, giving such material items is not the essence of love—the essence of love is the giving of oneself. (See Ephesians 5:25.)

Thought for the Day

Women need to have love expressed to them through affection, including tender words and gestures.

Reading: Leviticus 17–18; Matthew 27:27–50

February 16

Restoring Damage from the Fall

Husbands, love your wives and do not be harsh with them.
—Colossians 3:19

Why must husbands be *commanded* to love their wives? It is because the fall damaged the male's God-given natural love for the female, so that he wants *to rule over her* rather than *to love her as himself.* This is why, as the male is being restored to God's original design through redemption in Christ, he needs to be instructed to love the woman. For the same reason, the female's God-given natural *respect* for the male was damaged, and that is why she needs to be instructed to respect him. Thus, when God's purposes are restored, peace is reestablished between males and females. However, when the fallen nature is allowed free reign, there is discord.

When Paul said, "*Husbands, love your wives, just as Christ loved the church and gave himself up for her*" (Ephesians 5:25), he was saying, in effect, "Husband, above all else, love your wife. Don't worry about other things before that, because you can take care of those things in due course. If you love her, you will take care of many other problems and potential problems in your marriage. With love, she will function properly, because she was born to be loved."

A woman will reflect the love that she receives. When she is loved, she is better able to live a life of joy and peace, even in the midst of difficult circumstances. When she is unloved, it is as if there is a weight on her heart. Any man who violates a woman's need for love is misusing and abusing God's purpose for the woman.

Thought for the Day

When God's purposes are restored, peace is reestablished between males and females.

Reading: Leviticus 19–20; Matthew 27:51–66

February 17

Set Apart as Special

Husbands, love your wives, just as Christ also loved the church and gave Himself for her, that He might sanctify...her.
—Ephesians 5:25–26 (NKJV)

If a man is going to love his wife, he has to keep company with Christ. He has to find out how Christ loved His church. It will take a lifetime to study that manual on love! Christ *"gave Himself for her."* Then He sanctified her.

To sanctify something means to take it away from all else, set it apart in a special place, care for it every day, and value it as a priceless gem. To sanctify something means that you do not allow anything near it that would hurt or destroy it. It is set apart for special use. This means that you don't pass it around. It is not available to entertain other people. In Song of Songs, King Solomon speaks of the special love a man is to have for the bride he has set apart for himself:

> *You have stolen my heart, my sister, my bride; you have stolen my heart with one glance of your eyes, with one jewel of your necklace. How delightful is your love my sister, my bride! How much more pleasing is your love than wine, and the fragrance of your perfume than any spice!*
> (Song of Songs 4:9–10)

When a man really loves his wife, he considers her the crème de la crème. When she receives such love, she will reflect it in her countenance, the way she looks at life, and in her interactions with others.

Thought for the Day

If a man is going to love his wife, he has to keep company with Christ.

Reading: Leviticus 21–22; Matthew 28

February 18

Giving Affirmation

In the last several days, we have been discussing a woman's innate need to receive love primarily as expressed in the setting of the marriage relationship. Yet, how does this principle of a woman's need for love apply to women whom men may associate with through work or church?

Men can help build women's self-esteem by valuing them and treating them with kindness and Christian love. Women need the affirmation of men, just as men need the respect of women. Of course, this affirmation must always be given with wisdom, so that women never get the idea that the man is expressing anything more than a Christlike concern. These points are particularly important for men to understand, since they are often in positions of authority over women—in the church, in the workplace, and in other realms of life—and they influence women's perspectives and attitudes.

We can return to 1 Corinthians 13 as the man's guide to respecting and affirming women in any interaction or relationship he has with them. Men need to remember that females who are under their authority or supervision need to be treated with consideration so that the nature that God has given them will not be quenched. "*Love is patient, love is kind. It does not envy, it does not boast, it is not proud. It is not rude, it is not self-seeking, it is not easily angered, it keeps no record of wrongs*" (1 Corinthians 13:4–5). When men reflect the love and nature of Christ in their dealings with women, the women will reflect the love and nature of Christ in return.

Thought for the Day

Men can build women's self-esteem by valuing them and treating them with kindness and Christian love.

Reading: Leviticus 23–24; Mark 1:1–22

February 19

Five Vital Purposes of the Male

The Lord *God took the man and put him in the Garden of Eden to work it and take care of it.*
—Genesis 2:15

To become true men, males must reconnect to God's original concept of manhood in creation. The only way for a man to discover and live out his inherent masculine nature is to maintain a focus on purpose rather than roles that are related to a certain culture or time in history. Purpose is the key to manhood.

What do we know of God's plan for the first man? First, God *put* Adam in the garden of Eden. He didn't allow the man to wander around in an attempt to find it. He also did not leave Eden as an option, which means that "Eden" is a requirement for a male. God made the man and told him, "This is where you belong."

After placing him in Eden, God commanded the man to work. Note that work was given to the male even before the female was created. Work also came before the fall. Just to set the record straight, work is not a part of the curse. We can cause it to be a curse if we make it an idol and become workaholics. But work itself is a gift from God. The man was also instructed to "*take care*" of the garden. The Hebrew word translated "*take care*" denotes guarding, watching over, preserving, and protecting it.

During the next week, we will discuss five vital purposes of the male that men need to know to bring restoration to their own lives and to their families. These five purposes are natural outcomes of who God has created men to be.

Thought for the Day

Work came before the fall; work itself is a gift from God.

Reading: Leviticus 25; Mark 1:23–45

The Male's Purpose, Part 1: To Dwell in God's Presence

The first thing God did after creating the man was to put him in Eden. His first purpose for the male, therefore, is that he dwell in His presence. The word *Eden* in Hebrew is written with five strokes, each stroke a symbol representing a word or a character. When I studied the five strokes, I saw that they indicated *spot*, *moment*, *presence*, *open door*, and *delightful place*. Here is my interpretation of the word *Eden*. God took the man and put him in a spot, for the moment, where the presence of God was an open door to heaven.

The Scripture says the Lord planted, or established, the garden. He established a spot on the earth that His presence literally came down from heaven and touched so that it was a door of open access to heaven. Adam didn't have to do anything "religious" to enter the presence of God. He walked and talked directly with God in the cool of the day.

Why did God give the male Eden first, before the female? Because He wanted the male to have access to God first so he could always know the will of God for those who came out of him. In other words, Eden is for leadership access.

The first thing God gave Adam was *His own presence*. Likewise, the first thing you need in your life—whether you are a policeman, a politician, a CEO, a mechanic, an IT specialist, a doctor, or a carpenter—is the presence of God. A man needs God's presence before he needs the presence of a woman. Adam was already in Eden when God presented Eve to him. Eve met Adam in Eden where he was dwelling in the presence of God.

Thought for the Day

The first thing you need in your life is the presence of God!

Reading: Leviticus 26–27; Mark 2

February 21

God's Presence Is Life

"*Do not cast me from your presence or take your Holy Spirit from me*" was David's cry in Psalm 51:11. For a male, the presence of God is like water to a fish or soil to a plant. If you take the fish out of water or the plant out of soil, it malfunctions and dies. If you take the male out of God's presence, he will malfunction and die. This is why Satan will do anything possible to keep a man away from the presence of God. Satan wants the men to drop the women off at church and then go to play or watch sports or do some other activity.

Yet, when a man falls in love with God's presence, that man begins to truly function. The Bible says God dwells in the praises of His people. (See Psalm 22:3 KJV.) In Israel, the priests were the ones who led the worship—and all the priests were men. But today, when you bring a man into a worship service, he sits there as cool as a cucumber. He's too cool to say amen, too cool to clap, too cool to lift his hands, too cool to sing to God. He doesn't realize Satan has him cold, because he doesn't want him to get into God's presence.

At home, many men make their wives lead family devotions. The devil doesn't want men to start leading devotions because, if they do, the presence of God will come to their homes. During the years when my children were growing up, every morning I would say to them, "We are going to sing praises to God." I was blessed to lead them into God's presence. "*Blessed are those who have learned to acclaim you, who walk in the light of your presence, O Lord*" (Psalm 89:15).

Thought for the Day

When a man falls in love with God's presence, that man begins to truly function.

Reading: Numbers 1–2; Mark 3:1–19

The Male's Purpose, Part 2: To Manifest What God Put inside Him

The LORD God took the man and put him in the Garden of Eden to work it and take care of it.
—Genesis 2:15

The second purpose for a male is *work*. I researched the word *work* and found that in one sense it means "to become." Work is not something you do; it is something you become. It is manifesting what God has put inside you. What are you becoming?

Many people are poor and struggling because they have found a job but have not found their true work. A fulfilled man is someone who has discovered who and what he is supposed to become. There's some work God wanted manifested on earth that He buried inside you. He wants you to reveal it. You are not a mistake.

When you go to your job every day, are you becoming what you dreamed of? Perhaps you are in the right place with your employment and you thank God for it. But too many people's jobs stop them from becoming. There's no room for them to become, and their manhood is stifled by a job they hate.

Work reveals the potential God has placed within you. Suppose I have a mango seed, and I plant it and say to it, "Work." I'm telling it that I want to see a tree with mangos that have their own seed in them and can nourish people. Notice what happens when the mango tree fulfills its purpose. No mango tree eats its own mangos. The fruit is not for the tree's own benefit but for the benefit of others. You, too, were born with something "trapped" in you that the world is meant to benefit from, and that's your work.

Thought for the Day

God buried inside you some work He wants manifested on earth.

Reading: Numbers 3–4; Mark 3:20–35

February 23

Do You Have Just a Job?

Many men are afraid to talk about their dreams, but God is saying to you, "Manifest yourself! I want to see what I put into you."

I don't have a "job" anymore, but I used to. I worked for the Bahamas government for twelve years. I taught junior high school for five years. I worked in a food store before that, packing shelves. I worked in a warehouse lifting boxes. I worked in an ad firm, doing advertisements, drawings, and so forth. These were learning experiences. Then I found my true work of helping others understand how to manifest their God-given leadership potential. I don't wake up in the morning and "go" to work. I wake up and become what God created me to be.

Jesus said, *"Let your light so shine before men, that they may see your good works, and glorify your Father which is in heaven"* (Matthew 5:16 KJV). When other people see your work, when they see you manifesting what God put into you, they will glorify God. You were born to do something so awesome that only God could get the credit for it. Purpose is the reason for your being born; it's why you exist.

While purpose is why you were born, vision is when you start seeing it yourself. I believe most men have already been seeing or sensing their purpose, but it is so big that they're afraid of it. That's why they settle for jobs they hate. A God-given purpose can be fulfilled only through His guidance and strength. *"Now to him who is able to do immeasurably more than all we ask or imagine, according to his power that is at work within us"* (Ephesians 3:20).

Thought for the Day

You were born to do something so awesome that only God could get the credit for it.

Reading: Numbers 5–6; Mark 4:1–20

The Male's Purpose, Part 3: To Be a Cultivator

The Lord God took the man and put him in the Garden of Eden to work it and take care of it.
—Genesis 2:15

God placed Adam in the garden not only to work it, but also to take care of it. This leads us to the third purpose of the male: to be a cultivator. Men, I want you to fully realize that you do not just cultivate—you are cultivators by nature. You are cultivators designed by God. This means you improve things, maximizing the potential of the people and resources around you.

You are designed to bring out the best in everything under your care. This is why God will not give you a finished product. For example, He won't give you a business. Instead, He'll give you an idea and say, "I want you to bring the best out of that. Cultivate it." I built my organization from seven people to one hundred full-time workers with the potential of reaching millions of people every week. People see the organization for what it is today, but I had to cultivate it every single day of the last thirty years.

God hid products and resources in the physical world and watched to see what we would do with them. You will never be given a finished product by God. He'll only give you raw material. God won't even give you a completed woman. The perfect woman that many men are looking for does not exist. They get divorced because they are disappointed in the women they married. They don't understand that you have to cultivate your wife. It is your job to love her as God loves her by helping her maximize her potential, improve her life situation, and be the best she can be.

Thought for the Day

You are designed to bring out the best in everything under your care.

Reading: Numbers 7–8; Mark 4:21–41

Cultivating Your Wife

When I first married my wife, Ruth, she was so introverted that I had to encourage her to talk *to me*. Four people were too much of a crowd for her. She was afraid of expressing herself. When I discovered being a cultivator was part of my purpose as a husband, I began to draw out of her what she really had inside her. Today, my wife travels around the world ministering and speaking to thousands and tens of thousands of people. This is the woman who was afraid to be in a room with four people. God wants you to help your wife fulfill the plans He has for her.

The Scripture says,

> *Husbands, love your wives, just as Christ loved the church and gave himself up for her to make her holy, cleansing her by the washing with water through the word, and to present her to himself as a radiant church, without stain or wrinkle or any other blemish, but holy and blameless.* (Ephesians 5:25–27)

Jesus Christ is a Husband. His wife's name is *Ecclesia* (the church, the bride of Christ). He will minister to her and develop her until she is "*radiant*" and everything He desires her to be. He will present her as a glorious bride. This is the way husbands are to love their wives. In other words, if you are not proud of your wife, you are the failure. If you are ashamed of your wife, you should be ashamed of yourself. The more you criticize her, the more evidence there is of your failure. Instead, the longer your wife lives with you, the better she should become. A godly man brings out the best in his wife.

Thought for the Day

The longer your wife lives with you, the better she should become.

Reading: Numbers 9–11; Mark 5:1–20

February 26

The Male's Purpose, Part 4: To Be a Protector

The fourth purpose of the male is *to protect*. Men, even though many women may feel they are able to protect themselves, you are still called to be the protector of your family. Remember that God told Adam to guard everything in the garden. You were designed to guard and defend, and to cover everything under your care and in your sphere of influence. That includes your wife, your children, your neighbors, and your community.

Many men don't think about protecting others—they think about how they can use them. If you are a single man on a date with a young lady, you are supposed to protect her from even your own sexual desires. She is supposed to feel safe in your automobile. You are supposed to guard her virginity, not destroy it. Real men protect; they don't seduce. God designed you with physical strength in order to defend women, not to use your strength to overpower them. That is abuse of power. You are supposed to be the safest place any woman can be.

Many men use their gifts to destroy women. Christ protected women! He was a guard for them. Children were safe with Him. He blessed them. He didn't abuse them. A godly man always leaves a woman better when she leaves his presence. Let this be the last day you abuse or misuse a woman. Say, "Lord, forgive me for any time that I have used, manipulated, or abused a woman. Forgive me, and may they forgive me. Today, I am a guard, a protector, and a preserver. Amen."

Thought for the Day

Men, you were designed to guard, defend, and cover everything under your care and in your sphere of influence.

Reading: Numbers 12–14; Mark 5:21–43

The Male's Purpose, Part 5: To Be a Teacher

A fifth vital purpose of the male is *to teach* the instructions God gave him. Adam was formed first. God put him in the garden and gave him instructions concerning it. (See Genesis 2:15–17.) He was meant to pass along those instructions to Eve and other family members who would come after him.

Men need to learn the Word of God so they can be in a position to teach it. Whatever God creates something to do, He builds in the capacity to do it. God built men with the teacher psyche. Men in all countries are wired to be teachers. God created the husband to give instruction and the wife to receive his teaching and then command the children.

You are the teacher in your home. You are the one who is supposed to have the information, the instruction. It starts with you. That means you have to hear from God first. Perhaps you have never read the Bible. You may have read a few verses from Psalms, but you've never read the Bible from Genesis to Revelation. You're forty years old and you've never read the Bible, but you're attempting to be the head of the home!

Can you teach your wife the Word of God? Do you know enough of the Word to become the teacher of your children? If the answer is no, get busy and make a commitment to read the New Testament first. We need men who know the Word, not men who know the football scores and the names of every player on their favorite basketball team. I challenge you to read and study the Word of God for yourself and your family!

Thought for the Day

Men need to learn the Word of God so they can be in a position to teach it.

Reading: Numbers 15–16; Mark 6:1–29

February 28

The Marks of a Man of Purpose

To sum up the five vital purposes of a male, here are the marks of a man of purpose:

1. He loves Eden. He *loves* God's presence. He possesses a true self-image based on his knowledge that God created him in His own image. He knows who he is.
2. He desires to work. If you meet a man who doesn't like work, he's not a real man, a man of purpose.
3. He is able to cultivate.
4. He commits to protect everything under his care.
5. He knows the Word of God, and he teaches it.

What a beautiful picture of a true man. What a picture of fatherhood that reflects the Father God. If I was a woman, I'd marry that man right away! He knows who he is, where he is, and what he's supposed to be doing. He's able to cultivate, protect, and teach God's Word. Many women are confused today because they can't find that man. They meet men who have high-paying jobs, wear nice clothes, and own expensive houses, but who don't know what really matters. Or they meet men who are wandering aimlessly in life, unable to support themselves because they have no clear purpose. Women are asking, "What's happening?"

Men, I want to see you change things in your life, family, job, ministry, and community by understanding and fulfilling your God-given purpose. You will discover your true image and your true purpose only in your Creator.

Thought for the Day

A man of purpose knows who he is, where he is, and what he's supposed to be doing.

Reading: Numbers 17–19; Mark 6:30–56

February 29

Principles of the Male's Purpose

Today, review these principles of the male's purpose and reflect on how you can apply them in your everyday life—directly for yourself, if you are a man, and in your relationships with men, if you are a woman.

1. The only way for a man to discover and live out his inherent nature is to maintain a focus on his God-given purpose rather than on roles that are related to a certain culture or time in history.
2. Five vital purposes of the male are (1) to dwell in God's presence, (2) to manifest what God put inside him, (3) to be a cultivator, (4) to be a protector, and (5) to be a teacher.
3. When a man gets into God's presence, he begins to function again.
4. Work reveals the potential God has placed within you. You were born with something "trapped" in you that the world is meant to benefit from.
5. God doesn't give the finished product but the raw material with which to cultivate.
6. Men are designed to guard, defend, and cover everything under their care and in their spheres of influence.
7. The male must know God's Word in order to teach his wife and children.

The Lord God took the man and put him in the Garden of Eden to work it and take care of it. (Genesis 2:15)

Father God, You have given us Your Word as a light to guide us in our way. We have been created with a purpose that comes directly from You. You have designed the male with the inherent ability to be a protector, cultivator, and teacher. Please help us to see Your design clearly so that we can walk in it and fulfill our purpose on this earth. In Jesus' name, amen.

Reading: Numbers 20–22; Mark 7:1–13

March 1

Is Your Marriage an "Experiment?"

Do you know what most marriages are today? Big experiments. Some men think, "I don't really know what a wife is for, but I'm old enough to get married, so I'm going to have one." They get married just because they're twenty-five. All right, then what? Do you know what you have? After three weeks, you realize your wife doesn't agree with you on everything. The experiment isn't working. She begins to ask for things like time. She wants love and affection and attention. She wants appreciation. If you are in this situation, you may say, "Hey, I didn't bargain for all that." Well, my friend, marriage is not a trial run. *"The two will become one flesh....So they are no longer two, but one"* (Matthew 19:5–6).

God knew exactly what He wanted when He thought of the male and female. This means that He is the only One who knows how humanity is intended to function. *"Is he not your Father, your Creator, who made you and formed you?"* (Deuteronomy 32:6). If you have any questions about your relationship with your spouse, you should check the Manual. If you don't know the purpose of something, all you can do is experiment. Everybody who doesn't know his or her purpose is just experimenting with life.

Because God's purposes for us are so essential, over the next week we will explore the consequences of experimenting with life, as well as the blessings of living in the purposes for which God has called us, especially in our relationships.

Thought for the Day

God is the only One who knows how humanity is intended to function.

Reading: Numbers 23–25; Mark 7:14–37

March 2

We Are Not Divine Experiments

Do you begin building a house when you dig the foundation? No, you begin building it when the idea is conceived. This means that the finished house is in the unseen. People pass by the property, and they don't see it. However, to you who understand and know what is going to happen, it is already finished. Digging the foundation is the beginning of the implementation of your purpose. So, after you dig the foundation, when somebody asks you, "What are you doing?" your answer is very definite. You point to the architect's rendering of the house and say, "I am building this."

Likewise, God in His wisdom *is not guessing* about His plans for us-for humanity as a whole or for each of us individually. God has already decided on His purpose. He has the complete picture. It's on His drawing board. It's His vision for us. It isn't an afterthought. In Genesis 1, we read how He began to dig the foundation of humanity: *"Let us make man in our image, in our likeness"* (v. 26). Genesis was not the beginning of a supernatural experiment with an unknown outcome. Genesis was the beginning of the production of something that was sure.

What we need to understand is that when God created the male and the female, He had already predetermined what we were supposed to be and do. We are not divine experiments! Together, males and females are an intentional divine project with a predetermined purpose.

Thought for the Day

God in His wisdom is not guessing about His plans for us.

Reading: Numbers 26–27; Mark 8:1–21

March 3

Being Sincerely Wrong

Moses told the Israelites that it is possible to commit a wrong unintentionally. He offered them God's forgiveness for such a case: *"The priest is to make atonement for the whole Israelite community, and they will be forgiven, for it was not intentional and they have brought to the LORD for their wrong an offering made by fire and a sin offering"* (Numbers 15:25).

Remember, if you don't know the purpose of something, you will misuse or abuse it in some way. That's why it's possible to be *sincerely wrong.* It's possible to be *faithfully wrong.* It's possible to be *seriously wrong.* You're serious, but you're wrong, because you don't know the purpose for the thing you're involved in. This principle holds true for everything, including people.

How many people go into marriage very seriously? Most people do. They go to the church, stand at the altar, and say to their betrothed, "I will love you until I die." They're very serious. But then they "die" in six months. At least their love dies. Then their family and friends try to figure out what happened. Their marriage failed because they didn't understand the purpose of marriage, the purpose of a mate, or the purpose of family. Because they didn't understand these things, they abused their union.

People abuse things because they just don't know their purposes or they disregard their purposes. When males and females don't know God's intentions, they end up abusing each other, even if they don't mean to. If men and women are going to solve their current identity crisis and fulfill their purposes as husbands and wives, and as fathers and mothers, they must rediscover God's plan for them. Otherwise, they will hurt those around them, even if it's unintentional.

Thought for the Day

If you're sincere yet don't know your purpose, you will be sincerely wrong.

Reading: Numbers 28–30; Mark 8:22–38

March 4

Experimenting with Life

In the last few days, we have seen that whenever you don't know the purpose of something, you're experimenting. Many people today—especially young people—are experimenting with life. They don't know what education is for, so they treat school like an experiment. They skip classes and spend their time partying, then they flunk out. They experiment with sex and sexual identity, and they end up with all kinds of problems. They experiment with drugs and hurt their bodies.

When I was a boy, I was tempted to experiment in order to find out about life. I'm grateful God protected me from much of that. But many of the young people with whom I grew up did not make it through their experimentation. The experiment blew up. Some are dead. The bodies of others are contaminated and wrecked from using destructive substances. They didn't know the purpose of the elements they were using. "*There is a way that seems right to a man, but in the end it leads to death*" (Proverbs 14:12).

I'd like to say to the young people reading this devotional: if you want to know why you were born, the worst people to ask are your friends, because your friends are trying to figure out why they're here, too. If you want to know the reason for your existence, don't ask another product; ask the Manufacturer. Everyone else is guessing.

What we've been doing all these years is asking the product why it exists. Because the world doesn't understand much about the reason for the existence of things, it functions like one big experimental lab. All of us seem to have been assuming the position of scientists. We have imagined that we have the time and intelligence to discover the reason for our existence through experimentation. Then we find out that life is short and that we're very poor researchers.

Thought for the Day

If you want to know why you were born, ask the Manufacturer.
Everyone else is just guessing!

Reading: Numbers 31–33; Mark 9:1–29

March 5

Life Is Precious

Life is too precious to be treated like a trial run. The only way to avoid the cost of trial and error is to learn the purpose of your life. Think about a car mechanic. If he's just experimenting, he won't last long in the automotive business. If he says, "I wonder what this part is for? Let me guess what section of the engine I should attach it to," that's experimentation. He doesn't know what the manufacturer had in mind.

Well, if you wouldn't let an inexperienced mechanic work on your car, what about your life? No university professor knows people well enough to write a definitive book about what makes us tick. No psychologist or psychiatrist truly knows me. God wrote a Manual on His product, and the product is me. Tell yourself, "I'm an expensive product. I won't let anyone experiment with me." It's a dangerous thing for us to experiment with this precious commodity called life.

In the Psalms, we are reminded that God's Manual, the Word, directs our way. *"Your word is a lamp to my feet and a light for my path"* (Psalm 119:105). *"Your statues* [Word] *are my heritage forever; they are the joy of my heart"* (v. 111). *"The unfolding of your words gives light; it gives understanding to the simple"* (v. 130). If we look to ourselves or others, rather than to God and His Manual, to learn our reason for living, we will travel an unreliable and hazardous course in life.

Thought for the Day

It's a dangerous thing for us to experiment with this precious commodity called life.

Reading: Numbers 34–36; Mark 9:30–50

March 6

Unaware of Purpose

Everyone on earth has a purpose, but most people are unaware of their purposes. When Adam and Eve turned their backs on God and His ways, they ended up losing their knowledge of His intent for themselves and for the world. Rejecting God was the equivalent of buying a sophisticated and intricate piece of equipment and then throwing away the user's manual. If you get something to work under those circumstances, it is only by chance. The more likely scenario is that you will never get it to function properly. It will never fulfill its complete purpose.

Likewise, humanity has not respected the fact that God's creation and His directions for living were established for a specific reason. If that purpose continues to be abandoned, males and females will never function properly as human beings. This dangerous situation leads again to one of our key principles for understanding life and relationships: *whenever purpose is not known, abuse is inevitable.*

Suppose I'm Henry T. Ford. I'm going to add a motor to a carriage and build a product called a motorcar. I know the purpose before I build this vehicle. It will enable people to be more mobile on land. Now suppose you decide, "I want to use this motorcar as a boat," and you drive it off a cliff and into the water. What will happen? You're probably going to drown, and the car is going to be ruined. Why? The car was built to fulfill a specific purpose, and if you do not use it according to its purpose, then you will likely be harmed in the process. We need to keep from driving off the cliff of life by understanding and fulfilling our purpose as human beings.

Thought for the Day

If God's purpose continues to be abandoned, males and females will never function properly as human beings.

Reading: Deuteronomy 1–2; Mark 10:1–31

March 7

Only One Life

God desires that all men and women find their purpose and fulfill it. If a man wants to know who he is in order to live fully in that reality, he must first understand God's principles of purpose. He has to learn these anchors for living from the Word of God. Otherwise, he will fall into a trap of confusion—where many of us are right now.

Proverbs 19:21 is our foundational verse in regard to understanding God's purpose: *"Many are the plans in a man's heart, but it is the Lord's purpose that prevails."* This crucial truth tells us that we can make all the plans we want to in life, but if we don't make our plans according to the purposes for which God created us, then our plans will be in vain. We won't live up to our full potential, and we will be unfulfilled. We may even pursue goals and engage in practices that are harmful to us. We have only one life, and we have to make that life count if we are ever to fulfill our purpose.

What value do you place on your life? Do you know that one of the most dangerous things in life is wasting time? It is said that time is a commodity that you never are able to recapture. Once you've lost time, it's gone forever. So the best thing to do with time is to use it in a way that will bring the greatest results. The best way—the only way—to use time effectively is to do *what* you are supposed to do *when* you are supposed to do it. Effectiveness does not mean just doing good things but rather doing the *right* thing.

Thought for the Day

You have to make your life count if you are ever to fulfill your purpose.

Reading: Deuteronomy 3–4; Mark 10:32–52

March 8

Stopped in the Middle of Traffic

It is dangerous to live without God! If you don't know God, you'll never know your reason for existence. And if you don't know why you were born, you could live a completely wrong life.

One of the reasons Jesus knew His purpose was that He was continually seeking God and in constant communication with Him. That is the pattern each of us needs to follow. Why? There are many good people who are pursuing relationships, careers, and goals in life that are not best for them. What we have to concern ourselves with is living effectively. The only way to live a fulfilled life is to know why you were born. The only way to know why you were born is to learn it from the One who created you.

Have you ever had a new car break down on you right in the middle of traffic? You got out and kicked one of the tires. You just wanted to curse at it because the car wasn't fulfilling its purpose. It was brand-new. It looked sleek. It had a nice paint job. But you couldn't drive it. What made you angry at the car? It's simple: the car's purpose was to transport you, to make you mobile; but the car was not taking you anywhere. No matter how great the car looked, it wasn't right; it wasn't fulfilling its purpose.

Many men and women are like that car. They're stopped in the middle of traffic, and they don't even realize it. They're spending their lives doing things that look good, but they don't know God—or they know too little about Him and His ways.

Thought for the Day

Knowing and fulfilling your purpose is the only way to do what is right.

Reading: Deuteronomy 5–7; Mark 11:1–18

March 9

Fighting against Our Best Interests

This is the plan determined for the whole world; this is the hand stretched out over all nations. For the Lord *Almighty has purposed, and who can thwart him* [stop, interfere with, or cancel His purpose]*? His hand is stretched out, and who can turn it back?*

—Isaiah14:26–27

In this passage, God is saying, in essence, "My purpose will be accomplished. No one can interfere with it or hinder it. When I give a purpose to something, your plans, ideas, opinions, perceptions, and prejudices about what you think its purpose should be are inapplicable. What you think about what I have purposed is not going to change My purpose and design. And before My purpose could change, I would have to stop being God."

Let me ask you, if it comes to a contest between you and God, who do you think is going to win? If God sets a purpose for something, there isn't anything we can do to change it. God made the female and the male for certain purposes, and He designed them to fulfill those purposes. We cannot alter His design. What we need to keep in mind, however, is that if we try to change His plans, we're working against ourselves, because He created us for good and has our best interests in mind. "*'For I know the plans I have for you,' declares the* Lord*, 'plans to prosper you and not to harm you, plans to give you hope and a future'*" (Jeremiah 29:11).

Thought for the Day

God created us for good and has our best interests in mind.

Reading: Deuteronomy 8–10; Mark 11:19–33

March 10

God's Training Center

God's directive to the male and female was, *"Fill the earth and subdue it"* (Genesis 1:28). He was telling them, in essence, "Have dominion over this spot right here so that you become used to ruling on a smaller scale at first." The implication is that He intended for this man and woman to grow in dominion ability by learning to dominate the garden of Eden, the area in which they were initially placed. This is one of God's clear principles: If you've been faithful over a little, then your rulership will be expanded to much more.

Jesus explained this concept clearly in the parable of the talents. To the servant who has been faithful over a little, the Master says, *"Well done, good and faithful servant! You have been faithful with a few things; I will put you in charge of many things. Come and share your master's happiness!"* (Matthew 25:23).

God is so good to us. He doesn't give us more than we can handle. He always gives us just enough to train us for the rest. I hope you understand this principle. God will always give you just enough so that you can get used to the idea of more. Many of us want everything right now. We short-circuit God's plan because we grasp for everything at once. God is saying, in effect, "You'll get everything, but not right at this moment. You have not yet developed the character and the experience and the exercising of your potential to enable you to handle more."

Thought for the Day

God always gives us just enough to train us for the rest.

Reading: Deuteronomy 11–13; Mark 12:1–27

What Is a Man's Assignment?

I hope you are convinced that you need to be in God's purposes in order to be fulfilled in life! What God gave Adam to do still holds true for men today because, as a God of purpose, He has a reason for everything He does. He is teaching us His plan for mankind in the account of creation.

"The LORD God took the man and put him in the Garden of Eden to work it and take care of it. And the LORD God commanded the man..." (Genesis 2:15–16). Whom did the Lord command? He commanded the male. What did He tell him? *"You are free to eat from any tree in the garden; but you must not eat from the tree of the knowledge of good and evil, for when you eat of it you will surely die"* (vv. 16–17). In an earlier devotional, we saw that one of the male's purposes is teacher. God wanted him to be the initial recipient of His plan for mankind. He showed him the whole garden, the whole environment of Eden, a vision of everything He had created, and then He gave him instructions for living.

Recall that the female wasn't formed until after the events of the above Scripture passage. Thus, the male was given the charge of being the *visionary* and *leader*, the one who would guide those who came after him in the ways of God. This doesn't mean that women don't also have the capacity to be visionaries and leaders. However, the male is the one to whom God first entrusted His plans and purposes for the world. This indicates a major purpose of his existence.

Thought for the Day

The male was given the charge of being the visionary and leader.

Reading: Deuteronomy 14–16; Mark 12:28–44

March 12

The Male's Leadership Responsibility

Men have been entrusted with God's purposes. The male is to be responsible for everything under his jurisdiction. This is a serious assignment from the Lord. If something goes wrong in your family, you are accountable. You may say, as Adam told God when mankind fell, *"But the woman...."* (See Genesis 3:12.) No, not the woman—*you* are responsible. God went straight to Adam even though Eve was the one who first ate the fruit. When God asked him, *"Where are you?"* (v. 9), the question was not one of location, but of position. "You are not fulfilling your purpose of leadership, Adam. What has happened to your family?"

The male's purpose was not chosen by the male but by God. Whatever your purpose, that's where your position comes from. Purpose, rather than social expectation, should determine position. The male is not elected the head of the family. You don't canvas for votes in the family to become the head of the home. If you are a man, you *are* the head of the family.

You are the responsible one, whether you like it or not. If you run from this responsibility, it will run after you, because it's not just a role; it's a God-given purpose. However, it needs to be understood in light of God's Word and not in the context of many societies' definitions of what "head of the household" means. It never means domination, abuse, or misuse. It means godly leadership.

Thought for the Day

Everything that is necessary to lead the family is built into the male.

Reading: Deuteronomy 17–19; Mark 13:1–20

March 13

The Male as Visionary

God wants men to understand their dominion assignments and then to develop the qualities that are required in order to carry them out. This is the way that men can pursue God's purpose for their lives and grow in true manhood, for God's purpose is the key to our fulfillment.

The first responsibility that brings fulfillment and spiritual rewards to the male is that of visionary. This is a foundational responsibility because, without it, he can't fulfill the other assignments of leader, teacher, cultivator, protector, and provider.

Being a true visionary is a lost art in our times. The average male can't say who he is because he has no real vision for his life. He is either floundering without purpose or he is diligently pursuing a false vision based on the values of contemporary society, which are often the opposite of what God values. God wants males to have a vision for their lives that comes from Him and belongs to them personally—not something dictated by the cultural environment, current trends, man-made religion, or someone else's image of what their lives should be.

We can know that God has a vision for every male because the male was *created* to be a visionary. Remember that one reason the man was formed first was so that he could be the initial recipient of the information, revelation, and communication God desired to share regarding humanity's relationship with Him and its purpose for being. Then He created the female to enable the man to fulfill this vision. God's priority has not changed.

Thought for the Day

Being a true visionary is a lost art today.

Reading: Deuteronomy 20–22; Mark 13:21–37

March 14

What Does It Mean to Have Vision?

Where there is no vision, the people perish.
—Proverbs 29:18 (KJV)

Vision is necessary for life. The word "*vision*" in the Hebrew means a "dream, revelation, or oracle." Obviously, a vision that is connected to God's purposes is something that needs to be revealed by God Himself. You need His revelation of your life's vision. The only way you can discover this vision is to listen to what God is saying to you.

To have vision means to be able to conceive of and move toward your purpose in life. A man shouldn't get married and then say to his wife, "What are we going to do? Well, you know, we'll just wait on the Lord. We'll see where we're going when we get there." That's not vision. While God does want us to wait for His guidance and direction, He doesn't want us to abuse this principle by not earnestly seeking His particular vision and plan for us.

Now, it's true that we might not always see the whole picture right away, as Abraham had to trust God to lead him to an unfamiliar land in which he would become a great nation. (See Genesis 12:1–2.) However, Abraham had a clear vision that he was going to the place God had promised him, and he moved steadily toward that goal. Having vision means that you can already see the end of your purpose. It means that you have faith in God and what He has told you to do, so that you are continually moving toward your vision as it is moving toward you. Your responsibility is to support and sustain the vision until it comes to fruition.

Thought for the Day

To have vision means to conceive of and move toward your purpose.

Reading: Deuteronomy 23–25; Mark 14:1–29

March 15

Sharing the Vision

What vision did God give to Adam? He said, "Here's the garden: subdue it, work it, cultivate it. Make it better than it is. Develop it, and produce more of it." In other words, "Take this planet and make it richer than it is. There is seed in this ground that hasn't yet born fruit. Make it a harvest. There is gold in the mountains. Dig it out. There are diamonds in the rough. Mine them."

After God had given the man responsibility and work in the garden, He said, "I'm going to create a helper for the man to get this done." Therefore, one of the purposes of the woman is to share in the vision and responsibilities of the male.

Again, the dominion assignment was given to both men and women.

> *Male and female he created them. God blessed them and said to them, "Be fruitful and increase in number; fill the earth and subdue it. Rule over...every living creature that moves on the ground."*
>
> (Genesis 1:27–28)

This means that the woman is meant to help the man fulfill this vision in all areas of life. However, when the man sees the woman coming into the corporate office, he often becomes jealous. "What is she doing here?" he says. "Her place is in the home." Where did that idea come from? It did not come from God. This beautiful, precious gift of the woman was given to men so that they wouldn't be alone. Yet do you know what men do to women? They view them as trespassers or competitors in life's journey. They despise the very thing that was given to them for companionship and help. Woman was made to share the man's vision and to help him fulfill it.

Thought for the Day

The dominion assignment was given to both men and women.

Reading: Deuteronomy 26–27; Mark 14:27–53

March 16

Equal Responsibility

Two are better than one, because they have a good return for their work.
—Ecclesiastes 4:9

If man didn't need woman, God would not have created her. The woman enables the man to accomplish the vision and purpose for which they were both created. She shares in this vision, encourages the man along the way, and helps him to accomplish it. If a man has a vision, a woman should do everything in her power to see that it comes to pass. Women, when you help a man, it doesn't mean you are putting him down or putting yourself down. It means that you both have equal responsibility, each in the proper position.

A male was not meant to carry out his ministry by himself. His vision was not supposed to be fulfilled by himself. This means that a woman was not made to fulfill a vision by herself, either. Everything that the female has—her talents, gifts, expertise, experience, and education—was given to her to help the male fulfill God's vision. This is the reason why women have so much talent.

The problem is that men and women don't understand their purposes, and so they end up using their talents against one other. The woman uses her talents to prove that she doesn't need the man, instead of using them to help the man. The man hates this use of her abilities because he feels intimidated. When this happens, both of them lose their purpose in life, and both of them are dissatisfied, because she can't fulfill her purpose without him, and he needs her to help him fulfill his purpose. They need each other, but they end up working against each other.

Thought for the Day

The woman enables the man to accomplish the vision and purpose for which they were both created.

Reading: Deuteronomy 28–29; Mark 14:54–72

March 17

Where There Is No Vision

A man needs a clear vision of three things: (1) who he is in God, (2) what his overall purpose as a male is, and (3) what his purpose as an individual man is. In this way, he can know where he is going in life and can lead those under his care and responsibility. Again, "*where there is no vision, the people perish*" (Proverbs 29:18 KJV).

First things have to come first. Before God gave the man a helper, He gave him a vision for what he should be doing. That is also the order we need to follow today. If a man has no vision, or if his wife has the only vision, the man and his whole family will have a difficult time. This is because God has designed the male to carry others with him in his vision. Our society is in trouble because wherever the man goes, he brings everybody else along. Right now, most men don't know where they're going, and the women and children who are following have no direction.

It's dangerous for a woman to marry a man who doesn't know God, because she won't know where he's taking her. Even if he does know God, he needs to learn to live in God's presence, because some men who know Him don't talk to Him enough. No man has the right to lead a woman if he doesn't have the ability to truly hear God.

A man cannot ask a woman to follow and help him if he isn't really doing anything. The woman is looking for somebody who is doing something to which she can contribute. All the potential, all the energy, all the excitement, and all the creativity within her has to be applied to something.

Thought for the Day

Before God gave the man a helper, He gave him a vision for what he should be doing.

Reading: Deuteronomy 30–31; Mark 15:1–25

March 18

Jesus Had a Clear Self-Image

Many men don't have a vision for their lives because they are not committed to God and to seeking His will in this area. If a man does not have a relationship with God, he cannot fully function in his purpose.

The greatest example of someone who had a vision for His life is Jesus. He constantly repeated and affirmed who He is. Jesus was able to live in the confidence of His purpose from an early age. Remember what He said to His parents when He was only twelve years old? *"I must be about My Father's business"* (Luke 2:49 NKJV). Jesus knew His identity as the Son of God and as God the Son. He said, *"Before Abraham was born, I am!"* (John 8:58). He knew His reason for being and His purpose in life: *"The Son of Man came to seek and to save what was lost"* (Luke 19:10).

The example Jesus set for us by His life shows us our need for these important elements related to purpose: (1) a clear self-image and (2) a life consistent with one's purpose and calling. Jesus lived a life that was totally consistent with who He said He was. He had complete integrity; He always kept and fulfilled His own words.

John the Baptist is another excellent example of a man who knew his identity. *"I am the voice of one calling in the desert, 'Make straight the way for the Lord'"* (John 1:23). He had a sense of confidence in who he was and what he was called to do.

Thought for the Day

If a man does not have a relationship with God, he cannot fully function in his purpose.

Reading: Deuteronomy 32 –34; Mark 15:26–47

March 19

Know Your Identity

Yesterday, we saw how Jesus and John the Baptist knew their purposes in life. The apostle Paul also clearly had a vision for his life. He had a strong self-image and exhibited clarity of purpose. How frequently he began his letters with such statements as, *"Paul, a servant of Christ Jesus, called to be an apostle,"* or *"Paul, an apostle of Christ Jesus by the will of God."* (See, for example, Romans 1:1, Ephesians 1:1.) He also made these statements of purpose: *"For this purpose I was appointed a herald and an apostle"* (1 Timothy 2:7), and *"Of this gospel I was appointed a herald and an apostle and a teacher"* (2 Timothy 1:11). Paul received God's vision for his life through his encounters with Him. He was a man who understood the importance of staying in communion with God. True vision can be found only in God's presence.

Jesus was given to prayer and reflection during His entire earthly life. He was in constant contact with the Father in order to know how to fulfill His life's purpose. After a day of particularly busy ministry in which He had healed the sick and demon-possessed, He got up early the next day and went to pray in a quiet place. When Peter and the other disciples found Him there, they exclaimed, *"Everyone is looking for you!"* (Mark 1:37).

Jesus could have basked in the people's praise, but He continued to follow His life's purpose. God had shown Him the next step when He was in prayer. He said, *"Let us go somewhere else–to the nearby villages–so I can preach there also. That is why I have come"* (Mark 1:38).

Thought for the Day

We receive God's vision for our lives through our encounters with Him.

Reading: Joshua 1–3; Mark 16

March 20

THE KINGDOM OF GOD IS WITHIN YOU

I will ask the Father, and he will give you another Counselor to be with you forever–the Spirit of truth....You know him, for he lives with you and will be in you.

–John 14:16–17

You aren't fulfilling your purpose as a man or a woman until you can hear the voice of God. You aren't fulfilling your purpose until you start speaking and affirming the Word of God in your life. To do this, you need to be in the same "garden environment" that Adam and Eve were first placed in.

We need to get back to the place where the glory can flow between God and man, where we can hear the voice of God, and God can give us direction. Because the Holy Spirit has been poured out into the hearts of believers, the garden is no longer just one spot on the earth–it is within the heart of every person who belongs to Christ. That is why Christ said, "*The kingdom of God is within you*" (Luke 17:21). It is not within you of its own accord; the kingdom of God is within you because God's Spirit lives within you.

The kingdom of God–God's Spirit and will ruling in our hearts–has come to us through Christ, and it is through Him that we can fulfill the dominion mandate. We are called to spread the gospel message of reconciliation with God through Christ and of the gift of the Holy Spirit, who brings us power for living, working, and creating to the glory of God. If we want to fulfill our dominion responsibilities and assignments, we have to do so through the Spirit of God as we follow His will.

Thought for the Day

You aren't fulfilling your purpose until you can hear the voice of God and affirm His Word in your life.

Reading: Joshua 4–6; Luke 1:1–20

March 21

Principles of the Male as Visionary

Today, reflect on these principles of the male as visionary and begin to apply them in your daily life—directly for yourself, if you are a man, and in your relationships with men, if you are a woman.

1. Being a visionary is a foundational responsibility for the male because, without it, he can't fulfill his other assignments of leader, teacher, cultivator, provider, and protector.
2. To have vision means to be able to conceive of and move toward your purpose in life.
3. The male was *created* to be a visionary. He was given the first vision of God's plan for humanity.
4. A man needs a clear vision of (1) who he is in God, (2) what his overall purpose as a male is, (3) what his purpose as an individual man is.
5. If a man has no vision, this will negatively affect those who are to follow him, especially his family.
6. Before God gave the man a helper, He gave him a vision.
7. A male cannot ask a female to follow and help him if he has no vision.
8. God always provides for the vision He gives.

Now faith is being sure of what we hope for and certain of what we do not see. (Hebrews 11:1)

Heavenly Father,
Thank You for not leaving us on this earth without a Helper or Counselor. Your Holy Spirit reveals the vision for our lives and gives us the ability to fulfill the purposes for which You have created us. You have designed the male to be the visionary and the female to work with him hand-in-hand to see the vision accomplished. Help us to live out this mission for our lives in a way that brings You glory. In Jesus' name, amen.

Reading: Joshua 7–9; Luke 1:21–38

March 22

What a Woman Can Do

While the husband is called to be the leader of the family, the wife's response to him can determine how successful his leadership is. Sometimes a husband will say, "I think we should do this," and right away his wife will say, "Do *what?* You've never done anything right yet!" She just wiped out the man's ego. Her answer tells him she doesn't trust him.

Women, even if your husbands have failed in the past, and even if you aren't sure about their ideas, you can say, "Well, let's try it that way, then." When you say, "try," he hears "trust." "Let's try it" means you're going to trust him in this undertaking. Then, if he messes up, you can say, "We all mess up." A woman can protect her husband's dignity, realizing that she also makes mistakes.

"Each one of you also must love his wife as he loves himself, and the wife must respect her husband" (Ephesians 5:33). Feed your husband's need for leadership respect. When he gets to the point where it is strong and effective, then it will become a great blessing to both of you. He will learn to lead because he will know that you support him.

Men need to remember that women are here to help them. I believe that one of the reasons God took the woman from the man's side, or rib, is to emphasize her nature. The word *rib* means "sustainer" or "supporter." That's what the rib does. It supports the whole upper frame with the vertebrae. So a woman is a support system. If she functions in her purpose, she helps the male to function in his.

Thought for the Day

Women need to feed their husbands' need for leadership respect.

Reading: Joshua 10–12; Luke 1:39–56

March 23

Delicately Designed

Husbands, in the same way be considerate as you live with your wives, and treat them with respect as the weaker partner and as heirs with you of the gracious gift of life.
—1 Peter 3:7

The word "*weaker*" in this verse isn't referring just to physical strength, because some women are stronger than some men. In addition, women can put up with much emotional adversity and physical stress and still survive. Many men couldn't handle what women handle. I like to translate the word "*weaker*" as "more delicate." Peter was saying, "Husband, treat your wife with consideration and respect, because God designed her in such a way that she is delicate. She is very, very fine."

Remember that God took a scoop of dirt with which to fashion the male, but He built the female a little more elegantly. Her shape is a little more refined than a man's. He designed her delicately. I believe this also refers to the delicacy of her soul. The expression of a woman's soul is very refined because of her purpose; she is more sensitive than her male counterpart.

I believe that the definition of "*weaker*" should go even deeper to indicate that the woman is more "absorbent." She can absorb things more easily than a man, because she was created to absorb. That is why God told the husband to be careful how he treated her. Why? She is so delicate that she absorbs everything around her.

Thought for the Day

God took a scoop of dirt with which to fashion the male, but He built the female a little more elegantly.

Reading: Joshua 13–15; Luke 1:57–80

March 24

Would You Like Unfading Beauty?

Your beauty...should be that of your inner self, the unfading beauty of a gentle and quiet spirit, which is of great worth in God's sight.
—1 Peter 3:3–4

A woman has a spirit-man inside; this makes her a free and responsible spiritual being. You can't imagine the power that you will have when you understand the spirit that is inside you. Spiritually, men and women are equal; they have the same spirit-man within. God called both male and female "man." I like the way the Word of God expresses it: *"There is neither...slave nor free, male nor female"* in the body of Christ (Galatians 3:28).

First Peter 3:4 says that a woman's beauty *"should be that of* [her] *inner self."* It is this *"inner self"* that is a woman's spirit. What the woman is physically is different from what she is in her inner self. The spirit-man inside every woman is the being that relates to God. The next time you women run into somebody who is confused about this concept, just tell them, "Look, I have a female body, but I have a spirit-man inside. I deal directly with God through my spirit."

Jesus said, *"God is spirit, and his worshipers must worship in spirit and in truth"* (John 4:24). A woman has her own spirit-being with which to worship God. She can bless the Lord and love the Lord and receive from the Lord herself. A woman who loves and worships the Lord and reflects His nature has unfading beauty in God's sight.

Thought for the Day

Spiritually, men and women are equal; they have the same spirit-man within.

Reading: Joshua 16–18; Luke 2:1–24

God Honors Women

God honors and respects women. He loves and identifies with the spirit-man inside the female, and so He takes special care in regard to her. Because a spirit-man lives within the woman, the treatment of the woman by the man has to be taken very seriously. When you have offended the spirit-man, you have offended God. You have to be careful what you do to the spirit within either the male or the female.

Some men forget that there is a spirit-man inside of women. If a man impatiently tells a female, "I don't like your moods," he should check to whom he is speaking. There is a spirit inside that precious body. One reason why the Bible tells us not to go to sleep without resolving our anger (see Ephesians 4:26) is that it's very important to treat well those who have been created in the image of God. James reinforced this theme: "*With the tongue we praise our Lord and Father, and with it we curse men, who have been made in God's likeness....My brothers, this should not be*" (James 3:9–10). You see, anger or resentment is a spiritual matter.

"Husbands, in the same way be considerate as you live with your wives, and treat them with respect...so that nothing will hinder your prayers" (1 Peter 3:7). God is saying to men, "Wait a minute. The woman isn't just a body of flesh. She has a spirit. The way you treat her will affect your prayer life." Therefore, if you don't treat a woman with consideration and respect, it could block your relationship with God. God won't hear your prayers until you go back and make things right with her because you have interfered with the spirit-man in the woman.

Thought for the Day

God loves and identifies with the spirit-man inside the female, and so He takes special care in regard to her.

Reading: Joshua 19–21; Luke 2:25–52

March 26

Get Out of the Wilderness

In order for a woman to become what God intends, she needs to be filled with the Holy Spirit, submitted to the Word, and learning to follow the leading of the Spirit. Do you remember what happened when Adam and Eve rebelled against God? What did God do? He put them out of the garden. A garden is a specifically manicured, prepared place. Outside the garden is wilderness. Wilderness people are wild; they devour one another. God wants us to be transformed by the renewing of our minds and to get out of the wilderness. (See Romans 12:2.)

Women, you must develop an ongoing, intimate relationship with God. You can't just read popular women's magazines or watch talk shows and expect to get revelation from God. These sources are usually headed deeper and deeper into the wilderness. They're leading you into perversion and depravity. The wilderness mentality of women is, "I don't need anybody else. I'm going to make it on my own. I don't care what anyone says; I don't need any man." I believe you know that's wilderness talk because, deep inside, you have a garden desire. You need to be in relationship with God, and you need to be in relationship with men—with a husband or with your brothers in the Lord—in order to be who you were created to be.

This is the ideal, and God wants you to work back to it. He wants you to have the spirit of the garden so that you will be in continual fellowship with Him. Then you will be able to experience fulfillment both as a spiritual being created in God's image, and as a female, created for God's good purposes.

Thought for the Day

God wants us to be transformed by the renewing of our minds and to get out of the wilderness.

Reading: Joshua 22–24; Luke 3

March 27

A Drive to Excel

With your help I can advance against a troop; with my God I can scale a wall.
—2 Samuel 22:30

God gave the male what psychologists call *ego.* I like to call it *a drive to excel.* The man's ego is simply a spirited attitude to win. God gave him this attitude to help him overcome obstacles in life. Every male is supposed to have this spirit. When he doesn't, he's not fully functioning.

A male always wants to outdo. This is one reason why men are so competitive. Sports are usually more attractive to males than females because they provide a release for this drive to excel. A man isn't meant to release his drive to excel just on the basketball court. There are men who can shoot a three-pointer but who don't bring up their children to rely on the Lord. There are men who have all kinds of sports trophies but who haven't learned to take their drive and channel it properly through the Word of God. The mark of a man who knows God is, "I know I can make it, and nobody can stop me."

Ego, in itself, is not a bad thing. Having a drive to excel is good because it's part of a man's equipment for leadership. When a man has to bring his family through a difficult situation, he'd better have some ego. He'd better believe in himself to the point that he can say, "This thing can't overcome me. My God will supply all my needs." He can be confident because He trusts in God's provision. He can be strong because He believes he is everything that God says he is in Christ. That's the definition of a redeemed ego.

Thought for the Day

God gave the man a drive to excel to help him overcome obstacles in life.

Reading: Judges 1–3; Luke 4:1–30

March 28

Mistaking Power for Strength

Because men have lost the knowledge of what God created them to be, they often mistake power for strength. Much of a man's tendency to control comes from a false understanding of how his own nature is to function in dominion.

Men have a deep desire to prove they are strong. It is one of the underlying issues every male faces, whether he is a ten-year-old boy or a ninety-year-old man. Men's internal passion to prove their strength is inherent in their nature. All men have it in some form or another because of the purpose for which they were created. It is built in by God in order to give them the ability to fulfill their purpose of leading, protecting, and providing. The problem is that the male's passion to prove his strength has been perverted and abused by Satan and the sinful nature.

Because of this desire to prove their strength, there is nothing more frightening to most men than to be perceived as weak. Again, this fear is a result of the fall. Because his true relationship with the female has been distorted, he feels vulnerable in this area of strength. He doesn't want to be perceived as being helpless or out of control by either males or females. This fear drives the man to feel as if he has to constantly prove himself. It is the source of his aggressive spirit and his often overly competitive nature. It is also the source of some men's tendency toward violence. A lot of men have muscle but are weak in their minds, their hearts, their discipline, their responsibility, and their spirits.

> *Some trust in chariots and some in horses, but we trust in the name of the* LORD *our God.* (Psalm 20:7)

Thought for the Day

Men's internal passion to prove their strength is built in by God to give them the ability to fulfill their purpose of leading, protecting, and providing.

Reading: Judges 4–6; Luke 4:31–44

March 29

A Truly Strong Man

Men need a picture of what a truly strong man looks like. A strong man is a man who understands his God-given strength. To be a strong man is to maximize all your potential for the purpose for which you were created. Jesus was the strongest Man who ever lived, yet He is also described as meek. Someone has said that meekness is power under control. That is what true strength is. It is power that is ready to be channeled into good and constructive purposes rather than irresponsible or selfish ones. *"Be strong in the Lord and in his mighty power"* (Ephesians 6:10).

Males didn't choose their position; God gave it to them. However, the problem is that many males have taken another position that they weren't given. If we voted for a man to become the president or prime minister of a country, but instead he took over by force and became a dictator, he'd be taking a position he wasn't given. The first position was given to him by legal authority; the other was seized.

Whenever you take your position by force, you've moved out of your legal standing. The difference between an elected head of state and a dictator is very simple. The first has authority and the second merely has power. To have authority means to have a right to govern. Therefore, if a man slaps his wife, kicks his children, and then says, "I'm the man of the house; I do what I want," that's an abuse of authority; it's merely wielding power over others. Whenever you abuse your power, you no longer have legitimate authority. Any time a man starts to dominate another human being, he is out of God's will.

Thought for the Day

To be a strong man is to maximize all your potential for the purpose for which you were created.

Reading: Judges 7–8; Luke 5:1–16

March 30

Strong and Courageous

A leader has been designed to take risks and meet challenges. God often gives men assignments that seem too big for them—and they are. They can be accomplished only through God's help. Yet the qualities of courage, strength, and daring enable men to take the necessary steps of faith that bring God's intervention.

It is impossible to be the leader of the family and of society if you are not strong and courageous. After Moses died, the Lord said to Joshua, *"Be strong and courageous, because you will lead these people..."* (Joshua 1:6). Joshua had a "family" of three million people to lead! God gave this young Israelite a job designed for a man. God added something to His command to Joshua. He said, "Be careful to obey all the commands." (See Joshua 1:7.)

A strong man has to be submitted to God's authority. No man can be strong if he is not accountable to someone else. A real man doesn't ignore authority. He remains in the garden of God's presence, praying and reading God's Word, so that he may understand and obey His commands. As a man of God, you must realize that you were not put in a leadership position because you are big, strong, or overbearing. You are put in that position because of your purpose. Your strength is meant to support that purpose.

Some men take their courage and strength and use them recklessly. When a man turns from God, takes his life into his own hands, and doesn't combine courage with common sense, he can cause himself and his family many problems. True courage and strength come only through confidence in the faithfulness of God and belief in His Word.

Thought for the Day

The qualities of courage, strength, and daring enable men to take the necessary steps of faith that bring God's intervention.

Reading: Judges 9–10; Luke 5:17–39

March 31

A Servant's Heart

A real man, a true leader, is a servant. He is not a ruler. He takes care of others before himself. Jesus said,

> *You know that the rulers of the Gentiles lord it over them, and their high officials exercise authority over them. Not so with you. Instead, whoever wants to become great among you must be your servant, and whoever wants to be first must be your slave–just as the Son of Man did not come to be served, but to serve, and to give his life as a ransom for many.* (Matthew 20:25–28)

The apostle Paul echoed this theme when he wrote, "*Each of you should look not only to your own interests, but also to the interests of others*" (Philippians 2:4), and "*Husbands, love your wives, just as Christ loved the church and gave himself up for her*" (Ephesians 5:25). How did Christ love His church? First of all, by giving Himself for her. This means that a man should give up his personal, private, ambitious, egotistical desires in order to serve his wife and family. He needs to emulate Christ's nature.

A true leader has *humility*, so that he is willing to learn from others and be corrected when need be. Some of the greatest moments in my life are times when my wife corrects me, gives me ideas, or provides insight on something that I haven't been able to do right. My wife has awesome resources within her. It takes a real man to submit to help. It takes a fool to avoid it. God is looking for a leader who makes himself fruitful by being pruned when necessary in order to yield a healthier and greater harvest.

Thought for the Day

A true leader has *humility,* so that he is willing to learn from others and be corrected when need be.

Reading: Judges 11–12; Luke 6:1–26

April 1

Created to Provide

The L*ORD God took the man and put him in the Garden of Eden*
to work it and take care of it.
—Genesis 2:15

Work was given to the male (1) to advance the purposes of God, (2) to bring the male fulfillment while using the skills and abilities God has given him, and (3) to enable the male to provide for his own needs as well as the needs of those for whom he is responsible.

A male's first priority is to remain continually in God's presence. It is through worship and communion with God that the man receives his life's vision, vocation, and work. Some men have forgotten that worship takes precedence over work. When your work interferes with your worship, you cease to fulfill the purpose of a real man.

Remember that the man was given work before the woman was created. This means that before a man needs a woman, and before he is ready for marriage, he needs work. He needs to find out what God is calling him to do. Then he can use his vocation and work to provide for his future wife and children.

God gave the man the responsibility for being the main provider for the family. A male is made for this purpose. In general, he's built physically stronger than the female, particularly in his upper body, because of God's command that he should work. A woman is supposed to marry someone who is already able to provide. If you look at the Old Testament, the way in which God's people married indicates what God instructed them to do regarding matrimony. The prospective groom would have to show that he could meet the standard of living prescribed by the bride's father, or he would have to earn the money before he could have her hand in marriage.

Thought for the Day

It is through worship and communion with God that the man receives his life's vision, vocation, and work.

Reading: Judges 13–15; Luke 6:27–49

April 2

Designed to Work

Whatever you do, work at it with all your heart, as working for the Lord, not for men, since you know that you will receive an inheritance from the Lord as a reward. It is the Lord Christ you are serving.

—Colossians 3:23–24

The nature of the work the male was given to do was not mindless labor—it was cultivation. Remember, to *cultivate* means to make something grow and produce a greater yield. *Cultivate* also means to make something fruitful, to develop it into its perfection. The man is to be a developer and a fruit producer. Since God gave this assignment to the male before the female was created, and before the first child was born, the purpose of the male is to develop and cultivate both people and things to God's glory.

God Himself worked when He created the world, and He still works to carry out His purposes. Paul said in Philippians 2:13, "*It is God who works in you to will and to act according to his good purpose.*" Because you are made in God's image and likeness, you are designed to work. Work is meant to include creativity and cultivation, not drudgery. It is also supposed to be kept in its proper place. In Genesis 2, the Bible says that God worked hard and completed His work, and then He stopped His work and rested. He didn't burn the midnight oil or work seven days a week just for the sake of working. He stopped working when it was appropriate. He told us to do the same. (See Exodus 20:9–10.)

Thought for the Day

Work is meant to include creativity and cultivation, not drudgery.

Reading: Judges 16–18; Luke 7:1–30

April 3

The Significance of Work

What is the significance of work? First, work exposes a man's potential. You cannot show what you have inside unless demands are made on it, and demands are placed on it by work.

Second, work allows a man to reflect God's nature. God gave the male work because it is related to his purpose. His purpose is to stay in the presence of the Lord and learn to rule and manage what God has given him to do. In this way, he can eventually fulfill God's complete plan for him, which is to have dominion over the earth.

Third, as we have discovered, work enables a man to provide for those for whom he is responsible in his position as visionary and leader. *Provide* comes from a Latin word meaning "to see ahead." The male should be a visionary. He should have a vision for his life, and he should work to see that it is accomplished—for himself, his family, and others under his care.

I once asked God, "Lord, with all the responsibilities you gave us men, how do we know we can fulfill them?" His answer was very, very simple. He said, "Whatever I call for, I provide for." God is the ultimate Provider. It is so true. God will provide whatever we need to fulfill our responsibilities. *"I can do everything through him who gives me strength"* (Philippians 4:13).

Thought for the Day

Work exposes your potential.

Reading: Judges 19–21; Luke 7:31–50

April 4

Fundamental to His Being

Many women don't understand the mental, emotional, and spiritual effect that losing a job has on a man. They cannot fully understand, because they are not designed to be providers; they are designed to be producers. When a man loses his job, it's as if his life has fallen apart. Some men actually end up losing their minds after they lose their jobs. Why do they have such an extreme reaction? It's because it's not just a job to them. It's their means of providing. One of their purposes for being has been taken away from them.

Some men can't handle the pressure to provide, so they run from responsibility. Maybe the man has six kids and can't feed them. He feels useless; he feels like a failure, so he leaves. We call his behavior neglectful or irresponsible. Although this behavior is very wrong, we must realize that the man is dealing with something internal that he may not understand, something fundamental to his being.

Suppose a man calls his wife and says, "Sweetheart, I have some bad news for you. I just got laid off from my job." This is how some women would react: "I'm not surprised. You haven't been able to hold a job for the last six months." What has she done by saying this? He feels humiliated and unwanted. Instead, she should say something like, "Well, honey, God says that He's our Source. I've always believed that if God made you my covering, He'll provide for you so you can provide for us. I love you for who you are, not because of the job you have."

> *Love...bears all things, believes all things, hopes all things, endures all things. Love never fails.* (1 Corinthians 13:4, 7–8 NKJV)

Thought for the Day

A man needs his wife to respect his desire to provide.

Reading: Ruth; Luke 8:1–25

April 5

Created to Protect

The male is like God's "security guard." When he shows up, everyone is supposed to feel protected and safe. Remember that the atmosphere of God's garden is His presence. Therefore, God essentially told Adam, "Protect the garden, but also protect the presence that is in it. Don't let anything disturb My presence here." It is up to males to maintain God's presence—at their homes, jobs, or any other place in society. They are to be protectors.

I hear some men saying, "I can't wait until I get married so I can practice what he's teaching." Don't wait until then. A man doesn't need to be married to be responsible for women. Start being the protector of every female who comes into your presence, because you were created to be responsible for her.

Any woman should feel safe with you when you understand that your purpose is to protect and guard her and to lead her into the things of God. What should happen if a woman comes to you destitute, broken, depressed, sad, or vulnerable, and she confides in you? The spirit of protection should come upon you. Lead her straight to God. Show her Jesus. Then exemplify His character by treating her in a fatherly or brotherly way.

Men, when you are dating, you don't protect a woman by throwing away your own armor. You don't take her for a drive at night and park in a secluded place. Keep the lights on bright. Keep the tape playing the Word of God. Keep the conversation in His light. It takes a real man to keep his hands to himself. That's true strength.

Thought for the Day

A male should be the protector of every female who comes into his presence.

Reading: 1 Samuel 1–3; Luke 8:26–56

April 6

A Natural Protector

A male is a natural protector. His bone structure and upper body strength are designed to defend, protect, and guard. Now, even if a man isn't tall or extremely muscular, he seems to have inner physical resources that enable him to defend. A man's wife should be able to run to him any time trouble comes.

The safest place for a woman should be in the arms of her husband. Yet one of the saddest things I've seen is men abusing their strength. Instead of using it to protect women, they use it to destroy them. When I think of a man hitting a woman, my whole body turns into a boiling pot of indignation. God gave him muscles to protect her, not to hurt her. *"Husbands ought to love their wives as their own bodies"* (Ephesians 5:28).

A man's wife and children are supposed to feel totally at peace in his presence. As soon as he shows up, everything is in order. When they hear his voice, everything is all right. When a daughter gets hurt, her father's presence makes her feel better. When a son goes away to college, becomes homesick, and feels as if his life is falling apart, he can call his father and hear him say, "Son, it's going to be okay." Suddenly, everything comes into place because Dad spoke a reassuring word. When a wife becomes frustrated or emotional about what's happening in the family, her husband can say, "God says He'll be here for us, and I will be here for us, too." That's a man's responsibility.

Thought for the Day

A male seems to have inner physical resources that enable him to defend.

Reading: 1 Samuel 4–6; Luke 9:1–17

April 7

Territorial Protectiveness

Males often exhibit a fighting spirit, which was given to them by God to protect and defend those for whom they are responsible. Jesus exhibited a strong, protective nature. In Matthew 18:6, He spoke of protecting those who believe in Him. He said, in essence, "If anyone tries to take My children away from Me, it would be better for him if he tied a rope around his neck, put a stone on the other end of the rope, walked down to the ocean, and jumped in. It would be better for him to do that than for Me to get My hands on him."

A man has a spirit in him that says, "I have to protect what is mine." He speaks in terms of "my wife," "my house," and "my car." This possessive attitude isn't negative in itself; it's from God. However, when it is not submitted to His purpose, it is often used to overpower or control others.

Some young men don't know what to do with their spirit of possessiveness and competition, so they end up forming gangs and competing against other neighborhoods or those who don't wear the same hat or jacket as they do. They need strong male role models who can teach them what to do with their territorial protectiveness.

Jesus got angry, but His anger was aimed at ungodliness and hypocrisy. The Bible says, *"For this purpose the Son of God was manifested, that he might destroy the works of the devil"* (1 John 3:8 KJV). Men aren't supposed to fight against other men, but against the spiritual forces that try to steal what God told them to protect.

Thought for the Day

Men are meant to fight against sin and Satan,
not flesh and blood.

Reading: 1 Samuel 7–9; Luke 9:18–36

April 8

Blessed to Be a Safeguard

Nothing in the world can bless a man like feeling responsible for his family's safety. Something happens within a man when he can provide his wife and children with a house. He has kept them safe from the elements. He's built a place for them, and he feels proud. When a man provides his wife with a car and the car breaks down, he feels instantly protective. He can't stand to think of her out there in the elements, so he immediately takes care of the situation.

It hurts a man to feel as if he has no part in protecting his wife and children, to feel as if he's just visiting in his own home—eating and sleeping there but not contributing to his family's welfare. It is important for men to participate in solving family problems. When something happens in the home or to the children, a wife should tell her husband. Why? He needs to fulfill his dominion purpose as protector.

Some men have lost sight of their responsibility to protect to such an extent that they check on their investments more often than they check to see if their families are all right. These men are using their natural gift of protectiveness, but they're using it on the wrong objects. A man should call his wife every day, making sure everything is okay. He should also call to see how his children are doing, so they can know their father is there for them. A man's spirit of territorial protection is to be used primarily to safeguard his family and others under his care.

Thought for the Day

Nothing in the world can bless a man like feeling responsible for his family's safety.

Reading: 1 Samuel 10–12; Luke 9:37–62

April 9

Reflecting God's True Nature

There are also celestial bodies and terrestrial bodies; but the glory of the celestial is one, and the glory of the terrestrial is another. There is one glory of the sun, another glory of the moon, and another glory of the stars; for one star differs from another star in glory.

—1 Corinthians 15:40–41 (NKJV)

When we think of "*glory*," we often think of a cloud filled with light. Yet glory in the sense that we are talking about here has to do with the nature of something. In its larger meaning, the word *glory* can be ascribed to every single thing. *The glory of something is its best expression of itself.*

One of the definitions of *glory* is "a distinguished quality or asset." You can see a flower in its true glory when it is in full bloom. You can see a leopard or a lion in its true glory when it is at its prime strength. You can see the sun in its true glory at twelve noon; after that, its light begins to fade. The glory of a thing is when it is at its full, true self. Therefore, glory refers to the manifestation, or the exposure, of the true nature of something.

When the Bible says that the purpose of humanity is to manifest the glory of God, it does not mean just lifting one's hands and saying, "Hallelujah!" That is praise, but it is not glory in the sense in which we are speaking. *Reflecting the glory of God means reflecting His true nature.* God's glory is often best manifested when we respond in a Christlike way in a difficult situation. At that moment, God is saying to you, "Let the glory come out now. Let people see what God is like under pressure."

Thought for the Day

Reflecting the glory of God means reflecting His true nature.

Reading: 1 Samuel 13–14; Luke 10:1–24

April 10

Different Kinds of Glory

A man ought not to cover his head, since he is the image and glory of God; but the woman is the glory of man.
—1 Corinthians 11:7

The female and the male each have a different kind of glory. The male is to reflect the "image and glory of God," while "the woman is the glory of man."

The Word of God is stating a profound truth. The women are reflecting the men, and it's not always a positive image. Of course, each individual is responsible before God for his or her own actions. For example, a woman may reflect her own selfishness rather than her husband's kindness. Solomon said, "*A wife of noble* ["*excellent*" NKJV] *character is her husband's crown, but a disgraceful wife is like decay in his bones*" (Proverbs 12:4). This verse shows the powerful influence a woman can have in a man's life. Yet men have a great responsibility to reflect the glory of God so that this can be reflected to the women in their lives, and the women can reflect God's glory in turn.

You can tell what the men in our society are like by observing the women. Look at our homes; who is running them? The women are often heading them by themselves. What does this tell you about the man? He is not being spiritually responsible because he is not fulfilling his purpose and position as head of the household. Look at our children; what is their hope for the future? Many of them are directionless. What do they tell you about the man? He is not providing them with vision. Look at the women; more of them are employed than are the men. What does this tell you about the man? He is not fulfilling his purpose as provider. The female—and often the children, as well—show you what the male is like.

Thought for the Day

The female and the male each have a different kind of glory.

Reading: 1 Samuel 15–16; Luke 10:25–42

The Bride Reflects Jesus

A new command I give you: Love one another. As I have loved you, so you must love one another. By this all men will know that you are my disciples, if you love one another.
—John 13:34–35

Jesus has a bride who is meant to reflect His nature. In the original Greek, her name is *Ecclesia*. The English translation of this word is "church." Jesus sent the church into the world to be a reflection of Himself. He said to His Father, "*I have given them* [the church] *the glory that you gave me, that they may be one as we are one*" (John 17:22). Jesus said to His bride, "The world will know who I am and that I was sent by the Father by the way in which you act, by your unity with one another. The world isn't going to come to Me to find out what I'm like; the world is going to come to the bride. If you don't love one another, they'll never know what I'm like."

Do you know why the people of the world aren't coming to Jesus as much as they should? It is because the church as a whole is often a terrible witness, and it is because many Christian marriages aren't reflecting God's glory. We are not living in the love and unity that Christ said would reveal His nature to the world. Therefore, while the church is to reflect Christ as His bride, it often does not do so. The Bible tells us that this is unnatural. Jesus is the perfect Husband and deserves to have His true nature reflected in His bride. The glory of the Lord is meant to be in the church.

Thought for the Day

Jesus sent the church into the world to be a reflection of Himself.

Reading: 1 Samuel 17–18; Luke 11:1–28

Reflecting God to the World

And we, who with unveiled faces all reflect the Lord's glory, are being transformed into his likeness with ever-increasing glory, which comes from the Lord, who is the Spirit.
—2 Corinthians 3:18

It has often been said that a marriage is a church within the church. If the world isn't seeing the nature of Christ through the church in the way that it should, perhaps we should begin to correct this problem by first looking at the relationships between husbands and wives, fathers and daughters, brothers and sisters in our homes. We should then look at the nature of the relationships between men and women in the church.

The woman's role as reflector of the man's love and nature can powerfully reveal God's remarkable love for humanity. She can show her family, her community, and the world what it means to be loved by God and to bear the image of the Creator. She can be a witness to the world of God's compassion and sacrifice for man, and of the joy and healing we can receive through His love.

Jesus said to His disciples of those in the world who are lost, "*Open your eyes and look at the fields! They are ripe for harvest*" (John 4:35). If men and women realize the powerful impact of their relationships on the salvation of the world, they will prayerfully and seriously consider how the dominion mandate can be fulfilled as they give and reflect God's love and nature in their day-to-day relationships.

Thought for the Day

If men and women realize the powerful impact of their relationships on the salvation of the world, they will give and reflect God's love in their day-to-day relationships.

Reading: 1 Samuel 19–21; Luke 11:29–54

April 13

God's Good Idea

God did not create the woman as an afterthought but as an integral part of His plan in creation. As such, He designed and built her in His love and with particular care. Her uniqueness is a reflection of God's purposes and design for her.

Women, you don't understand how special you are. Adam hadn't even imagined the woman, but God had her particularly in mind. In Genesis 2:18, God said, "*It is not good for the man to be alone. I will make a helper suitable for him.*" Adam was fumbling around in the bush thinking up animals' names. God said, "This is not good. This man needs help." So it was God who said that the man needed the woman. You are God's good idea and His unique creation.

A woman is a product of God; this makes her God's property. If you handle her, you are handling God's idea. If you curse at a woman, you are cursing at God's idea. If you slap a woman, you are slapping God's idea in the face. If you abandon a woman, you are abandoning God's idea.

Women, no matter what men might say about you, no matter what you might think about yourself, you are a good idea. God's mind thought of you, and God's Spirit brought you into being. You are the result of His idea, and that makes you very valuable to Him.

Thought for the Day

God created women as an integral part of His plan in creation.

Reading: 1 Samuel 22–24; Luke 12:1–31

April 14

The Woman Was Placed in the Garden

Then the man and his wife heard the sound of the LORD God as he was walking in the garden in the cool of the day.
—Genesis 3:8

God specifically placed the woman in the garden of Eden along with the man. In Genesis 3:8, we read that God walked in the garden in the cool of the day in order to meet with Adam and Eve. The garden represents man's relationship with God, the place of fellowship.

You cannot be the kind of woman you are supposed to be outside of God any more than a man can be anything outside of God. Any woman who is outside a relationship with the Lord is a dangerous woman, just as a man who is outside a relationship with the Lord is dangerous. You can be who you were created to be, and you can fulfill the purpose you were meant to fulfill, only as long as you remain in the garden of fellowship with God. Paul admonishes in Ephesians 5:17–18, *"Therefore do not be foolish, but understand what the Lord's will is....Be filled with the Spirit."*

The female cannot become what God intends unless she is continually in fellowship with Him, filled with His Spirit, learning His will, and obeying His Word. Many women today are not living godly lives. They have rebelled against God's plan. They are living outside the garden in the wilderness. If this describes your life, return to the garden of fellowship with God today. Your heavenly Father is waiting for you. *"I will give them a heart to know me, that I am the LORD. They will be my people, and I will be their God, for they will return to me with all their heart"* (Jeremiah 24:7).

Thought for the Day

A woman cannot fulfill her purpose unless she is in relationship with God.

Reading: 1 Samuel 25–26; Luke 12:32–59

April 15

Was the Woman Cursed?

After Adam and Eve rebelled, God made some specific statements to the woman. I want to strongly emphasize that these statements were not curses. The Bible does not say that God cursed either the man or the woman. God said, *"Cursed is the ground because of you; through painful toil you will eat of it all the days of your life. It will produce thorns and thistles for you, and you will eat the plants of the field"* (Genesis 3:17–18). In other words, God said to Adam that the earth would suffer from their disobedience, and they would have to struggle to survive in it. Moreover, God did not curse the woman by making her a child-bearer. (See verse 16.) He didn't say, "Just for that, now you're going to have children, and it's going to hurt."

Adam and Eve were always meant to have children. Eve already had the ability to bear children so that humanity could reproduce after its kind. That ability was established before sin came into the picture. So bearing children is not a curse. Rather, when you bear a child, you are fulfilling part of God's purpose for humanity. However, God told Eve that, because of sin, she was now going to experience pain in childbearing. God made it clear that pain—not the ability to have the child—was the product of the fall.

Many women today consider childbearing and child-rearing to be a burden because they do not receive enough support in this from their husbands. The Scripture says in Genesis 1:28, *"God blessed them and said to them, 'Be fruitful'."* Both female and male were supposed to be fruitful. That meant that any babies Eve would bear would belong to both of them—to love and to be responsible for.

Thought for the Day

When you bear a child, you are fulfilling part of God's purpose for humanity.

Reading: 1 Samuel 27–29; Luke 13:1–22

April 16

Principles of Woman's Uniqueness

Review these principles of the woman's uniqueness in creation and reflect on how they apply to your everyday life—directly for yourself, if you are a woman, and in your relationships with women, if you are a man.

1. Reflecting the glory of God means reflecting His nature to the world.
2. The male and the female each have a different kind of glory. The male is to reflect the "*image and glory of God,*" while "*the woman is the glory of man*" (1 Corinthians 11:7).
3. The woman's role as reflector of the man's love and nature can powerfully reveal God's remarkable love for humanity.
4. God did not create the woman as an afterthought but as an integral part of His plan in creation.
5. God specifically placed the woman in the garden of Eden, the place of fellowship with Him. A woman cannot fulfill her purpose unless she is in relationship with God.
6. God did not curse the woman or the man; He cursed the ground.
7. Child-bearing is not a curse. Adam and Eve were always meant to have children.
8. Before the fall, Eve already had the ability to bear children so that humanity could produce after its kind. Having children is fulfilling part of God's purpose for humanity.

So God created man in his own image, in the image of God he created him; male and female he created them. God blessed them.

(Genesis 1:27–28)

Heavenly Father, You have created woman as a reflector of love and as an integral part of Your plan for humanity. May the women who love You seek out Your best for their lives. May they long to dwell in Your presence as in the garden. Help them to see their uniqueness as a gift from a loving Father to be used for His good purposes and glory. In Jesus' name, amen.

Reading: 1 Samuel 30–31; Luke 13:23–35

April 17

Desire and Domination

After the fall, God told Eve, "*Your desire will be for your husband, and he will rule over you*" (Genesis 3:16). This was a change from their former relationship. This statement emphasizes the fact that the male and female were originally created to rule together. They were designed to function together equally. God had said to them, "*Fill the earth and subdue it*" (Genesis 1:28). Both of them were supposed to be rulers.

Though both the man and the woman would still rule, their relationship became distorted. First, God said to Eve that because of sin, "*Your desire shall be for your husband.*" Once a woman gets married, she has a desire, a longing, for her husband. Sometimes this desire can become controlling. Most women would not like to admit that they have this desire. However, many marriage counselors can confirm that it exists. They have counseled women who are being abused by men, and they have wondered how these women take it. While many women have a limit to their tolerance of abusive behavior, a woman's *tendency* is still this longing for her husband, this desire to please him at all costs.

God also told Eve that the man would develop an attitude of rulership over her. "*He will rule over you.*" He would feel as if he had to dominate her. This was not part of God's original plan. However, because of sin, the man's twisted perception of life would cause him to want to dominate the woman.

In God's creation plan, He never said that the male was to dominate the female. He said that man—as male and female—was to dominate the earth!

Thought for the Day

After the fall, the man developed a distorted desire to dominate the woman.

Reading: 2 Samuel 1–2; Luke 14:1–24

April 18

Restored by Redemption

For he has rescued us from the dominion of darkness and brought us into the kingdom of the Son he loves, in whom we have redemption, the forgiveness of sins.
—Colossians 1:13–14

Jesus Christ restored humanity to God's purpose and plan. I define the plan of God very simply. The first two chapters of Genesis are a depiction of God's perfect program for the spirit-man and his manifestation as male and female. Chapter 3 reveals how and why this program fell apart. Genesis 3 to Revelation 21, the last chapter of the Bible, explains what God has done and is still doing to restore humanity to His original program (and even beyond). The Bible is an account of God's restoration program, which He effected through various covenants with His people.

Christ's life, death, and resurrection accomplished the redemption of man. The sacrifice of the perfect Man made atonement for the sins of fallen man and restored humanity to the fellowship with God it had enjoyed in the garden of Eden. This means that the curse of sin is removed from people's lives when they receive Christ's redemptive work and are born again. Christ's own Spirit comes to dwell within them, they are restored to God's purposes, and they are able to love and serve God again.

Under the redemptive work of Christ, the woman is restored not only to fellowship with God, but also to the position of partner with her male counterpart. Therefore, she is not to be dominated or ruled by the male, because, if she were, it would mean that the redemptive work of Christ had not been successful.

Thought for the Day

Under the redemptive work of Christ, the woman is restored not only to fellowship with God, but also to the position of partner with her male counterpart.

Reading: 2 Samuel 3–5; Luke 14:25–35

April 19

Speaking the Truth from the Father

When the Counselor [Holy Spirit] *comes, whom I will send to you from the Father, the Spirit of truth who goes out from the Father, he will testify about me. And you also must testify, for you have been with me from the beginning.*
—John 15:26–27

From the Father *through* the Son *by* the Spirit, we are taught the truth, which we, in turn, teach others. This is part of man's dominion assignment carried out by redeemed men and women. The only instruction we are supposed to speak comes from the Father. The Father, through Jesus, gives instructions by the Holy Spirit to the bride, the church. Then the church takes the instructions from her Lord, Husband, and Everlasting Father, and speaks them out with authority as commands.

This is the principle behind Jesus' statements to believers regarding authority. He has given His Bride, the church, the authority to use His name to command sickness, disease, demons, and mountains. "*When Jesus had called the Twelve together, he gave them power and authority to drive out all demons and to cure diseases, and he sent them out to preach the kingdom of God and to heal the sick*" (Luke 9:1–2). (See also, for example, Matthew 17:20; Mark 16:17–18.)

As the bride of Christ, the church has the Father's instruction, authority, and power to speak and act with boldness in the world. The bride of Christ is empowered to declare things. "I bind you" is a command, not an instruction. "I loose you" is a command. (See, for example, Matthew 16:19.) "Come out of him" is a command. The church binds, looses, heals, and delivers, not as teachings, but as commands under the authority of our Teacher and Husband, Jesus Christ.

Thought for the Day

The Father, through Jesus, gives instructions by His Holy Spirit to the bride, the church.

Reading: 2 Samuel 6–8; Luke 15:1–10

April 20

Male as Founder

In Scripture, there is no such thing as the son of two fathers. God always speaks of lineage in terms of one man—the father. Why is that important? Because the minute you start bringing in another ancestry or lineage, you split the fatherhood. There can be only one source. That is why the Bible says, *"For this reason a man will leave his father and mother..."* (Matthew 19:5). It doesn't say the woman leaves because, when she marries, she inherits another "father." The husband becomes responsible for his wife 100 percent. He provides, sustains, nourishes, upholds, and supports.

The word *father* also implies authorship, as well as the legitimate authority of something. "Father" possesses inherent authority.

In addition, the concept of father includes "founder" or "foundation." That's why companies, institutions, and movements use the word *father* to describe the person who established the organization, institution, or movement. The men who established the United States of America are referred to as the "Founding Fathers." Nelson Mandela is known as the "Father of the New South Africa." If someone founded something, he is called the father of it. Why? He generated it. God built the male to found future generations and to be the foundation on which they develop. For the next few days, we will be exploring these essential characteristics of the male as founder and foundation.

Thought for the Day

God built the male to found future generations.

Reading: 2 Samuel 9–11; Luke 15:11–32

April 21

The Father of Human Society

In God's creation plan, the male is the father of human society and social relationships. Out of man came the woman and marriage. Out of marriage came children. So then we have a family. When families gather together, we have a community. When a multiplicity of communities comes together, we have a nation and a society.

The male is the source of the human family. This puts an awesome responsibility on the man as a husband and father. The male is the source, sustainer, nurturer, and protector of the female because God took the woman out of the man.

God did not go back to the soil to produce a woman. Why? He did not want the soil to support the woman. God made Adam to be a father. God wanted a father to represent Him on earth. Out of a father—Adam—was produced a woman to be sustained and nurtured by the man. So God created man to be a father like Himself. Together, the man and the woman come together in marriage. Again, the Scripture never said that the wife leaves her father. Why? Her husband is to be her "father" in the sense of being her source and sustainer.

In our society, too many women are called upon to do a father's job. Women were not created to be sustainers. Too many men have abandoned their women and left them alone to sustain themselves and the offspring that the men have given them. Whatever is produced by a father must be sustained and nourished by him.

Thought for the Day

The male is the source of the human family.

Reading: 2 Samuel 12–13; Luke 16

The Foundation of the House

Men were created to be the source and sustainer of the human family. They are the underpinning not only for their homes, but also for their churches, communities, and nations. Men, being the source and sustainer doesn't mean that you lord it over others, or that you necessarily run things. It means you are *responsible* for everything.

The kingdom of God teaches that the man is the foundation of the house—he carries everything. As a husband, you are the foundation of your marriage. As a father, you are the foundation of your home. As a pastor, you are the foundation of your ministry.

Fatherhood is God's way of building and sustaining the human family. His plan is to fulfill His vision of the earth as an extension of His heavenly kingdom. This happens as the male functions as the foundation of the home, allowing all those he is responsible for the protection and freedom to grow and prosper as God intended.

Human beings are ignorant about the nature of their true purpose, and this includes fatherhood. King David described the root cause of our confusion: "*They know nothing, they understand nothing. They walk about in darkness; all the foundations of the earth are shaken*" (Psalm 82:5). Darkness implies ignorance. A lack of knowledge and understanding promotes ignorance, which jeopardizes the very foundations of society. When people lack knowledge and understanding of the basic, fundamental laws of God, all life goes off track and ends in failure. True fatherhood is the answer to resecuring the foundations of our societies.

Thought for the Day

As the foundation, men are responsible for everything.

Reading: 2 Samuel 14–15; Luke 17:1–19

April 23

Just as the Father Is Faithful

As I travel around the world, I see evil everywhere. At times, I ask the same question Jeremiah did: *"Why does the way of the wicked prosper?"* (Jeremiah 12:1). There are drug pushers, pimps, thieves, and dishonest businesspeople everywhere who have big homes, nice cars, boats, and lots of money. What is the ultimate source of all that they have? How do they sustain their lives?

The answer to those questions is generally the same answer as to why the righteous prosper. The Father (Sustainer) sends the rain upon the just and the unjust because everyone and everything is from Him. (See Matthew 5:45.) Why? Because God is a good, faithful, and patient Father; He sustains, nourishes, and protects. He *"is patient with you, not wanting anyone to perish, but everyone to come to repentance"* (2 Peter 3:9).

Jesus understood that with God continually as His Source, only good things could come from Him. The religious leaders criticized Jesus for doing miracles, saying that He was from the devil. Yet He answered His critics by saying, *"Which of you fathers, if your son asks for a fish, will give him a snake instead? Or if he asks for an egg, will give him a scorpion? If you then, though you are evil, know how to give good gifts to your children, how much more will your Father in heaven give the Holy Spirit to those who ask him!"* (Luke 11:11–13).

What has Jesus taught us? Simply this: God's sustenance does not depend on behavior or how it is received. He sustains what He creates because of His goodness. Our heavenly Father gives men a remarkable example for their role as sustainers and nurturers of their families.

Thought for the Day

God is a good, faithful, and patient Father; He sustains, nourishes, and protects.

Reading: 2 Samuel 16–18; Luke 17:20–37

April 24

"Dad Is Destiny"

Dad is destiny." The words sprang from the page in *U.S.News & World Report*[1] and exploded in my mind like an atom bomb. I could not believe what I was reading. Even more surprising was the source from which I was reading those words—words that seemed to spring from the heart of one of my seminars.

For thirty years, I have lectured and counseled thousands of individuals on the subjects of relationships, family development, and marriage. One of the greatest concerns I have carried over these years is the male crisis facing most of our communities. I emphatically believe that the key to the restoration and preservation of a sane and healthy society is the salvaging of the male, especially as a responsible father. Reading those words in such a popular news magazine gave me great encouragement.

It is a source of enormous comfort and relief to see that contemporary behavioral scientists, psychologists, and government bodies are finally agreeing with what Christian leaders have known all along.

The statement "Dad is destiny" embodies both the problem and the solution for the majority of society's ills. In it lies the key to the salvation and restoration of mankind. About twenty-five hundred years ago, the prophet Malachi spoke of the work and purpose of the coming Messiah, declaring, *"He will turn the hearts of the fathers to their children, and the hearts of the children to their fathers"* (Malachi 4:6). In this Scripture we see the divine assessment of man's fundamental problem—a fatherless society!

Thought for the Day

The statement "Dad is destiny" embodies both the problem and the solution for the majority of society's ills.

Reading: 2 Samuel 19–20; Luke 18:1–23

[1] Joseph P. Shapiro, Joannie M. Schrof, Mike Tharp, and Dorian Friedman, "Honor Thy Children," *U.S.News & World Report*, February 27, 1995.

April 25

A Foundational Problem

The church cannot fix society's problems when the foundation is out of place. As we read in the Psalms, "*When the foundations are being destroyed, what can the righteous do?*" (Psalm 11:3). No matter how much the church works at correcting social ills, if the foundation that God laid for the family is not in place, even the work of the righteous will not be successful. The devil does not care as much if the church is filled with women, because as long as men do not come back to their heavenly Father, then the women and their children are fatherless. Fatherhood is the foundation of the family, the church, and the culture.

If societies and nations have problems with drugs, unwed mothers, teenage pregnancy, corruption, and violence, then they must go back to the foundation in order to solve these problems. If they have a national problem, then they must go back into the communities to find the problem. Community problems are rooted in the families that make up each community. When we check to see what the families' problems are, we must look at marriages. When we examine the condition of our marriages, we discover that husbands and wives are divorced, mothers have been abandoned, and men are not sustaining their families.

What does all this boil down to? Brothers, we are at the root of the problem affecting the nations! The foundational source has a problem: men are not being the fathers God created them to be.

Thought for the Day

The church cannot fix society's problems when the foundation is out of place.

Reading: 2 Samuel 21–22; Luke 18:24–43

Who Is the Rock?

When I was in London for a speaking engagement a few years ago, I noticed a foundation being dug for a new hotel not far from the Millennium Dome. From my own hotel room, I could look down at the construction site. I took a photo of it because I thought it was such a striking reminder of what it takes to build a tall building, and I wanted to use it as an illustration in my seminars.

When you construct a building, what do you do first? You build *down*. That's remarkable, isn't it? As I watched the men at that construction site, they kept digging and digging, and I thought, *My goodness, that hole is equivalent to about five floors below ground level.* What were they looking for? Solid rock.

In a similar way, although a man is to be a stable foundation for his family, who is actually carrying the whole structure? A physical building rests on its foundation, but the foundation is resting on rock. Therefore, if you're going to be a real man, you have to be resting on the solid Rock.

If you are thinking that being a foundation is too much responsibility for you, you are right. It is not enough to know your function as a man; you have to know who to lean on in order to weather the storms. Now, the male is the foundation, but the male is not the Rock. Who is that Rock? It is Jesus Christ.

Unless the LORD builds the house, its builders labor in vain.

(Psalm 127:1)

Thought for the Day

The male is the foundation, but the male is not the Rock!

Reading: 2 Samuel 23–24; Luke 19:1–27

April 27

Hold On to the Rock

Jesus said you can't build your house on sand or your house will collapse. (See Matthew 7:24–27.) You can't say, therefore, "I'm a man. I have this, and I am that, so everything's going to be okay." That isn't enough.

I'm a pastor, a businessman, a government advisor, an investor, a speaker, a facilitator of seminars, and an author, but when my storm comes, I have to grab onto a Rock that is mightier than I. As King David's said, *"From the ends of the earth I call to you, I call as my heart grows faint; lead me to the rock that is higher than I"* (Psalm 61:2). No matter how successful you are, you had better find the Rock because your family depends upon you for survival.

As you hold on to the Rock in the midst of whatever crisis you face, your foundation will remain sure. Then, as Paul said, you will be able to build a temple to God on it. *"In* [Christ] *the whole building is joined together and rises to become a holy temple in the Lord"* (Ephesians 2:21). In Jesus, the whole building is held together.

If your building is pure, who dwells in it? God comes to dwell in a well-built life and a well-built family. If He's your Rock, He lives in you. And if you are a strong foundation in Him, He lives in whatever you're holding together—whether it's a marriage, a family, a church, or a business. It becomes a holy dwelling place for Him.

Thought for the Day

As you hold on to the Rock in the midst of whatever crisis you face, your foundation will remain sure.

Reading: 1 Kings 1–2; Luke 19:28–48

Watch Out for Cracks

In him [Jesus] the whole building is joined together and rises to become a holy temple in the Lord.
—Ephesians 2:21

We have seen that the key to constructing any building is the structure's foundation, because the foundation carries the weight of the building. The quality of a foundation determines the stability and value of what is built upon it. Having the characteristics of a strong foundation is therefore essential for every man.

A building can have a number of problems and not be condemned. But if a crack is discovered in the foundation, it doesn't matter how nice the interior is, the building will need serious repair and may well be condemned. Men, we need to be careful not to allow any cracks in our character. If you see a crack developing, fix it immediately! Do not let it get any bigger, or the whole structure may collapse. You may think that character lapses affect only you, but they also affect those entrusted to your protection, teaching, and care. Strengthen your character, and you will strengthen your entire family.

> *Make every effort to add to your faith goodness; and to goodness, knowledge; and to knowledge, self-control; and to self-control, perseverance; and to perseverance, godliness; and to godliness, brotherly kindness; and to brotherly kindness, love. For if you possess these qualities in increasing measure, they will keep you from being ineffective and unproductive in your knowledge of our Lord Jesus Christ.*
>
> (2 Peter 1:5–8)

Thought for the Day

Character lapses affect not only you, but also those entrusted to your protection, teaching, and care.

Reading: 1 Kings 3–5; Luke 20:1–26

April 29

A Sure Foundation

He will be the sure foundation for your times, a rich store of salvation and wisdom and knowledge.
—Isaiah 33:6

The most important part of a building is the part you can't see. You can see the walls, the doors, the lighting, and the furnishings of a building, but you can't see the foundation once it is laid and the building is built upon it. Likewise, men are to be like Jesus as a "sure foundation" for their families. And they are to do what they have to do for those around them without drawing attention to themselves.

You don't see a foundation. Why? It's too busy carrying everything. Real men do not advertise their responsibility. Real men do not go around telling everyone including their wives what they're doing for them. Real men do not announce to the community what they're doing for their families. You just see the family functioning well and working together. The English word *husband* is derived from an Old Norse word meaning *householder*. We can say that the husband is meant to "hold the house" intact. He's the glue that keeps his family together. Likewise, a good pastor doesn't tell the church members everything he's doing for them; the community just sees or experiences the results of his work.

Real men are quiet. They just carry the responsibility. Become a man that your family, community, and nation can stand secure on, knowing that, in Christ, you won't collapse beneath them, regardless of what forces come against you.

Thought for the Day

Become a man that your family, community, and nation can stand secure on.

Reading: 1 Kings 6–7; Luke 20:27–47

April 30

Principles of the Male as Foundation

Today, review these principles of the male as foundation and reflect on how you can apply them in your everyday life—directly for yourself, if you are a man, and in your relationships with men, if you are a woman.

1. The concept of father includes "founder" and "foundation."
2. The male is the father of human society and social relationships.
3. The kingdom of God teaches that the man is the foundation of the house—he carries everything.
4. The divine assessment of man's fundamental problem is a fatherless society. (See Malachi 4:6.)
5. The male is the foundation, but he is not the Rock. Jesus Christ is the Rock.
6. A man needs to be careful not to allow any cracks in the foundation of his character, which could lead to disaster for his family.
7. A foundation functions without being seen. As the foundation, men are to do what they have to do for those around them without drawing attention to themselves.

In [Christ] *the whole building is joined together and rises to become a holy temple in the Lord.* (Ephesians 2:21)

Heavenly Father,
Thank you for giving Jesus as the Rock and sure foundation for our lives on this earth and for eternity. Help us always to hold on to Him as the Rock that is higher than we are. Help us to develop His character so we can be solid foundations for our families. In His precious name, amen.

Reading: 1 Kings 8–9; Luke 21:1–19

May 1

Good versus Best

Men and women can fulfill their God-given purposes by understanding how to be effective in life. We have seen that effectiveness does not mean just doing good things but rather doing the *right* thing. Wouldn't it be sad to be serious and committed and faithful—to the wrong thing? It would be terrible to be busy doing the wrong things your entire life.

It is possible to do good things but not the things that are best based on God's purposes for you. One of the devil's greatest weapons against my life is to get me busy doing things that are good but that are not right and best for me.

God created each of us with a purpose. That purpose is what's right for us. Suppose Jesus had become a priest in the Sanhedrin, the highest council and tribunal of the Jews. That would have been a good thing. Suppose He had become a member of the Pharisees and been one of the leaders in the social structure of Galilee and Judea. That would have been a good thing. Suppose He had become a social worker, helping the poor, feeding multitudes of people every day with bread and fish. Would that have been a good thing? Sure. Suppose He had devoted every hour to healing the sick and raising the dead. That would have been a good thing, wouldn't it? Yet none of these things would have been the right thing for Him in fulfilling His chief purpose of being the Savior of humanity.

Jesus was always able to say, in effect, "I know the purpose for My life. Don't distract Me with things that are merely good. I must pursue the highest purpose."

Thought for the Day

It's possible to do what is good but not what is right.

Reading: 1 Kings 10–11; Luke 21:20–38

May 2

Sidetracked in Life

Isn't it time to stop wasting your life? Discovering our purpose enables us to stop wasting our lives and start fulfilling our potential. We must be careful not to become sidetracked along the way. The greatest way to destroy someone is to distract the person from his or her true purpose.

In the Old Testament, Nehemiah fulfilled an important purpose in life, but he might have been sidetracked. He was in exile serving as cupbearer to the king of Persia when he heard that Jerusalem was still in a broken-down condition. He was distressed and determined, "I've got to repair the city." So he prayed, and he obtained permission from the king to rebuild the wall of Jerusalem. God's favor was on his plans because this was the purpose for which he had been created. He went and started to rebuild the wall with the help of the remnant of Jews in Jerusalem.

Some men near Jerusalem didn't like what Nehemiah was doing, and they tried to stop him. They ridiculed and slandered him, but he kept on with the work. They conspired to kill him, but he armed some of the workers and thwarted the plot. They tried to fill him with fear and make him flee for his life, but he remained steadfast. One of the last things they tried is usually the most effective means of sidetracking people. They said, "Come, let's have a meeting; let's discuss what you're doing. Maybe we can help you." (See Nehemiah 1–6.) Yet Nehemiah wasn't fooled. He told them, *"I am carrying on a great project and cannot go down. Why should the work stop while I leave it and go down to you?"* (Nehemiah 6:3).

Don't be distracted from your purpose in God!

Thought for the Day

Discovering our purpose enables us to stop wasting our lives and start fulfilling our potential.

Reading: 1 Kings 12–13; Luke 22:1–20

May 3

PARENTS AND PURPOSE

Did Jesus have an adolescent problem? The answer is, very simply, no. Why? One reason is that His purpose was reinforced by His earthly father and mother from birth. Somehow I believe that God would love for all parents to know Him so well that they would have an idea of the life purpose of their children.

The angel Gabriel said to Mary, "*You will be with child and give birth to a son, and you are to give him the name Jesus. He will be great and will be called the Son of the Most High*" (Luke 1:31–32). An angel of the Lord told Joseph, "*You are to give him the name Jesus, because he will save his people from their sins*" (Matthew 1:21). When Jesus was born, Joseph and Mary could talk to Him about His purpose. Even though, at the time, they didn't fully understand the implications of His name, they could tell Him, "You're going to be a Savior." The Hebrew meaning of the name Jesus is "Jehovah-saved," or "the Lord is salvation." In essence, Jesus' name means "Savior."

I can't emphasize strongly enough that knowing your purpose is crucial for your life's course. Every young person comes to a time when he or she leaves childhood and enters adulthood. This is the time in which young people are trying to discover who they are and why they are. This is also often the time when we lose them or gain them—lose them to a destructive lifestyle and a wasted life or gain them for a positive, fulfilling future. Purpose, therefore, is a key to a young person's effectiveness and happiness in life.

Thought for the Day

Jesus' purpose was reinforced by Joseph and Mary from birth.

Reading: 1 Kings 14–15; Luke 22:21–46

May 4

Don't Give Up on a Purposeful Life

All who heard Him were astonished at His understanding and answers....His mother said to Him, "Son, why have You done this to us? Look, Your father and I have sought You anxiously." And He said to them, "Why did you seek Me? Did you not know that I must be about My Father's business?"

–Luke 2:47–49 (NKJV)

When Jesus was twelve years old, He went to Jerusalem with His parents to celebrate the Feast of the Passover. When the feast was over, His parents started for home, thinking that Jesus was among the large group of relatives and friends traveling with them. When they didn't find Him, they went back to Jerusalem and finally found Him in the temple courts. They said, "Why did you leave us, Son? Why did you do this to us?" His answer was very powerful. At twelve years of age, He was able to say to His parents, *"I must be about My Father's business."*

Are you still questioning what you are about? Are you still wondering what kind of business your Father is in and which part you are to play in the company? Are you still "changing your major" in life every three years? Do you find you can't graduate from God's preparatory school into God's work world?

I know it's not easy to take a hard look at yourself, but it's necessary if you're going to discover your true purpose in life. You will be busy doing meaningful work when you learn why you are here. At twelve years of age, Jesus was busy with His purpose. Isn't that an exciting way to live? Don't give up on having a purposeful life, no matter what your age. Get busy with the right thing.

Thought for the Day

Don't give up on having a purposeful life, no matter what your age.

Reading: 1 Kings 16–18; Luke 22:47–71

May 5

Individually Responsible

Doing the right thing in life always starts with a relationship with God. As we have seen, God deals with the spirit-man inside us because *"God is spirit, and his worshipers must worship in spirit and in truth"* (John 4:24). We worship God with our spirits, not with our genders. Therefore, spiritually, it does not matter to God whether you are male or female. He is concerned with the spirit-man.

That means if you are a woman, before God, your spirit does not depend on your husband. If you are a man, before God, your spirit does not depend upon your wife. Many men seem to have this impression. They drop their wives off at church because they believe their wives are going to cover for them. *She's the spiritual one in the house,* they think. *She'll pray for the kids, and she'll pray for me. I'll just go and play baseball.* Yet the man within the male and the man within the female are each responsible to God.

Many women misunderstand this truth, also. They seem to be waiting for their husbands to become Christians before they will worship God. If their husbands don't care about God, that fact has nothing to do with their own worship of Him. The Bible says that every person must stand on his own feet before God. He is going to deal with us Spirit to spirit. (See Romans 14:10.)

To live in your purpose, you must make your own decision to develop a consistent and deep relationship with God through Christ. *"Make every effort to be found spotless, blameless and at peace with him....Grow in the grace and knowledge of our Lord and Savior Jesus Christ"* (2 Peter 3:14, 18).

Thought for the Day

Doing the right thing in life always starts with a relationship with God.

Reading: 1 Kings 19–20; Luke 23:1–25

May 6

WHAT IS AN ANCHOR?

We have this hope as an anchor for the soul, firm and secure.
—Hebrews 6:19

Merriam-Webster's 11th Collegiate Dictionary defines *anchor* as "a reliable or principal support: mainstay" and "something that serves to hold an object firmly." Another definition is "anything that gives stability and security." You need stability and security in an environment that is unstable and insecure. This is a description of the world we live in.

Men serve not only as the foundation, but also as the anchor of the human family. As a verb, *anchor* means "to fasten, to stop, or to rest." Men are supposed to "fasten" the society—to secure it with beliefs and principles that don't change. The male is also supposed to stop things from happening that are harmful to others. I am amazed at what men allow to happen—in their homes, with their children, in their communities. As anchors, men can stop their families from being swept away by the currents of immorality, stabilize uncertain youth, and bring safety and order back to communities. An anchor also brings rest: when people have a true anchor present in their lives, they experience an inner peace.

Men, you should think of your family as a ship, and you as the anchor of that ship. A ship has no foundation of its own. The hull, the masts, the sails, the rigging, and even the helm can't fulfill that function. Your boat may look beautiful on the outside; yet, by itself, it contains no foundation. The only thing that secures a boat is an anchor. When the anchor is in place, the entire hull comes to rest. Even if the ship is beaten, twisted, and torn by waves, a strong anchor keeps it from breaking apart and allows it to weather the storms.

Thought for the Day

Men are supposed to "fasten" society—to secure it with beliefs and principles that don't change.

Reading: 1 Kings 21–22; Luke 23:26–56

May 7

Is Your Anchor Strong Enough?

When I was growing up in the Bahamas, where I still live, my friends and I had a little boat called a Boston Whaler. We worked during the summers and bought our own boat with our earnings. We would go out and water ski every day after school.

One day, we were skiing when we decided to do a little diving off a reef. We fastened the anchor to a rock. But the current was so strong that it pulled the anchor and actually broke it. Now we were in danger; we had a boat without an anchor in a current. Fortunately, the current carried the boat to where we were able to get home safely. But the experience emphasized for me that having an anchor is not enough. Your anchor must be able to handle the rough currents of life.

The only way an anchor will be truly tested is during intense pressure. Men, you must realize that if you break under pressure, your "ship" will become a victim of life's currents and storms. Just as it is not enough merely to say your boat has a strong anchor, it is not good enough merely to say, "I am a man." You have to ask, "What kind of man am I? What currents and storms am I really able to handle?"

The Scripture assures us, "*God is faithful; he will not let you be tempted beyond what you can bear. But when you are tempted, he will also provide a way out so that you can stand up under it*" (1 Corinthians 10:13). Maybe your plans for your life or your family have fallen apart. Keep in mind God's promise that the storm will not be beyond what you can handle with Him. God will verify your quality as an anchor by the tests He allows to come to you.

Thought for the Day

What currents and storms am I really able to handle?

Reading: 2 Kings 1–3; Luke 24:1–35

May 8

A Key Principle of Testing

We have learned that an anchor can be truly tested only when it undergoes intense pressure. In learning to follow God's purposes for our lives, we must understand a key principle of testing: our tests are designed by our declarations. The moment you make a declaration that you're going to do something, life will test your resolve.

If a man says, "I am not going to have sex before marriage," every old girlfriend of his will appear in his life within the next week. And he will wonder what happened. He just invited the test by his declaration. Or perhaps you say, "I'm going to start a business!" That declaration will be tested by obstacles and setbacks to see if you really mean it.

Remember the declaration Peter made to Jesus: *"Lord, I am ready to go with you to prison and to death"* (Luke 22:33). In other words, "Lord, I don't know about the other disciples, but as for me, I will never leave You or forsake You." Jesus replied, in effect, "Peter, Satan has just demanded you to appear for trial on what you said. I have prayed that your faith won't fail in the midst of it, that you will still believe what I told you." (See verses 31–32.)

An anchor is tested by storms; it is only as good as what it survives. For some of you, God is going to bring you through something big, and He wants you to remember these instructions. You must learn to survive the little storms so you can weather the larger ones in fulfillment of the vision. If God is going to trust you with something and use you to accomplish it, He has to test you first.

Thought for the Day

God will test before He entrusts.

Reading: 2 Kings 4–6; Luke 24:36–53

May 9

The Anchor Must Hold

Anchors are designed to secure a ship; that's why they must be tested. It's too late to test them in an emergency. When a ship is heading toward a rocky shore, its anchor must hold. Similarly, when men's families run into problems, *they* must hold. They have to hold those families together.

If you are a male living at home with your mother and sisters, and your father is absent, you are the "father" of that house. Your mother wasn't designed to fill that purpose. Jesus took over His family's leadership after Joseph died. And He made sure with His last breaths that His mother would be secured in John's household after He was gone. He said to His mother, "*'Dear woman, here is your son,' and to the disciple, 'Here is your mother'*" (John 19:26–27). He was being the sustainer of His mother.

When the anchor of a family fails, disaster is inevitable. If you walk out on your marriage, you will not only destroy your family, but you will also damage the community. If you're a pastor and things aren't going right and you abandon the pulpit before God calls you to leave, you will cause problems in the body of Christ. That's not a personal decision anymore because you're called to be the anchor.

Remember that storms are only for a season. You are being tested to insure your strength. You will come back from the storms better than ever, in a way others have never seen you before. Your best years are still ahead of you. Let God refine you, and a new man will emerge. You are an anchor. Protect your ship throughout the journey so that it can arrive at its destination safely.

Thought for the Day

When the anchor of a family fails, disaster is inevitable.

Reading: 2 Kings 7–9; John 1:1–28

May 10

Anchored on the Rock

The word *Bahamas* means "shallow waters," but there's a place where the sea drops off about six thousand feet, which is called the tongue of the ocean. Once my associates and I had gone spear fishing, and we were diving at a reef right next to the tongue. As long as our boat stayed in the shallow area, the anchor held because it could reach rock at the bottom. But then the anchor got into some sand, and the current from the tongue of the ocean started dragging the boat.

When the boat drifted over the tongue, the anchor had nothing to hold on to; it was thousands of feet above the bottom of the ocean. When we noticed what was happening, we were on the reef yelling for the captain to come, and he was trying to start the engine, but the engine wouldn't start! He was drifting over the depths of the ocean.

That was a moment I'll never forget. We were about fifty feet from the tongue where there were massive sharks. We were stranded on the reef, there was a strong current that could pull us toward the tongue, and our only refuge was that boat. At that point, the boat's anchor was useless as our security because it had nothing to hold on to. After being out all night in the darkness, we were finally rescued. Our families had contacted the equivalent of the Coast Guard in the Bahamas, and a ship came and found us.

You are not strong enough to keep your family's "boat" secure if you as the anchor have nothing solid to hold on to. If you can't hold steady and you get "lost at sea," what will they do? Make sure you are holding "*firm and secure*" to Jesus Christ. (See Hebrews 6:19.)

Thought for the Day

As heavy as an anchor is, it needs to rest on something heavier to enable it to hold steady.

Reading: 2 Kings 10–12; John 1:29–51

May 11

The Female as Life-Giver

It has been said that the pressure exerted on a woman's body during delivery would kill a man. Apparently, the pressure is so strong that a male's body could not physically hold up under it. This phenomenon sheds new meaning on the verse, *"I praise you because I am fearfully and wonderfully made; your works are wonderful, I know that full well"* (Psalm 139:14). When God created the woman to be able to carry a baby to term and to deliver that baby, He gave her extraordinary capabilities! He built her so that she could do what He had designed her to do. The woman was designed to be able to gestate—to conceive, carry a baby to term, and bring forth this new life into the world.

After the fall of humanity, but apparently before the man and woman were banished from the garden, the man gave the woman a name. *"Adam named his wife Eve, because she would become the mother of all the living"* (Genesis 3:20). The name Eve in the Hebrew is *Chavvah*, and it means "life-giver." It is significant that God did not cause the man and woman to leave the garden before Eve was named. As was mentioned earlier, her ability to bear children, her role of life-giver, was part of God's original design and is not a result of the fall in any way.

In the month of May, the United States and other countries celebrate Mother's Day. This is appropriate for a number of reasons, but certainly so because the woman is in essence a life-giver. She was given the ability to receive the seed of the male and to reproduce after their kind. This is an awesome capability. God gave the female a powerful responsibility in the world.

Thought for the Day

God gave the female the powerful responsibility of being a life-giver.

Reading: 2 Kings 13–14; John 2

May 12

The "Incubator": Transformation and Multiplication

Pregnancy is a remarkable process that shifts the focus and effort of the woman's entire body to the task of developing the new life within her womb. Yet the woman's dominion role of life-giver is not limited to carrying and delivering a human child. God's design for the woman as life-giver goes beyond her physical abilities. It permeates her entire makeup as a female.

We could call the woman an "incubator," because her very nature reflects her inclination to develop and give new life to things. This purpose for the woman is not surprising, because there is often a reflection of the spiritual in the physical world, as Paul told us in Romans 1.

Since God created the woman's gestational ability as an integral part of her nature, this ability permeates all areas of her life. She has a physical womb, but she also has an emotional "womb," a mental and instinctual "womb," and a spiritual "womb." She brings forth life in all these areas of her makeup. She receives things into herself, nurtures them until they mature, and then gives them back in fully developed form.

Everything goes back to the purpose and design of God. The woman's nature is to be a receiver, and that is why she can receive the seed of the man in order to create a new human life. Yet it is not only a matter of receiving, but also of being able to transform what she has received in a remarkable way, that makes her an incubator. A womb will never give back to you just what it has received. It will always take what you have given it and multiply it.

When a woman receives an idea and incubates it, therefore, it becomes something greater—something bigger, stronger, and more dynamic.

Thought for the Day

Whatever you give a woman, she's going to multiply it.

Reading: 2 Kings 15–16; John 3:1–18

May 13

A Woman's Creative Processes

As part of her dominion role, the woman is meant to conceive, develop, and give new life to or "incubate" what she receives into herself. She is gifted with many creative abilities that can assist her loved ones, herself, and the world. A woman incubates in these ways:

- She sees possibilities and potential.
- She ponders words, actions, and relationships between things.
- She processes words, ideas, needs, and problems.
- She conceives and invents.
- She develops ideas, plans, and programs.
- She protects what she has received while it develops.
- She produces something new from what she receives.
- She multiplies what she is given.

You could say that the woman is an entire research and development department all in one. In this, she reflects the nature of her Creator, who *"gives life to the dead and calls things that are not as though they were"* (Romans 4:17). Just as God created man out of Himself, a woman brings forth new life from within herself.

Thought for the Day

The woman is gifted with many creative abilities that can assist her loved ones, herself, and the world.

Reading: 2 Kings 17–18; John 3:19–36

Emotional Incubation Can Hurt

A woman has the capacity to receive and incubate not only what is good, but also what is unhealthy for her emotionally, psychologically, or spiritually.

Suppose a man tells his wife during a heated argument, "I wish I had never married you!" The woman becomes angry when she hears it, but she locks herself into her emotional room. That one sentence goes into her heart, penetrating it just as the single sperm out of millions penetrates the egg at conception. Do you know what she does with it? She incubates it. Nine years later, he says to her, "Honey, you're the sweetest woman I ever could have married." She says, "You didn't think so nine years ago." She is still carrying the emotional pain.

Many men display domineering or antagonistic attitudes toward the women in their lives over long periods of time. A woman can become "pregnant" with the bitterness that a man has been presenting to her for years. At some point, her long-suffering will come to an end, and she will be full-term. She might say to the man, "That's it! I've had it. I want you to leave." The man will say, "What happened? I'm doing the same things I've been doing for the last ten years." "Well, that's it; I've had enough. Get out. Take your clothes, everything, and get out of my house." He wonders what has gotten into her, but the "baby" of emotional pain has been in her for a long time, growing and developing.

The Bible tells us in many places to watch our tongues. Solomon gave wise advice that can be applied in all our relationships: "*Reckless words pierce like a sword, but the tongue of the wise brings healing*" (Proverbs 12:18).

Thought for the Day

A woman can become "pregnant" with the bitterness that a man has been presenting her for years.

Reading: 2 Kings 19–21; John 4:1–30

May 15

Words Can Go Deep

Yesterday, we talked about how a woman has a natural capacity to incubate the words she receives. If a man knows that a woman is an incubator, then he can be more considerate about what he says to her. Suppose a husband tells his wife that he notices she has put on a few pounds. To him, it's just a casual statement, but it becomes something that the woman incubates. All of a sudden he sees her getting up early and jogging when she never jogged before. He wonders what brought this on, but it is because she has conceived his comment. Every time he mentions it, she feels more and more under pressure. Then she begins to feel insecure. She starts to wonder if he is looking at other women and comparing her to them. This builds internally until one day she hears him say something nice about another woman. Then, get out of the way, because here comes "the baby"!

Single men also have to be careful about what they say to single women. If a man says to a woman, "Hey, beautiful, you look great," he is probably going to have a "baby" in a little while. I'm not talking about a physical baby. He will conceive an emotional baby. The woman will tell him, "I thought you said you loved me!"

Again, Solomon provides us with a truth that is especially applicable to male/female relationships: "*Even a fool is thought wise if he keeps silent, and discerning if he holds his tongue*" (Proverbs 17:28).

Thought for the Day

If a man knows that a woman is an incubator, then he can be more considerate about what he says to her.

Reading: 2 Kings 22–23; John 4:31–54

May 16

A Spiritual Incubator

When the Sabbath was over, Mary Magdalene, Mary the mother of James, and Salome bought spices so that they might go to anoint Jesus' body.
—Mark 16:1

Why is it that few men attend prayer meetings? I noticed this at my church and started to wonder about it. Then I realized, "It is because women are incubators. If they are presented with an idea, a need, or a problem, they will take it to heart and will work through it until they arrive at a solution."

Just as a womb nourishes a fetus during development and an incubator protects premature or sick babies, a woman has a nurturing instinct that can be a powerful source of encouragement in the lives of others. If a man wants something prayed about, he should tell a woman. She'll take the circumstance into her spiritual womb, where she meets with God in her inner being, incubate it for months, if necessary, and bring forth a solution. She won't give up until she receives an answer from God.

Jesus didn't say that it was a man who kept knocking at the judge's door in order to obtain justice. (See Luke 18:2–8.) It wasn't a man who persisted with the Lord Jesus for a healing for her daughter, saying, "*Yes, Lord,...but even the dogs eat the crumbs that fall from their masters' table*" (Matthew 15:27). Do you know to whom God first gave the resurrection message? Women. It was the women who first saw the resurrected Christ and went to tell the men. Why? Because the men had locked themselves in their room! Note also that Jesus gave the woman at the well a message, and she turned it into an entire evangelistic team. (See John 4:4–30.) Women are spiritual incubators who birth spiritual results in God.

Thought for the Day

A woman won't give up in prayer until she receives an answer from God.

Reading: 2 Kings 24–25; John 5:1–24

May 17

Develop Your Gifts

A woman was made to give life. This means that if you need some life in your life, get a life-giver. Some men today are walking around trying to be self-reliant, keeping women at arm's length. They don't know the life they are missing.

God made the female to be the life-giver, so that whenever you need to give life to something, she can do it. Have you ever been in the apartment of a man who is living by himself? The colors are drab. Everything is out of place. People tell him, "You need a woman's touch." When the man gets married and his wife moves in, she changes the drab look. She puts up colorful curtains, hangs pictures on the walls, rearranges the furniture, and, in no time, makes it into a beautiful place. When a woman walks into a room, she changes the countenance of that room. She gives life to a place.

Ladies, your husbands might not be able to provide you with a castle right away, but you can take what they provide for you, incubate it, and give life to it. When you have finished with it, the house will have become a home.

Many women have been so beaten down by life that they have rarely used their gifts of incubation. They have been told by others that they have nothing to contribute. Women, I believe that God wants to set you free to develop the gifts He has placed within you and the ideas and visions He will give you. Don't be afraid. God has given you tremendous ability, and you can be a blessing to many as you reflect the nature of your Creator, the Life-Giver.

Thought for the Day

God wants to set women free to develop the gifts He has placed within them.

Reading: 1 Chronicles 1–3; John 5:25–47

May 18

PRINCIPLES OF THE WOMAN AS LIFE-GIVER

Today, review these principles of the woman as life-giver and reflect on how they apply to your everyday life—directly for yourself, if you are a woman, and in your relationships with women, if you are a man.

1. A major aspect of the female's dominion role is that she is a life-giver.
2. The woman is an "incubator" because her very nature reflects her inclination to develop and give new life to things.
3. The woman's incubational ability permeates all areas of her life. She has a physical womb, but she also has an emotional "womb," a mental and instinctual "womb," and a spiritual "womb."
4. When a man knows that a woman is an incubator, then he can be considerate about what he says to her.
5. A woman has a nurturing instinct that can be a powerful source of help and encouragement in the lives of others.
6. God wants to set women free to develop the gifts He has placed within them and the ideas and visions He will give them.

Adam named his wife Eve, because she would become the mother of all the living. (Genesis 3:20)

Heavenly Father,
You are the true Life-Giver. It is because of You that we walk in a fruitful life today. Please enable us to develop our gifts to the fullest as we seek Your will for our lives. We want to be used by You and to develop the things You have given us in a way that will bless Your kingdom. In Jesus' name, amen.

Reading: 1 Chronicles 4–6; John 6:1–21

May 19

Love the Mother of Your Children

After loving God, the most important thing a man can do for his children is to *love their mother.* Many men buy gifts for their children, such as bicycles and computers, when what the children want and need most is to see their fathers truly love their mothers. There is nothing more precious than for a child to see his parents being affectionate with one another. I believe children get a feeling of security when they see that.

Men, showing consideration and respect for your wife is extremely important. "*Be kind to one another, tenderhearted, forgiving one another, just as God in Christ forgave you*" (Ephesians 4:32). Are you demanding and impatient with your spouse, or do you treat her with kindness and understanding? What are you modeling for your children about what it means to be a husband? Children take in everything they see, and your children observe the way you treat your wife more than you know. A child will often lose respect for his father if he doesn't see him giving his mother the consideration and love she deserves.

As we have seen, the way men treat their wives affects how God views them, also. The Word says that if a husband doesn't treat his wife with respect, his very prayers will be hindered. (See 1 Peter 3:7.) When you love the mother of your children, you bring peace and happiness into your home, and you teach your children what it means to be a real man.

Thought for the Day

There is nothing more precious for a child to see than his parents being affectionate with one another.

Reading: 1 Chronicles 7–9; John 6:22–44

May 20

Love Your Children

The Lord disciplines those he loves, and he punishes everyone he accepts as a son.
—Hebrews 12:6

Love is not buying gifts. Love is *you being a gift.* The Bible tells us that our heavenly Father so loved the world that He became a revelation of that love in Jesus Christ. Therefore, if a man is really a father, he doesn't just send gifts. He sends himself. That's the essence of love.

Love also means correcting, chastening, and reproving your children when they need it. Some children are begging to be corrected, but their fathers don't have any sense to realize it. Some children hate their fathers because they let them do whatever they want. The fathers imagine the children will do fine on their own. They think, *My children are old enough to handle it,* while their children are thinking, *I need help, Daddy! I don't know the right values in life. I don't have standards to judge by. I'm looking to you to give me some guidelines, and you're telling me, "Decide for yourself."*

Loving your children means setting standards for them. Life today is very complex and confusing. Children need someone who can tell them, "This is the way in which to go." You need to give your children a love that instills eternal values. I've talked to parents who were concerned because their child was wayward. "We don't know what happened. We gave him everything he wanted," they said. That was the problem. You don't give your child everything he wants. You give him what he needs—unconditional love, godly discipline, and eternal values to live by.

Thought for the Day

Love is you being a gift.

Reading: 1 Chronicles 10–12; John 6:45–71

May 21

Be Responsible for Your Children

Our fathers disciplined us for a little while as they thought best; but God disciplines us for our good, that we may share in his holiness.
—Hebrews 12:10

Many fathers don't really want to take responsibility for their children, because children take time and energy. Therefore, they leave them to fend for themselves.

How much time do you spend with your children? Who is really bringing them up? Perhaps you and your wife leave for work early in the morning and don't return until late in the evening. Someone else has brought them up all day. Realize that everything that person represents goes into your children. They will learn their views of God, their concept of themselves, and their philosophy of life from their caretaker.

A father's responsibility also includes disciplining his children, but some men don't have the backbone for it. They are afraid to correct their children, so they leave it up to their wives. The Bible doesn't tell the mother to correct the children; it says the father is to discipline them. Yet how many fathers leave discipline up to the mothers? Some fathers don't correct their children because they want the children to like them. They don't realize the effect this has on their families. Their children think, *Daddy doesn't really love me.* They may also grow up believing a parent isn't supposed to discipline his children, so they don't become good agents of correction for their own children. There are times when love has to be tough. If you love your children, you will correct them.

Balancing all of life's demands can be difficult for a father, but your children should be at the top of the list, after your wife.

Thought for the Day

Who is really raising your children?

Reading: 1 Chronicles 13–15; John 7:1–27

Train Your Children

It was I who taught Ephraim to walk, taking them by the arms; but they did not realize it was I who healed them. I led them with cords of human kindness, with ties of love; I lifted the yoke from their neck and bent down to feed them.
—Hosea 11:3–4

"*It was I who taught Ephraim to walk.*" God was talking about His people. He was saying, "I have always been with you. From the time you were a 'child,' I was working with you. When you fell down, I picked you up. I was training you." Our heavenly Father takes a personal interest in our training. Likewise, we are to personally train our children.

Proverbs 19:18 says, "*Discipline your son, for in that there is hope; do not be a willing party to his death.*" This is serious business. The verse is saying, "Discipline and train a child now because there is hope in that discipline, hope in that training." You are giving hope to your child when you discipline and correct him because *you are giving him a value system for his entire life!*

The above verse makes the strong statement that if you don't do this, you may be a party to your child's death. Proverbs 29:15 says, "*A child left to himself disgraces his mother.*" Check out the children in the reform schools. Check out the inmates in the prisons. Look at the people living on the streets. Observe the young people who have little sense of direction or morality. Many of them were left to themselves as children, with no one to teach them character and values. If you don't correct or discipline your child when he needs it, then when he goes bad, you are responsible.

Thought for the Day

When you discipline and correct your child you are giving him a value system for his entire life.

Reading: 1 Chronicles 16–18; John 7:28–53

May 23

Condition Your Children

My heart goes out to single parents who have to fill the roles of both father and mother. I strongly want to encourage you not to let your children train you. Don't allow them to reverse the roles of parent and child. You may not know everything in life, but you know more than they do! And that's enough for you to be in charge. I don't care how old they are, when you're paying the mortgage, when you're providing for them, you make the rules. If they disobey the rules, you have to make sure they experience the consequences.

"Train up a child in the way he should go: and when he is old, he will not depart from it" (Proverbs 22:6 KJV). The word for *"train"* in this verse is the same word that is used for conditioning. The Bible is saying, "Condition your child in the way he should go." Why? He can't condition himself. He was born with a rebellious spirit. You don't have to teach your children to swear, lie, steal, commit adultery, or have bitterness and hatred. It's already in them. If you don't condition them, they will naturally become wayward. You have to train them. If you seek and trust Him, the Lord will provide everything you need to help you fulfill this role, whether you are in a two-parent family or are a single parent. *"A father to the fatherless, a defender of widows, is God in his holy dwelling"* (Psalm 68:5).

Thought for the Day

You may not know everything, but you know more than your children do!

Reading: 1 Chronicles 19–21; John 8:1–27

May 24

Disciplined by My Parents

No discipline seems pleasant at the time, but painful. Later on, however, it produces a harvest of righteousness and peace for those who have been trained by it.

—Hebrews 12:11

If you train your children, they will grow up to know God's ways and to have peace in their hearts. The things children learn from their parents never leave them. I still retain what my father and mother taught me. The same temptations that come to any young man came to me. What kept me on an even keel were the values and morals that were instilled in me. There were situations where, if it wasn't for the training of my parents, I would have gone under. What kept me safe was the character I learned from their teaching and correction. I love my parents because they disciplined me.

The King James Version uses the word "*chastening*" instead of "*discipline*" in Hebrews 12:11. The word *chasten* means "to correct," "to reprove," or "to discipline." Some children are punished but not corrected. Parents sometimes confuse the two. Your children need discipline. To discipline means to instill moral and mental character, to give values to a person. You don't give values just by punishing. You give values by correcting.

My parents had a wonderful way of sitting me down and saying, "Now, here is why we disciplined you." They didn't just punish me; they corrected me. They said, "If you keep this up, this will happen," and "If you keep this kind of company, this will be the result." Disciplining your children will be painful for both you and your children at times, but the results will be positive and healthy.

Thought for the Day

You don't give values just by punishing. You give values by correcting.

Reading: 1 Chronicles 22–24; John 8:28–59

May 25

Encourage Your Children

For you know that we dealt with each of you as a father deals with his own children, encouraging, comforting and urging [or warning] *you to live lives worthy of God, who calls you into his kingdom and glory.*

—1 Thessalonians 2:11–12

Children need encouragement. Some children never hear an encouraging word from their parents. Do you hear how some parents talk to their children? They act as if the children can't do anything right. They don't remember what it is like to be a child, and they expect their children to have adult skills. A ten-year-old boy is washing the dishes. His father comes in and says, "Can't you clean dishes better than this?" The little guy is at least trying. So encourage him. Maybe he leaves a little soap on the stove or counter. Don't look at what he left; look at what he cleaned up. Encourage him.

Maybe your child can't read quite as fast as you did when you were her age. Don't criticize her. Encourage her. Some children are really trying. Sometimes a child will try to help out with the chores and will unintentionally break something. His mother will run into the room and yell, "What are you doing?" He gets a lecture. So he goes to his room with a broken heart, a depressed spirit, and a hurt ego. He thinks, *I'm not going to help ever again!* Some parents don't see their child's intention. They see only their own anger and frustration. So correct and instruct your child with patience, and encourage his or her efforts.

Thought for the Day

Some children never hear an encouraging word from their parents.

Reading: 1 Chronicles 25–27; John 9:1–23

Comfort Your Children

Praise be to the God and Father of our Lord Jesus Christ, the Father of compassion and the God of all comfort, who comforts us in all our troubles, so that we can comfort those in any trouble with the comfort we ourselves have received from God.

—2 Corinthians 1:3–4

Children need comforting. You encourage them when they're doing something positive, and when you want them to improve in something. But there will be times when they become discouraged, hurt, confused, or disillusioned. That is when they need comfort.

How can you comfort your children? By letting them know they are loved, even when they make mistakes or don't live up to your expectations. By listening to their struggles and problems with kindness and understanding. By giving them warm embraces and loving words when they are sad. By remembering the times God has comforted you in your distress and giving that same comfort to them.

To be a comforter, you have to be accessible to your children. You have to know what's going on in their lives so you can know when they're going through struggles and loneliness. Children will be comforted to know you're available to them and that you make it a point to spend time with them. Your comfort will also help them to know that their heavenly Father is a Comforter, just as He is described in His Word: *"the Father of compassion and the God of all comfort, who comforts us in all our troubles."*

Thought for the Day

Comforting your children will help them to know that their heavenly Father is a Comforter.

Reading: 1 Chronicles 28–29; John 9:24–41

May 27

Warn Your Children

The Bible points out that conscientious parents warn their children *"to live lives worthy of God"* (1 Thessalonians 2:12). It is the parents' responsibility to warn their children of the consequences of rejecting God. "Son, there is an eternal hell. I warn you, whatever you sow on earth, you're going to reap in eternity." "Daughter, I warn you that whatever you become involved in can follow you in your memory forever." These are examples of spiritual warning.

Parents are to urge or warn their children to live righteously. Yet how many parents confuse warning with threatening? "I'm going to kill you if you don't stop that!" Some fathers don't have any kind of tact because they don't know any better. A child interprets a warning as love but sees a threat as hate.

Many parents warn their children, but their children don't listen to them because they aren't setting a godly example. If you are walking in God's ways when you warn your children, they will come to respect the God of their parents. They will say, "If I obey my parents, then I'm obeying my God. I know that my parents know what is best because I see God working in their lives. I'll obey my parents because I want God to work in my life, too."

Warn your children. It's your responsibility. *"Him* [Christ] *we preach, warning every man and teaching every man in all wisdom, that we may present every man perfect in Christ Jesus"* (Colossians 1:28).

Thought for the Day

Warn your children. It's your responsibility.

Reading: 2 Chronicles 1–3; John 10:1–23

May 28

Are You Moving Toward God or Away from Him?

Although they knew God, they neither glorified him as God not gave thanks to him....Therefore God gave them over in the sinful desires of their hearts....
—Romans 1:21, 24

Are you setting a good example for your children by walking in God's ways? What are they observing about the way you live your life and the consequences of your actions?

When humanity rejected God, He gave them what they wanted. He gave them over to their passions. That's not as simple as it might sound. If God had just given us over to what we wanted, the implication might have been that we could succeed in spite of Him. But when God gave us over, He also allowed us to experience the inevitable results of our actions. God didn't just say, "Okay, go, carry on." He said, "If you carry on, you're going to end up depraved, because that isn't the way I made you." (See Romans 1:28.)

The principle here is that you cannot move away from God and be successful. You cannot cut off your relationship with the Manufacturer and expect to find genuine parts somewhere else. Any part you find on your own will not function properly.

God says that when we reject His purposes, He gives us over to a depraved mind. In other words, He tells us, "Without Me, your mind isn't going to get any better; it will only get worse." Therefore, if we think we can find out how to be better women or men without God, we are in trouble, for the consequences are serious. When we believe that we don't need God, we get worse and worse. If you don't want to live in God's purpose for humanity, then you will end up doing yourself harm.

Thought for the Day

You cannot move away from God's plan and be successful.

Reading: 2 Chronicles 4–6; John 10:24–42

May 29

How Are You Using Your Life?

Even though humanity as a whole has turned away from God, He still creates us with gifts and talents that are intended to be used to fulfill His purposes. Yet since we don't understand how they are to be used, we take the talents He has given us and use them against ourselves and others.

For example, Romans 1:29 says that one of the manifestations of a depraved mind is unrighteousness or wickedness. Some of the wickedest people in the world are wise when it comes to information. They are sharp people; they can be wicked with class. Some people are gifted, but they use their gifts in such a wicked way that their victims don't know what hit them until it's all over. Our gifts, which God means for good, can be turned and used for evil purposes.

Some people blame the devil for the results of their actions. Don't blame the devil; he just takes advantage of your decisions. The devil cannot dominate you or force you to do anything. Instead, he waits for your decisions. When you make a bad one, he'll ride it to the end, or just as far as he can, and he'll try to bring you down with it. Satan is not the culprit. The culprit is your rejection or ignorance of God's purpose. You don't know God's purpose for living, and so you abuse your life. Be careful; that abuse can cripple or kill you.

We must discover God's purpose for our lives and use our gifts for His glory.

> *Every good and perfect gift is from above, coming down from the Father of the heavenly lights....He chose to give us birth through the word of truth, that we might be a kind of firstfruits of all he created.*
> (James 1:17–18)

Thought for the Day

God creates us with gifts that are intended to be used to fulfill His purposes.

Reading: 2 Chronicles 7–9; John 11:1–29

May 30

The Cause of Conflict

What causes fights and quarrels among you? Don't they come from your desires that battle within you?
—James 4:1

God's purposes are vital for successful lives and relationships. When we don't understand and appreciate God-given differences between people, we will inevitably have conflict with others.

The misunderstanding and discord between women and men may be illustrated by the way many people enter into marriage today. Most are unprepared for the marriage relationship. They approach it in the same way that they buy a car. When you want to buy a new car, you go to various car dealerships, compare the models and features, make your selection, sign the papers, and then drive your new car home. The mere act of getting married is like purchasing a new car; it is relatively simple to do. You look at the choices, find somebody you like, go to a minister or justice of the peace for the ceremony, receive your marriage certificate, and then go home with your new spouse.

However, buying a car is one thing; operating and maintaining it is something else. Likewise, getting married is one thing, while maintaining and growing in the relationship is another. Many husbands and wives have been trying to function without understanding or addressing the other's individual needs. Each spouse has been trying to operate based only on what he or she needs. That's why many relationships are at a standstill. To address the conflict between men and women, we must learn, understand, and appreciate each other's unique designs.

Thought for the Day

When we don't understand and appreciate our God-given differences, we will inevitably have conflict.

Reading: 2 Chronicles 10–12; John 11:30–57

May 31

The Why Dictates the Design

Yesterday, we talked about the importance of learning, understanding, and appreciating the unique designs of women and men in order to resolve the conflicts between them. We often assume that a man needs what a woman needs and a woman needs what a man needs. In many ways, this is not the case. Despite their similarities, each has a unique design and unique needs.

Consider these questions: Why are humans different from animals? Why is a bird different from a fish? Why is the sun different from the moon? Why are women different from men? Everything is the way it is because of *why* it was created. The *why* dictates the design. God created everything with the ability to fulfill its purpose. His purposes were always planned out ahead of time; everything was already "made" in the mind of the Maker before He created it.

Since God is a God of purpose, He never created anything *hoping* that it would turn out to be something viable. He first *decided* what it was to be, and *then* He made it. He always begins with a finished product in mind. What this means is that God never gives a purpose to something *after* He has made it; rather, He *builds* everything to fulfill the specific purpose He already had in mind for it. God designed everything to function in its purpose, and everything is the way it is because its purpose requires it to be so.

The unique designs and needs of males and females enable them to fulfill the purpose for which God created them. The next time you begin to have conflict with the opposite sex because of your differences, remember that the other person's unique design is God-given and vital to fulfill His purposes.

Thought for the Day

Everything is the way it is because of *why* it was created.

Reading: 2 Chronicles 13–14; John 12:1–26

June 1

My Parents' Roles

I am one of eleven children, and my family was typical of the not-so-distant past. My father rose in the morning before we children got up, and he came home after we had gone to bed. He spent his whole life working, trying to feed us and keep a roof over our heads and clothes on our backs. It was a twenty-four-hour-a-day job. My mother had to stay home, and her job was as hard as his. She had to take care of all eleven of us—cooking the meals, bathing us, washing our clothes, getting us off to school, disciplining us. It was a very hard life. It was survival.

Historically, the basic needs of survival required men and women to develop distinct roles and skills, which were passed along to succeeding generations. Up until your grandparents' time or even your parents' time, everybody knew his or her role and had skills that were equal to it. Husband and wife knew what they needed to do, and they did it.

Although survival was difficult, relationships were comparatively easy because there was no confusion over gender roles. A man and a woman didn't have to wonder whether one was infringing on the other's territory. Her role was to keep the house, cook the food, and care for the children. His job was to hunt or harvest the crops and build a dwelling in order to provide food and shelter for the family. Life was straightforward and so, in that sense, relationships were less complicated than they are today.

Hundreds and thousands of years of tradition have been set aside in just one or two generations. Let us have patience with one another as we sort out roles from purpose and learn to live as God intends.

Thought for the Day

The basic needs of survival required men and women to develop distinct roles and skills.

Reading: 2 Chronicles 15–16; John 12:27–50

Contemporary Roles

Life is completely different for men and women today because we are no longer utterly dependent on one another for security and survival. Our roles and strategies have really changed.

Men used to have a role that was very clear—one they didn't share with their wives. How was manhood measured? Young men were told, "Get a job, son, so you can provide for your family, and have some babies." Being the breadwinner and having the ability to procreate was the measure of a man. But the way society views men is in transition, and these are not considered the primary marks of manhood any longer. A number of families still follow the traditional pattern of the husband holding the job while the wife stays home with the children, especially while the children are young. However, even these marriages are usually influenced by contemporary rather than traditional ideas of how men and women are to relate to one another.

Biology doesn't determine male-female roles the way it used to. Today, because of the prevalence of both dual careers and birth control, a husband and wife might choose not to have children. If they do have a child, it doesn't necessarily mean that the wife will stay home every day to take care of the baby.

This change is bringing new kinds of stresses to the family. For example, since a woman's primary role of childbearing and child-rearing was what formerly brought her respect from her husband, the man now needs to honor his wife in different ways. Similarly, since the man's primary role of breadwinner was what used to bring a man respect from his wife, a working woman needs to understand how to honor her husband.

Twenty-first century relationships are difficult, but we can learn to live in a way that honors both God and one another.

Thought for the Day

Biology doesn't determine male-female roles the way it used to.

Reading: 2 Chronicles 17–18; John 13:1–20

June 3

What Does a Woman Want?

For the first time in recorded history, men and women look to one another primarily for love and companionship rather than survival and protection. Our priorities as human beings have changed. People are looking for something more: happiness, intimacy, and lasting passion are now requirements for relationships. Yet understanding how to provide these things for their wives often does not come easily to men.

The male's traditional roles are not enough to make his partner happy anymore. What can men do to make women happy today? That's the challenge. Have you ever heard a man say, "What does a woman want?" In the past, men used to tell their wives, "Woman, what else do you want from me? I put a roof over your head and food in the kitchen." Remember when men said that? Those days are over.

Nowadays, women want companionship and attention in order to be happy. My father couldn't take my mother for walks in the park or out to dinner at a restaurant. There was no time for it. He made my mother happy just by making sure that the family had food, shelter, clothing, and running water.

Women also want intimacy and communication. "Talk to me. You haven't told me you love me all day." Men, that's the way women think. "You looked at everybody else except me. You didn't notice my dress." Men are trying to figure out how to build intimacy and communication into their relationships. In this challenging time in our culture, women need to show understanding to the men in their lives. In coming days, we will look at specific ways to build intimacy and communication in relationships.

Thought for the Day

Happiness, intimacy, and lasting passion are now requirements for relationships.

Reading: 2 Chronicles 19–20; John 13:21–38

June 4

A Woman Who Knows Her Purpose

Many are the plans in a man's heart, but it is the Lord's purpose that prevails.
—Proverbs 19:21

Many are the plans, the opinions, the doctrines, and the concepts that are in our hearts, but it is God's purpose that counts. When we rely on our own understanding of our purposes, we run into difficulty. Yet when we understand God's purposes for us, we can address the needs that come with those purposes. In this way, we can live fulfilled lives.

Many men are having problems in their lives today for two reasons. First, they don't know their own purpose; second, they definitely don't understand the woman's purpose. When men do not know their own purpose or the woman's purpose, it has a negative effect on the woman, causing her both stress and heartache. Yet when a woman understands her purpose and how it relates to the man's purpose, she can bring much healing and fulfillment to her relationships. She may even be able to alleviate some of the situations of misuse and even abuse in her life. You'll be amazed at what a woman who knows her purpose can become. I've met very few men who can handle a woman who knows her purpose.

> *So God created man in his own image, in the image of God he created him; male and female he created them. God blessed them and said to them, "Be fruitful and increase in number; fill the earth and subdue it."* (Genesis 1:27–28)

> *For we are God's workmanship, created in Christ Jesus to do good works, which God prepared in advance for us to do.* (Ephesians 2:10)

Thought for the Day

When a woman understands her purpose and how it relates to the man's purpose, she can bring much healing and fulfillment to her relationships.

Reading: 2 Chronicles 21–22; John 14

June 5

The Purpose of Fatherhood

The priority of purpose has its origins in our Creator, and it has significant practical applications for us as human beings. When our Creator made humanity, He designed men and women to fulfill their specific functions and gave them qualities and characteristics to enable them to perform His intended purpose. The nature of a thing is determined by its purpose. If a man does not know, understand, or fulfill his God-given purpose, then problems will arise both in his identity and his relationships.

From Scripture, we can see that God created the male with a particular purpose in mind. We have already talked about some of his major responsibilities as the first human being created, such as foundation and anchor. Related to these ideas is the concept of fatherhood. God clearly intended men to be *fathers*; therefore, He designed them to be so. The nature of the male as father is providential, essential, and valuable for the fulfillment of his particular purpose in life.

"Fatherhood" has a much broader meaning than just the biological production of children. Fatherhood is not a choice for a male but is inherent in his very nature. Males are designed to provide for and protect everything within their sphere of influence. *Every* male is a father, and his personal fulfillment is linked to living out that purpose. Purpose is the source of all true fulfillment and defines one's existence.

We will examine fatherhood over the next several days, as well as in other months of this devotional, because of the vital part fathers are meant to play in the healing of our families, communities, and nations. I want to present to you the purpose of fatherhood according to the "Manufacturer's Manual" (the Bible). We will begin tomorrow with an understanding of God as Father.

Thought for the Day

The essence of the male is fatherhood.

Reading: 2 Chronicles 23–24; John 15

June 6

The Father of Life

Jesus taught us to pray, *"Our Father which art in heaven, hallowed be thy name"* (Matthew 6:9 KJV). The Father in heaven was not just Jesus' Father; He is ours, as well. Isaiah 63:16 declares, *"You, O LORD, are our Father, our Redeemer from of old is your name."* When we use the term *Our Father* in relation to God, we must remember that this is not so much a name but a title resulting from a function. We can say that God is our Father in two main ways: through creation and through redemption.

God is the Source and Sustainer of everything He created, which makes Him the Father of all things. Whether it is material or spirit, God is still the Father of it. He is Father by virtue of His creative will. James 1:17 reveals that God is *"the Father of the heavenly lights."* That means stars, suns, moons, and everything that exists in the universe came out of God. All creation came out of God. Everything came from Him, but He Himself did not come from any other source. The word *God* means self-sustaining, self-sufficient One. God is life and gives everything life.

God is also our Father through our redemption in Jesus Christ. Through His sinless life and sacrifice on the cross, Jesus restored fallen human beings to their heavenly Father. After Jesus' resurrection, He said to His disciples, *"I ascend unto my Father, and your Father; and to my God, and your God"* (John 20:17 KJV). We can call the Creator our Father again because of the reconciliation provided through Christ.

We need to keep in mind that the fatherhood of God is indicative of His nature; it is the way He desires to relate to us. *"But you received the Spirit of sonship. And by him we cry, 'Abba, Father'"* (Romans 8:15).

Thought for the Day

God is our Father by virtue of creation and redemption.

Reading: 2 Chronicles 25–27; John 16

June 7

Designed to Be a Father

From one man he made every nation of men, that they should inhabit the whole earth.
—Acts 17:26

From this Scripture we see that God created the male to function as father on earth. Genesis 1:27 tells us that man was made in God's own image, and that the general term man refers to both male and female. But Adam was created first (see Genesis 2:7–8, 18–23), and it was from him that all humanity, including Eve, came. That is why, in the genealogy of Jesus recorded in Luke 3, the lineage concludes with, "*...the son of Seth, the son of Adam, the son of God*" (v. 38). Adam came from God.

Recall that in Genesis, God created only one human being from the soil. He never went back to the soil to create Eve or any other human being. He placed all of mankind in that first man, Adam. This is a mystery. Everything God wanted for the human race was in that one man. God went to the soil, carved out one male, breathed life into him, created out of that male a female, and then said, "Now be fruitful." (See Genesis 1:28.)

Fatherhood is the design and destiny of the male. God wanted the male to be the source of all people. The male is father, not by vote or cultural positioning but by virtue of his disposition in the process of creation. This is because he was to represent God. God the Father is the perfect Model, Example, and Mentor for all men who desire to be true fathers. Just as God is the Father of all living things, He made the male to be the father of the human family.

Thought for the Day

Fatherhood is the design and the destiny of the male.

Reading: 2 Chronicles 28–29; John 17

June 8

What Is Father?

We must have a clear understanding of the meaning of "father" because one of the greatest dangers to society is a misconception of what true fatherhood is. Definitions determine interpretations; thus, we must start here. In the Old Testament, two Hebrew consonants spell "father"—*aleph* and *beth*, creating the word *ab*. *Abba*, meaning "Daddy," comes from this Hebrew word for father. In the New Testament, the Greek word for father is *pater*. So, you have *ab* and *abba* in Old Testament Hebrew and *pater* in New Testament Greek.

What do *ab* and *pater* mean? These words denote the following: source, nourisher, sustainer, supporter, founder, and protector. The source of a thing is its *ab* or father. As the source, the *ab* sustains and maintains. Another meaning of the word father is "upholder." Father is the source that upholds everything that comes from it.

You cannot be a true father unless you are willing to uphold that which comes out of you. God sustains everything that came out of Him. Through the Son, God the Father made the universe and upholds all things by the power of His Word. (See Hebrews 1:2–3.)

Other words that describe the nature of fatherhood are progenitor and ancestor. *Progenitor* comes from the Latin meaning "to beget forth." It also denotes "originator." A father is the initiator or source. God created man to be father—the progenitor, source, and supporter of generations. The words *ancestor* and *ancestry* ultimately come from the same Latin verb *antecedere*, meaning "to go before" or "precede." At the start of an ancestral line is the father. He begins the heritage for all his seed. This is very important. The man (father) was given the responsibility not only to start and provide the future generation, but also to give that generation an identity.

Thought for the Day

You cannot be a true father unless you are willing to uphold that which comes out of you.

Reading: 2 Chronicles 30–31; John 18:1–18

Fundamentals of Fatherhood

Men must understand the basic principles of fatherhood in order to be effective fathers. We have discovered that the father is the source that sustains, protects, nourishes, and provides identity for that which he produces. Let us review the principles that distinguish men in their role of father:

The male is the source of the female. First Corinthians 11:8 says, *"For man did not come from woman, but woman from man."* Therefore, the glory of the man is the woman. (See verse 7.) In other words, the man is responsible for what came out of him. Since woman came from man, men are responsible for women and how they treat them.

The male is the source of seed. The male is the host of the sperm. He is the initiator of human life, whereas the woman is the incubator of life. It is the woman who gives life to the man's seed.

The male is the nourisher of fruit. The seed of a tree gets planted, and then it becomes another tree that bears fruit. Whatever comes out of the seed is fruit; therefore, fathers are responsible for nourishing the fruit.

The male is designed to protect. God gave men physical strength and physique. Their bone structure is heavier and bigger than the woman's—not to beat her, but to protect her.

The male maintains his offspring. The fatherhood principle is to maintain. The male is responsible for the security, sustenance, and development of his seed. Fatherhood means maintenance.

The male teaches his seed. A male is a godly father when he takes responsibility for his seed and gives his seed knowledge. The source must train and instruct the resource. That is fatherhood.

Thought for the Day

The father is the source that sustains, protects, nourishes, and provides identity for that which he produces.

Reading: 2 Chronicles 32–33; John 18:19–40

June 10

In Need of Good Fathers

The month of June, during which many people celebrate Father's Day, is a good time to encourage men in their role as fathers. It seems that never before have we been as much in need of good fathers as we do today. When God created the male and gave him his dominion assignments, He included the responsibility of cultivating and protecting his offspring. Yet, today, there is a widespread lack of understanding about the nature of fatherhood. Men of all nations and races lack the skills of good parenting.

Certain men think that their ability to produce a child makes them a man. Any male can have a baby. Merely having a child is no guarantee that you are a real man—or a real father. These men don't know the meaning of being a covering, protection, and role model for their children.

Many men were never taught what it means to be a good father, and their own fathers did not provide good examples for them. When fathers are a negative influence on their sons, boys grow up with the wrong concept of marriage and fatherhood. Broken relationships and families are the result.

In a large number of homes today, fathers are absent due to separation, divorce, and the rising number of out-of-wedlock births. Other fathers live in the home but are absent from the family, for all intents and purposes. They have forsaken their responsibility because of career pursuits and selfishness, as they put their own pleasures ahead of their children's welfare. This means that many children don't have the benefit of a good father.

Good fathers are always in great demand. Men, will you commit to being the fathers you were created and designed to be?

Thought for the Day

Good fathers are always in great demand.

Reading: 2 Chronicles 34–36; John 19:1–22

A Tremendous Calling

Men, we have a tremendous calling ahead of us. Our task involves changing not only our own perspectives of fatherhood, but also those of our children, especially our sons. God intends every boy to grow up into fatherhood. As a matter of fact, buried in every boy is a father. Again, I am not just talking about the male's biological ability to father offspring. Being a "father" is rooted in God's image, because God is Father. He is not satisfied until the father comes out of the boy.

We have to communicate to our sons the standards of God, so that the trend I described yesterday can be reversed. But we have to start with ourselves. We must discover and put into practice what the Word of God says about fathers and to fathers. Then we can teach these principles to other men and boys. God's truth about fathers will be the salvation of our communities and nations.

God has always been very specific in His Word about the responsibilities of a father. This role is of particular importance to Him, because fathers are meant to represent Him to their children. When fathers fail to show His love and character to their sons and daughters, the children's concept of God suffers, affecting their relationships with Him. Now, no earthly father can ever be perfect. Yet God has provided a wealth of instruction on parenting in His Word. When men look to Him for guidance and strength, they can fulfill their responsibilities and be meaningful reflections of the fatherhood of God to their children.

Fathers, do not exasperate your children; instead, bring them up in the training and instruction of the Lord. (Ephesians 6:4)

Thought for the Day

Fathers represent God to their children.

Reading: Ezra 1–2; John 19:23–42

June 12

Know Your Heavenly Father

After Jesus rose from the dead, He made the wonderful statement, *"I am returning to my Father and your Father, to my God and your God"* (John 20:17). Because of Jesus' death and resurrection on our behalf, we can know God not only as our Creator, but also as our Father.

A man won't be able to understand what it means to be a good father if he doesn't know His heavenly Father. A man must also have faith in God as His Father—that He will love, protect, and provide for him. Trust and reliance on God is what a father needs to model for his children. They must see a strong walk of faith in their father's life, both when things are going well and when life is beset with difficulties. The greatest heritage a man can leave his sons and daughters is not money or property but faith. A house can burn down, or someone can sell or repossess it, but no one can destroy the faith you have instilled in your child. Besides, the child will be able to use his faith to obtain another house, because he has been taught to trust God as his Provider.

In the Bible, you will often see variations on the phrase "the God of my father." (See, for example, Genesis 26:24; 32:9; 2 Chronicles 17:4; Isaiah 38:5.) If your children have seen God reflected in you, then you have displayed His life and character to them. In doing so, you have given them a true spiritual heritage.

"I write to you, fathers, because you have known him who is from the beginning" (1 John 2:13).

Thought for the Day

The greatest heritage a man can leave his sons and daughters is not money or property but faith.

Reading: Ezra 3–5; John 20

June 13

What Kind of God Are You Representing?

The father shall make known Your truth to the children.
—Isaiah 38:19 (NKJV)

Why did the children of the patriarchs follow the God of their fathers? He kept His promises and took care of them. In Genesis 12:2, God said to Abraham, *"I will make you into a great nation and I will bless you; I will make your name great, and you will be a blessing."* Later, Abraham's servant reported, *"The LORD has blessed my master abundantly, and he has become wealthy. He has given him sheep and cattle, silver and gold, menservants and maidservants, and camels and donkeys. My master's wife Sarah has borne him a son in her old age, and he has given him everything he owns"* (Genesis 24:35).

Abraham's son, Isaac, saw firsthand that the God of his father was real, and he decided, "I'm going to serve my father's God, too." Today, many children are turning away from the true God because their fathers' faith is weak, and therefore they think their fathers' God is also weak.

If you are a father, your representation of God in the home will likely determine what your children believe about Him. Will they say, "I will serve the God of my father"? Or will they say, "The God of my father is not worth serving"? I want my children to see the faithfulness of God displayed in my life. I want them to say, "This God that my father and mother serve is real. I will follow the God of my parents because He is faithful."

Men, if you have one goal in life, let it be this: before you die, you will hear your children say, "I serve the God of my father."

Thought for the Day

Your representation of God in the home will likely determine what your children believe about Him.

Reading: Ezra 6–8; John 21

June 14

PRINCIPLES OF FATHERHOOD

Today, review these principles of fatherhood that we have learned over the last two months and reflect on how you can apply them in your everyday life—directly for yourself, if you are a man, and in your relationships with men, if you are a woman.

1. A good father loves the mother of his children; loves his children; is responsible for his children; teaches, trains, disciplines, encourages, comforts, and warns his children.
2. "Fatherhood" is much more than just the biological production of children. Males are designed by God to provide for and protect everything within their sphere of influence.
3. God is our Father in two main ways: through creation and through redemption.
4. The word *father* denotes one who is source, nourisher, sustainer, supporter, founder, and protector, and one who provides identity for that which he produces.
5. A good father knows the heavenly Father.
6. A father's representation of God in the home will likely determine what his children believe about Him.
7. A good father leaves a strong spiritual legacy for his children.

> *The overseer must be...self-controlled, respectable, hospitable, able to teach, not given to drunkenness, not violent but gentle, not quarrelsome....He must manage his own family well and see that his children obey him with proper respect.* (1 Timothy 3:2–4)

Heavenly Father, there is no one like You. You love us, sustain us, provide for us, and equip us to further Your kingdom on earth. We love You and place our complete trust in You. We pray that You will teach fathers how to represent You to their children, and that the children will desire to follow the God of their fathers. In Jesus' name, amen.

Reading: Ezra 9–10; Acts 1

June 15

Perfectly Complementary Designs

God created men and women with perfectly complementary designs. The male is perfect for the female, and the female is perfect for the male. It is when men and women expect each other to think, react, and behave in the same ways—that is, when they don't know or appreciate their God-given differences—that they experience conflict. Yet when they understand and value each other's purposes, they can have rewarding relationships, and they can blend their unique designs harmoniously for God's glory.

Many husbands and wives don't realize that the needs of their spouses are different from their own. Remember the principle that purpose determines nature, and nature determines needs? If a woman wants to help a man fulfill his purpose, she must learn his nature, how he functions, and what his needs are. She can't give him what she needs, because his needs are often different from hers. The reverse is also true. A man must learn a woman's needs and seek to meet them. Consider this illustration: you fill up your car's gas tank with gasoline so that it will run. However, you don't pour gasoline on your plants to make them grow. Each entity needs to be given what is appropriate for its own nature and needs. The same principle holds true for males and females.

God has given strengths to the female that the male does not possess, and vice versa. Until they recognize the natures God has placed within each of them, they will be weak in certain areas, because each was designed to supply what the other lacks. Males and females have different strengths, and neither can fully function without the other.

Thought for the Day

When men and women understand and value each other's purposes, they can have rewarding relationships.

Reading: Nehemiah 1–3; Acts 2:1–21

June 16

Meeting the Needs of Others

We have already determined that the designs of males and females govern the needs of each that must be met for them to be fulfilled, contented, and living in God's creation purposes. The problem is that many people are not fully aware of their own needs, let alone the needs of others. Again, many husbands and wives don't know that the needs of their spouses are different from their own.

Even when people are aware of their needs, they often live in frustration because their needs are not being met. They end up demanding that another person satisfy them or they suffer in silence, never expecting to live a completely fulfilled life.

In the next few days, we will explore the paramount needs of the female and the male that contribute to a fulfilling relationship: her need for love, conversation, and affection, and his need for respect, recreational companionship, and sexual fulfillment. Please keep in mind that the needs that are listed as female needs and the needs that are listed as male needs are also the needs of both. However, they will be discussed in the context of the *primary* needs of each.

As we come to understand one another's needs and work to fulfill them, our hearts and minds will be renewed and more of God's creation purposes will be restored to our lives. Women and men must understand that fulfillment can come only when they work together to address one another's needs. In this endeavor, Jesus' great principle, "*It is more blessed to give than to receive*" (Acts 20:35), is vital. As you give, meeting the needs of others, you will be blessed, and many of your own needs will be met in return.

Thought for the Day

Giving to others by satisfying their needs will bring true fulfillment.

Reading: Nehemiah 4–6; Acts 2:22–47

June 17

The Woman's Primary Need Is Love

Husbands, love your wives.
—Colossians 3:19

I cannot stress this point enough: The primary need of the female is love. We have learned that the woman was *designed* to receive love. This truth is so central to a woman's emotional needs that if it is the only one that men learn and apply, it will make a vast difference in women's lives—and consequently in their own.

A woman doesn't just want love; she truly *needs* it by design. This is why a man can give her a house and expensive gifts and she will still not feel satisfied. The man will say, "What's wrong with you? I can't do anything to please you. I'm giving you all these things, and you're still unhappy." She will answer, "It is not this mink coat or this house that I really want. I want *you.* I want you to tell me I'm important and special and unique to you, and that I am everything you've been dreaming of. I want you to tell me you love me."

You can't replace love. To love means to cherish, to care for, and to show affection. Cherishing a woman doesn't mean buying her expensive presents; it means calling her several times a day and telling her that you love her.

Caring means that you go out of your way to make sure that she has everything she needs. It means dropping everything you're doing just to make certain she is all right. Love doesn't say, "I'm busy right now. I'll talk to you later." Caring is making other people wait while you meet the needs of your wife.

Thought for the Day

A woman doesn't just want love; she truly *needs* it by design.

Reading: Nehemiah 7–9; Acts 3

June 18

The Man's Primary Need Is Respect

The apostle Paul emphasized the primary needs of men and women when he stated, "*Each one of you* [husbands] *also must love his wife as he loves himself, and the wife must respect her husband*" (Ephesians 5:33). As much as a woman needs to *feel* that she is loved, a man needs to *know* that he is respected. Being respected is at the core of his self-esteem, and it affects every other area of his life.

Some women think that because the culture has changed, they don't need to respect their husbands as the leader in the family. A woman may say to her husband, "Let me tell you something. I have a college degree, and you just have your GED. I could pay for this house by myself. I don't need you." Even if the husband is less educated or is making less money than his wife, he still needs her to show him respect as her husband.

A wife can meet her husband's need for admiration and respect by understanding his value and achievements more than anyone else. She needs to remind him of his capabilities and help him to maintain his self-confidence. She should be proud of her husband, not out of duty, but as an expression of sincere admiration for the man with whom she has chosen to share her life.

We should remember that a single man needs respect as much as a married man does. He needs the respect and affirmation of women because he is designed to need it. The women in a single man's life can meet his need by recognizing his value and accomplishments as a man and by encouraging him in his talents and lifework.

Thought for the Day

As much as a woman needs to *feel* she is loved, a man needs to *know* he is respected.

Reading: Nehemiah 10–11; Acts 4:1–22

June 19

Different Primary Needs

Each of you should look not only to your own interests, but also to the interests of others.
—Philippians 2:4

Because the female's primary need is for love, she often thinks that the male's primary need is for love, also. He needs love, but his need for respect is even greater.

If a female expresses love to a male, without fulfilling his need for respect, he might not respond in the way she expects him to. He might remain somewhat distant. For example, a woman may wonder why her husband doesn't seem satisfied in the relationship when she has been lovingly trying to help him by keeping the household running smoothly and providing for his material needs. A woman might even write her husband love notes and give him lots of affection, but notice that he still doesn't seem happy. She wonders, "What else can I do for this man?"

Yet a male feels about those things in the same way that a female feels about the male's provision of a house. He is grateful that his material and emotional needs are being taken care of, and he appreciates his wife's efforts. However, these things don't address his primary need. A husband is to love and cherish his wife. A wife is to respect and honor her husband. In this way, there will be a constant meeting of the other's primary needs.

Let us pursue the things which make for...the building up of one another. (Romans 14:19 NASB)

Thought for the Day

Build up your spouse by meeting his or her primary need.

Reading: Nehemiah 12–13; Acts 4:23–37

June 20

What Do I Do in the Meantime?

One of the problems a woman may face is that her husband doesn't know he's supposed to love her in the ways we've been talking about. Even though a woman might be honoring and esteeming her husband, he might not be showing her love because he really doesn't yet know how. This is a very real problem for many wives, who may wonder, *What do I do in the meantime?* While men and women need to understand and meet each other's needs, if the woman understands the needs of both men and women but her spouse doesn't, it is important that she have patience. She needs to respond to her husband according to what he knows.

If I know that a person is ignorant, I can't be angry at him. Jesus is the highest model of this for us. He said, *"Father, forgive them, for they do not know what they are doing"* (Luke 23:34). The difficulty comes when you know that a person is aware of what he's supposed to be doing but still doesn't do it. In this case, some kind of reproof is necessary. Depending on the situation, a woman might appeal directly to her husband; or she might appeal to the pastor, a trusted Christian friend, or even a family member to speak to her husband for her. Yet her best appeal is to pray for her husband and allow the Lord to change him.

You can reprove a person who has knowledge, but, again, you need to overlook the faults of a person who is ignorant. This will keep bitterness from taking over your heart. Avoid blaming the other person, live responsibly before God, and make sure you carry out your own responsibilities to your spouse. *"That they may be won over without words by the behavior of their wives"* (1 Peter 3:1).

Thought for the Day

Trust God to teach your partner how to meet your needs.

Reading: Esther 1–2; Acts 5:1–21

The Woman's Need for Conversation

In addition to love, a female needs conversation. She enjoys talking with others. This sounds so simple, but it is a real need based on her nature. A woman needs to have a man talk with her. Notice that I said *with* her and not *to* her. Because males have a leadership mind-set, sometimes their conversations with their wives amount to instructions rather than a give-and-take dialogue. A man should always make a point to converse with his wife. Costly gifts don't mean anything to a wife if her husband just leaves them with her and then walks away. She'd rather have the conversation.

The man can fulfill a woman's need for intimate conversation by continually making a point to communicate with her. To truly meet her need, he should talk with her at the *feeling* level and not just the knowledge and information level. She needs him to listen to her attitudes about the events of her day with sensitivity, interest, and concern. All of his conversations with her should convey a desire to understand her, not to change her. This means that he should not necessarily immediately try to solve her problems for her. He should offer his full attention and understanding rather than quick solutions.

After giving her plenty of time to express her feelings, he should conduct his end of the conversation with courtesy and openness, looking her in the eyes and telling her what he really thinks and feels. He should share his plans and actions clearly and completely, because he regards himself as accountable to her, and ask for her input. This will enable her to trust him and feel secure.

Thought for the Day

A man should show a desire to understand his wife, not to change her.

Reading: Esther 3–5; Acts 5:22–42

The Man's Need for Recreational Companionship

A man feels happy when a woman is involved in his recreational pursuits. I can't emphasize enough how important this is. Because of the man's design, he seems to have an inborn need to protect his "territory" from threats from the outside world. This is why he needs to feel as if he is always winning at life. (You women may have noticed this trait already!) This need translates into a desire to win over the competition in a sports event or to master a particular area of interest or expertise. It is his territorial nature that leads to his need for recreational companionship. He needs to be involved in challenging activities, and although he likes to win, he also likes to share these experiences with others.

If a woman takes part in whatever a man enjoys doing—playing tennis, visiting historical landmarks, playing an instrument, designing computer programs—and lets him tell her all about them, she can strengthen her relationship with him. He will feel good when she takes an interest in what he is interested in.

I've heard women say things like this about their husbands: "That old fool; he's always over at the ball field playing softball. I wish he would stop that and come home and be a husband." This attitude won't help the situation. He has a need that is being met out there on the ball field. Why would a man spend hours on something unless he has a need that is being fulfilled through it? Instead of fighting against what brings fulfillment to the man, the woman should find out why it is important to him. Then, if possible, she should participate in it so that they can experience it together, thus building understanding, companionship, and intimacy in their relationship.

Thought for the Day

A man feels happy when a woman is involved in his recreational pursuits.

Reading: Esther 6–8; Acts 6

Interrelated Needs of Affection and Sex

A woman needs affection. She doesn't just want affection—she needs it! Yet while one of her primary needs is affection, one of the male's primary needs is sex. If these two interrelated needs are not lovingly understood and balanced, they can cause some of the worst conflicts in a marriage.

What men and women need to understand is that *affection creates the environment for sexual union* in marriage, while *sex is the event.* Most men don't realize this, and so they immediately go after the event. They don't know what it means to create an environment of affection. They focus only on their need. Women need affection to precede sexual intimacy.

The man is the provider of the seed, and therefore his natural inclination is to provide this source. This is one of the reasons why he concentrates on the event of sex. The woman, on the other hand, is the one who gestates the new life. Her role is to provide a warm and secure environment in which the life can grow and develop. As an incubator, the woman's natural focus is on the sensory, intuitive, and emotional realms of life, and this is why she has a corresponding need for affection. She needs an environment of affection in order to feel loved and fulfilled.

The problem is that most males are not naturally affectionate. Many men simply do not understand how to give affection to their wives. How can a man give a woman what she needs when he feels he doesn't have what she needs? He can learn to be affectionate. He can come to know the woman's design and then meet her need for affection as it relates to this design. If a husband is not sure how to be affectionate, he should sit down with his wife and ask her—gently and sincerely.

Thought for the Day

Affection creates the environment for sexual union in marriage, while sex is the event.

Reading: Esther 9–10; Acts 7:1–21

June 24

Seasons of Love

Men are to be considerate and respectful to their wives in sexual matters. Paul wrote, "*Encourage the young men to be self-controlled*" (Titus 2:6), and "*Teach the older men to be temperate, worthy of respect, self-controlled*" (Titus 2:2). Peter wrote, "*Husbands, in the same way be considerate as you live with your wives, and treat them with respect*" (1 Peter 3:7).

Men need to be aware that the woman's design is related to her purpose. She is designed to reproduce, and therefore her body has a reproductive cycle. Even though the man is the one who plants the seed, he has to plant it during the right season for the female. God designed her differently from a man because of her purpose in reproduction. The man needs to cooperate with this purpose so that both parties can be blessed. At the same time, it is important for a woman to recognize and be sensitive to her husband's need for sex.

While a man is always sexually ready, a woman is not always ready for sexual relations. Many people believe that God designed women to be on a four-season cycle within each month: summer, winter, autumn, and spring. Her hormones determine when each of these seasons appears.

You can always tell when it's summer. The sun is at high noon—hot. God made her that way. Then comes autumn. Autumn is when the weather grows cooler and the woman begins acting a little more reserved. Then winter comes, and the man feels as if he's been left out in the cold. Yet winter passes and suddenly spring arrives, it gets warmer, and everything is new again. A man needs to understand about the seasons of a woman. He might be ready, but, for her, it might not be the right season.

Thought for the Day

Husbands need to understand about the seasons of a woman, and wives need to be sensitive to their husbands' need for sex.

Reading: Job 1–2; Acts 7:22–43

Principles of Primary Needs

Today, review these principles of the primary needs of women and men and reflect on how they apply to your everyday life.

1. The primary need of the female is love, while the primary need of the male is respect.
2. To love means to cherish, to care for, and to show affection.
3. If a woman's husband is ignorant of her need for love, it is important that she be patient and trust God to reveal this need to him while avoiding bitterness.
4. A primary need of the female is conversation, while a primary need of the male is recreational companionship.
5. To truly meet his wife's need for conversation, a husband should talk with her at the *feeling* level and not just the knowledge and information level.
6. A woman can create opportunities for conversing with her husband by developing an interest in his job, his activities, and his hobbies.
7. A primary need of the female is affection, while a primary need of the male is sex.
8. Affection creates the environment for sexual union in marriage, while sex is the event.

Each one of you also must love his wife as he loves himself, and the wife must respect her husband. (Ephesians 5:33)

Heavenly Father,
You have made men and women different in their primary needs, yet we are truly created to complement one another. Please guide us as we seek to meet each other's needs without always thinking of our own needs first. Help us to understand and walk in Your purposes for our relationships. In Jesus' name, amen.

Reading: Job 3–4; Acts 7:44–60

June 26

Knowing the Word

If a man doesn't have the knowledge and capability to teach a woman the Word of God, then he is not really ready for marriage. Getting past puberty doesn't make you ready for marriage. Getting a job or college degree doesn't make you ready. I'm talking about God's qualifications. As far as God is concerned, you are ready for marriage when you are able to teach your family His Word. If you are already married but don't know the Word, you should make it a priority to study and gain knowledge of the Bible. You should go to a church where you can learn the Scriptures, so you can follow up on what God has commanded you to do as a man. You can't teach what you don't know.

How can you teach the Word of God to your family if all you watch is television sitcoms or reality shows or ball games? How can you teach your family God's Word if all you read is *Superman* and *Fantastic Four* or *Time* and *Newsweek*? How can you teach the Word of God to your family if you haven't spent any time learning it yourself?

Many men know more about sports than they do the Bible. They can name every baseball team, who plays on them, and who is pitching in the series, but they don't know the Word. They can instruct their boys in how to play soccer, but they don't know how to teach them to be sanctified. Someone may claim, "The Bible is one thing, but I'm teaching my boy how to be a *real* man." What are you really teaching him?

It takes a true man to teach a boy the Word of God, to instruct him in the values and principles of life that will live on after the game is over.

Thought for the Day

If a man can't teach the Word, he's not really ready for marriage.

Reading: Job 5–7; Acts 8:1–25

Let the Lord Teach You

Blessed is the man who finds wisdom, the man who gains understanding.
—Proverbs 3:13

Men, you must get knowledge and understanding from the Word of God so you can lead your family with wisdom, integrity, and confidence. Remember that husbands and fathers are to teach and nourish. This means they provide "nutrients" and resources that develop, enrich, expand, and grow that which comes from them. One of man's major responsibilities is to teach. Many men are found lacking in this area of teaching and are intimidated by the women they marry, who seem more knowledgeable in spiritual things than they are.

Let me tell you something: the male is wired to teach, so you don't need to be overly concerned about teaching techniques. Males, by nature, love to give instruction. The fatherly instinct to teach is inherent within them. Incidentally, this is why men often resist the attempts women make to instruct them. Men are teachers, but they must have something worthwhile to teach. Get knowledge and understanding from God's Word so that you can teach His truth.

Ask God to instruct you in His Word through the power of the Holy Spirit. He desires to give us His wisdom, knowledge, and understanding: "*For the Lord gives wisdom, and from his mouth come knowledge and understanding*" (Proverbs 2:6). "*Get wisdom, get understanding; do not forget my words or swerve from them*" (Proverbs 4:5). Jesus said, "*But the Counselor, the Holy Spirit, whom the Father will send in my name, will teach you all things and will remind you of everything I have said to you*" (John 14:26).

Thought for the Day

God desires to give us His wisdom, knowledge, and understanding.

Reading: Job 8–10; Acts 8:26–40

June 28

Washing with the Word

Husbands, love your wives, just as Christ loved the church and gave himself up for her to make her holy, cleansing her by the washing with water through the word, and to present her to himself as a radiant church, without stain or wrinkle or any other blemish, but holy and blameless. In this same way, husbands ought to love their wives as their own bodies.

—Ephesians 5:25–28

In this passage, Paul was saying, "Jesus is a good Husband. A man ought to love his wife as Jesus loved the church. He gave Himself for her and cleansed her by the washing of water through the Word."

If a man is to wash his wife with the Word, just as Christ washes His bride with the Word, he certainly needs to be filled with the Word, just as Christ is filled with the Word. You can't wash if you don't have any water.

Jesus emphasized the importance of the Word in our lives. A male who wants to be a real man—the man God created him to be—has to be full of the Word of God. There's only one way to get clean water: go to the well. You can't wash with the muddy water of the world. When you fill your mind and heart only with things such as television or sporting events, that's mud. Some men are washing their wives in mud. If you want the water that the Manufacturer intended you to have, you need to stay connected to the well of God, which is filled with the Word. This means consistently reading, studying, meditating on, and obeying the Scriptures; it also means maintaining your relationship with Jesus and manifesting His nature and character, because Jesus is the Word. (See John 1:1.)

Thought for the Day

A male who wants to be a real man has to be full of the Word of God.

Reading: Job 11–13; Acts 9:1–21

June 29

SPEAKING A POSITIVE WORD

What does it mean for a husband to wash his wife with the Word? Christ is our example in this. Every time we have a negative experience, Jesus comes in immediately with a positive one and washes away the negative. Husbands are to do the same for their wives.

For instance, when the disciples were afraid, Jesus said, "*Be of good cheer*" (Matthew 14:27 KJV). Every time they became nervous, He told them to remain calm. Whenever they became frightened by a storm, He told them to relax. He was always there to wash away fear, to wash away doubt. When they wondered how they were going to feed the five thousand, He told them to have faith. When they told Him that Lazarus had died, He said, "Don't worry about it; he's sleeping." He was always washing His church with God's truth.

What kind of man do we need today? When your wife says, "We're not going to be able to pay the mortgage," you say, "Honey, we serve the God of Abraham, Isaac, and Jacob, the God of my grandparents and parents. Let's just keep standing on the Word. It's going to be all right." When your wife feels a little pain in her body and begins to imagine all kinds of things, such as cancer, you have to be there and say, "Honey, God is the God who heals you. Come here and let me pray for you." That's washing your wife.

God wants men who will stand up in their faith, saying, "A thousand may fall on my right, and ten thousand on my left, but in this house we're going to come through. My house is covered by the Word of God. As for me and my house, we're going to be all right." That's a man; that's a washer, filled with the Word of God!

Thought for the Day

God wants men who will stand up in their faith.

Reading: Job 14–16; Acts 9:22–43

June 30

Does God Know You?

Abraham was a man who took his responsibility as head of the home seriously. And the Lord said, "I know Abraham." (See Genesis 18:19.) I wonder—does God know you? Can He say about you, "I *know* that you will teach your family the Word of God"?

If you want God to consider you His friend, then become a teacher in your home. Again, you have to be filled with the Word in order to give it to your family. Many, many men still don't understand and appreciate the value of the Word of God for the fulfillment of their purpose.

We have talked about the fact that many men just drop off their wives and children at church because they don't want to be responsible for their spiritual training. Abraham knew the Word, and he taught it. Remember, God said, "I will not hide anything from Abraham." (See Genesis 18:17.) Wouldn't you like to be the kind of man to whom God says, "I'm going to tell you My secrets"?

A man who instructs his household in the Scriptures attracts God. No matter how much you pray and go to church and sing hymns, if you don't teach your household God's ways, if you don't give the Word of God prominence in your home, then God sees you as a weak man. God said, in effect, "If a man wants to be a leader in the church, first let him get his house in order." (See 1 Timothy 3:12.)

God doesn't measure your ability to lead by your religious or academic qualifications. He measures it by your domestic qualifications. If you can take care of your children, then God says, "All right, now you can lead My church." If you can manage your home, then you can manage the house of God.

Thought for the Day

Many men still don't appreciate the value of the Word of God for the fulfillment of their purpose.

Reading: Job 17–19; Acts 10:1–23

Designed to Adapt

The LORD God said, "It is not good for the man to be alone. I will make a helper suitable for him."
—Genesis 2:18

Another word for *suitable* is *fit*, which means "adapted to an end or design." The woman was designed at creation with the ability to adapt to the man. This means that she has the built-in energy and "circuits" to adapt to the man's vision in order to help him fulfill it.

A woman's adaptability also means that when she enters a new situation or environment, she is more prone to become like it than a man is. This trait can be a tremendous blessing, but it can also be dangerous. This explains why women have to be careful not to open themselves up to any and every environment they encounter.

A female is more emotional than a male because she is moved by environmental stimuli. For example, a woman will become excited when she enters a church service in which the Spirit of God is very strong. A man will walk in with her at the same time, sit in the back, and check it out. If she is asked if she would like to join the church, she will join in three weeks, while he might wait three *years*. The man is wired to be more logical than emotional, so he wants an explanation for everything.

These complementary traits, working together, enable the man and woman to accomplish their God-given vision. While the man sees the overall vision and the facts related to it, the woman sees the possibilities and gets right to work. The woman is able to see how the man's vision can be implemented and enthusiastically uses her gifts and abilities to make it become reality.

Thought for the Day

A woman has the built-in energy and "circuits" to adapt to a man's vision.

Reading: Job 20–21; Acts 10:24–48

July 2

Using Her Gifts to Help

God has given women many wonderful gifts, and He says, in effect, "I gave you all these things not only for your own enrichment and enjoyment, but also so that you can use these gifts in your position as coleader and helper with men."

If you are a woman, how are you using your gifts? You may be talented, educated, experienced, eloquent, and well dressed. Are you using these assets to prove to men that you are just as good as they are? That's not a help; that's competition. God's plan is for men and women to work together for mutual benefit.

Women often need to exercise special wisdom when helping men, however, because the last thing many men want to admit is that they *need* help. They don't understand how God has designed women to help them. When a woman tries to assist a man, therefore, the man may interpret her help as nagging. For example, a woman may be trying to say to her husband, "God's vision is for you to be the spiritual leader for me and for our children; however, you can't be a spiritual leader if you won't develop your spiritual life." So, the next day, she asks, "When are we going to pray?" He retorts, "Don't bother me right now. The Lord will tell me when to pray."

The man needs to appreciate the woman's role of helper, and the woman needs discernment when giving help. If the man messes up or fails, the woman shouldn't kick him when he's down. Helpers pick people up and dust them off. Do you know how many men are where they are today because their helpers made sure they got there? Your man might not yet be the best husband, he might not yet be spiritually mature, but encourage him and help him to become all God created him to be.

Thought for the Day

How are you using your gifts?

Reading: Job 22–24; Acts 11

July 3

A Spiritual Encourager

A woman can help a man greatly in his spiritual life. For example, if your husband doesn't pray, don't ask, "Why don't you pray?" Instead, pray *for* him. Then, encourage him whenever he shows an interest in spiritual matters. Don't make him feel as if he's not spiritual.

Many men try to move close to God, but their wives actually push them away from Him. I've seen some women who do not know how to help their husbands after their husbands receive the Lord. For example, a woman prays for her husband for twenty years, and he finally becomes a Christian. She praises God for this answered prayer. Then, all of a sudden, she becomes depressed. Why? Perhaps her husband hears a statement from the Scriptures, and he asks, "Where is that found in the Bible?" She's embarrassed about his lack of knowledge. Maybe he prays a little too loudly during the prayer meeting, and she feels ashamed because she thinks he doesn't know how to conduct himself. The best thing she can do to help him is to let him ask his questions, let him learn to pray, and be thankful about the wonderful things God is doing in his life.

Or perhaps a woman sees her newly converted husband reading the Bible, and she says, "Why don't you take out the garbage?" She's not helping. The garbage can wait a little while longer. She might even be jealous and say, "Now that you're saved, you sit and read the Bible for three hours at a time. Do you think you're more spiritual than I am?" Instead, she should say, "I'll help you take out the garbage, honey." Why? In this way, she will be helping him to become the spiritual leader of the home, and this will be a blessing to her. A wife needs to support her husband's spiritual growth.

Thought for the Day

A woman can help a man greatly in his spiritual life.

Reading: Job 25–27; Acts 12

July 4

Nothing to Adapt To

The world is filled with frustrated women who live with men who aren't going anywhere. The first question a woman should ask a man after he proposes is, "Where are you going in life?" If he can't answer this question, she should tell him to find a map and say that she'll talk to him later. A woman is too valuable a person to waste sitting in a house being frustrated for twenty years. It breaks my heart to see the precious, awesome potential of a female being suffocated by some male who doesn't know what he's doing.

God created the woman to be able to adapt to the man. Yet it's hard for a woman to adapt to someone who isn't leading. She cannot follow someone who isn't going anywhere—who doesn't know what he's doing. Therefore, if a man wants a woman to adapt to him, he has to give her something to adapt to. There are many men walking around who have nothing to do, and they're asking women to help them with it. In God's plan, that's illegal. God told the man, "You will be a provider. You will provide the vision." A man was made to have a vision. A female was made to help him fulfill it. But if he doesn't have a vision, how can she help him?

> *The shepherds have become dull-hearted, and have not sought the* LORD*; therefore they shall not prosper, and all their flocks shall be scattered.* (Jeremiah 10:21 NKJV)

Thought for the Day

The world is filled with frustrated females who are living with men who aren't going anywhere.

Reading: Job 28–29; Acts 13:1–25

Supporting, Not Comparing

The woman is meant to bless, support, and honor the man, and the man is meant to be a head, a covering, and a protection for her. In this way, they are helping each other to be all they were created to be. Yet these purposes break down when the man and the woman don't know or address each other's needs.

A woman who is struggling with her husband's lack of vision or spiritual immaturity may begin to compare him with other Christian men. The worst thing a woman can do is to compare her husband with another man. Ladies, please don't tell your husbands, "Why can't you be like our pastor?" or "Why aren't you like So-and-so?" That's the most dangerous—and ridiculous—thing a woman can say to a man. Every man is his own being and has his own image of himself. Again, you need to support him, even if he is not perfect; you need to be an encouragement to him in his life.

For example, a man always wants to feel as if he is a leader. Try to make your husband feel that he has contributed significantly to your family's success. When you make a man feel that he is important to what has been accomplished—that he is the one responsible for, or that his input was necessary for, the success of something—then you will have somebody who serves you, because a man feeds on respect. However, if you make him feel unimportant, you will run into trouble. He may even go elsewhere, to someone who believes he is everything.

Her husband has full confidence in her and lacks nothing of value.
She brings him good, not harm, all the days of her life.

(Proverbs 31:11–12)

Thought for the Day

The worst thing a woman can do is to compare her husband to another man.

Reading: Job 30–31; Acts 13:26–52

July 6

The Vulnerability of Adaptability

I have heard men say, "If my wife did to me what I do to her, I'd have been gone a long time ago." They are saying that there is something about women that makes them able to stay in uncomfortable situations longer than men would. The reason is a woman's spirit of adaptability.

It's difficult enough for a woman to have nothing to adapt to, but it's even worse if she adapts to something that isn't right for her. The word *adapt* could be translated "submit." The woman should submit only when she recognizes the man's moral authority over her. Some men don't deserve to be adapted to. They're not giving the adapter anything comfortable to adapt to. When this is the case, you will find women adapting in bitterness, hatred, deceit, or malice. They're being forced to adapt to something against their wills, and they resent and even hate it.

Whatever the male gives off or gives out, the female will generally adapt to. For instance, I have observed women whose husbands or boyfriends are prone to swearing. They eventually develop the habit of swearing themselves. Children also take in whatever comes from their source, and they end up producing the same kind of fruit.

Yet while a woman is designed to adapt, she isn't designed to adapt forever. Women have a tremendous ability to endure frustration and pain, but most won't allow abusive behavior to go on forever. Love may suffer long, but only long—not forever. The woman reaches a point at which she needs to adapt to some freedom and find something worthy of spending her life on. A man must be careful to treat a woman's spirit of adaptability with respect and sensitivity, and to consider it a valuable aspect of his unity with her.

Thought for the Day

A man must be careful to treat a woman's spirit of adaptability with respect and sensitivity.

Reading: Job 32–33; Acts 14

The Abuse of Purpose

Some husbands wonder why their wives spend so much time at church. It may be that the women don't have anything to help with at home. The men don't have visions, so the women go to church to help the ministers with *their* visions. They help with children's programs or music ministries because they have a need to contribute.

Some women even help men to do wrong things if they can't find any who are doing the right things. A man may tell a woman, "You wait in the car while I rip off this store," and she actually feels good about it because she feels she is doing something to help him. She feels valuable to this man. For the same reason, some women carry drugs and do deals for their kingpin boyfriends. You may wonder how they can do that. In a warped way, they are seeking to be fulfilled, to have their needs met.

Remember one of our key principles: Where purpose is not known, abuse is inevitable. When men and women misunderstand their purposes, these purposes will be abused in some way. "*Where there is no vision, the people perish*" (Proverbs 29:18 KJV).

A misunderstanding of purpose has pulled men and women away from God's original design in creation. As long as this misunderstanding persists, we won't live fulfilled lives as men and women, and our relationships will continue to suffer.

Thought for the Day

Some women help men to do wrong things in their attempts to feel fulfilled.

Reading: Job 34–35; Acts 15:1–21

July 8

A Good Word from a Good Woman

When God said He would make a helper for the man, I believe that He intended the woman to be the "*help meet*" (Genesis 2:18 KJV) for men in general, not just for her husband. This means that, if you are a woman, you are meant to be a spiritual help and encouragement to the men you encounter in life.

Please understand that I am certainly not saying a woman should submit to other men as she submits to her husband; rather, I am saying that she can be a tremendous influence for good in men's lives. Moreover, the helping nature of a woman can be exercised whether a woman is married or single, since it is a natural part of her makeup. Single women have male relatives and friends who need encouragement. A single woman has much to contribute in this way, and, if she marries, she can bring into her marriage this valuable experience of exercising her gift and understanding the nature and needs of men.

If a woman sees a man she knows destroying his life with drugs, she might go to him and say, "God has put so much potential inside of you. It breaks my heart to see you on drugs." Saying that will help him. You don't have to be married to give that type of help. Some men just need a good word from a good woman. They have been told negative things about themselves all their lives. They are looking for a woman to tell them something positive about themselves.

Let me caution you that this can require careful discretion on the woman's part so that the wrong impression is not given. Yet a woman can be a powerful force for good in a man's life by being a spiritual encouragement to him.

Thought for the Day

The helping nature of a woman can be exercised whether a woman is married or single, since it is a natural part of her makeup.

Reading: Job 36–37; Acts 15:22–41

July 9

Cultivate Adaptability

A woman is to be commended for her tremendous spirit of adaptability and its contribution to the lives of individuals, families, and communities. It is truly a gift from God. As we have seen, this gift must be treated with respect by both men and women because it can have a negative as well as a positive side.

Consider the following illustration. What determines the health of a plant? The soil in which it is rooted. If you put it in soil that is full of nutrients, it will likely thrive. Yet if you put it in soil that is high in salt content, it will become sickly and might even die. The plant adapts to what it receives from the environment to which it is connected. Therefore, you can usually determine the health of the plant based on the quality of the soil in which the plant grows.

Women and men who desire healthy personal relationships should cultivate a positive environment in which a woman's ability to adapt can thrive. A woman enhances the life of a man by being his companion, adapting to him, and sharing and helping in the vision. In all the ways in which the woman enhances the man's life, she is also enhancing her own, since she is a coleader and participant in the dominion vision that was given by God. When a woman and man learn to live together harmoniously within their purposes and positions, helping and supporting one another, they can live the lives they were created to live and find lasting contentment and fulfillment.

Thought for the Day

Cultivate a positive environment in which the woman's ability to adapt can thrive.

Reading: Job 38–40; Acts 16:1–21

July 10

Principles of Adaptability

Review these principles of a woman's spirit of adaptability and reflect on how you can apply them in your everyday life—for yourself, if you are a woman, and in your relationships with women, if you are a man.

1. God created the woman with the ability to adapt to the man's vision and to help fulfill it.
2. A female is more prone to adapt to her environment than a male is.
3. A female is more emotional than a male because she is moved by environmental stimuli.
4. God gave women many gifts, not only for their own enrichment, but also for their purpose as coleaders and helpers with men.
5. The man needs to appreciate the woman's role of helper, and the woman needs to use discernment when giving help.
6. The world is filled with frustrated women who live with men who aren't going anywhere.
7. Whatever the male gives off or gives out, the female will generally adapt to—whether it is positive or negative.
8. Women and men who desire healthy personal relationships should cultivate a positive environment in which a woman's ability to adapt can thrive.

The Lord God said, "It is not good for the man to be alone. I will make a helper suitable for him." (Genesis 2:18)

Heavenly Father, You have created women with much energy and giftedness. You have given them a spirit of adaptability that makes their role as coleader and helper invaluable to the men in their lives. Please protect them from adapting to the wrong environment. Give them the discernment they need to avoid any source that is not from You. Help men to provide positive environments in which women's gifts can thrive and bless others. In Jesus' name, amen.

Reading: Job 41–42; Acts 16:22–40

What Is Vision?

Men, you may be wondering how you can have a positive vision that your wife can adapt to and help you with. You don't want her to live with frustration, but you still don't really understand what vision is.

Vision is the capacity to see beyond your physical eyes into a preferred future. Vision is purpose in pictures. Have you been seeing pictures of your dream? When you turn off the TV and computer and everything is quiet, do you start thinking of your future? Your dreams are being drowned out by your music, your phone, and other people talking. In the Bible, whenever God wanted to speak to someone about his work, He always took him away from other people. God took Abraham to a mountain all by himself. He took Moses to the desert. David heard from God when he was out tending sheep in the hills. You need to disengage from the noise of life so you can see pictures of your future again.

Purpose produces a vision, and a vision produces a plan. Once there's a plan, it produces discipline in you. Write down your purpose and vision, and then get some pictures symbolizing that vision and what you need to fulfill it. I cut out pictures of my dream and put them where I could see them every day. I would say, "That's what I'm going to do."

"Many are the plans in a man's heart, but it is the Lord's purpose that prevails" (Proverbs 19:21). I have shared this Scripture often because I want it to be emblazoned on your heart. God's purpose for your life is already established; He's not worried about your future. Whatever you were born to do is already finished in Him. Cease worrying about it, capture His vision for your life, and start making plans to go there.

Thought for the Day

Capture God's vision for your life and start making plans to go there.

Reading: Psalm 1–3; Acts 17:1–15

July 12

The Great Challenge of Life

The unfolding of your words gives light; it gives understanding to the simple.
—Psalm 119:130

The great challenge of life is understanding life. When life throws us a curveball, we often just play games and fake it. Many times, we have to guess and then wonder endlessly if our guesses will work.

What we lack is understanding. I want to repeat an observation made by David, the great king of Israel, regarding this very issue. By divine inspiration, he spoke of the moral and social chaos in his community and described the root cause of mankind's confusion, frustration, and self-destruction: "*They know nothing, they understand nothing. They walk about in darkness; all the foundations of the earth are shaken*" (Psalm 82:5).

This text declares that the reason why the people of the earth are so confused and filled with problems is not because there are no answers but because we don't understand our Creator. We don't know His principles, His purpose, His nature, or His precepts.

The greatest enemy of mankind is *ignorance of self.* Nothing is more frustrating than not knowing who you are or what to do with what you have. All of mankind's problems are a result of this major dilemma. Essentially, the dilemma is that we lack understanding. Without understanding, life is an experiment, and frustration is the reward.

Thought for the Day

God's Word teaches us about who we really are.

Reading: Psalm 4–6; Acts 17:16–34

Faking It Leads to Failure

I'll never forget bringing home my algebra homework during junior high school. Remember all those formulas? Trying to understand those many formulas made algebra a horrible experience for me. I remember just sitting there, staring at those problems. Since I did not understand the formulas, I could not solve the problems. So, what did I do? I faked it! I wrote down whatever figures came to my mind. Having numbers written on the page may have looked good, but all the answers were incorrect!

This is more than just an interesting story. When it comes to the issues of life, we often do the same thing I did with my algebra assignments. When problems arise, we don't understand the problems, much less life itself, so we fake it. Although I tried to make the figures work out the way I wanted, they were wrong because I didn't understand the formulas. When test time came, my lack of understanding brought me the final result of faking it: failure.

One day I decided I had better learn those formulas, so I took a tutoring course after school with my teacher. It took me hours to learn them, but I put forth the time and effort until I understood and was able to do them. Algebra finally made sense to me, and my fear was replaced with confidence.

Godly principles are very much like formulas. They are set laws that govern life and are constant in the face of change. Understanding and applying God's principles helps us to handle any situation in life.

Thought for the Day

Understanding and applying God's principles helps us to handle any situation in life.

Reading: Psalm 7–9; Acts 18

July 14

Three Problems in Life

They know nothing, they understand nothing. They walk about in darkness; all the foundations of the earth are shaken.
—Psalm 82:5

The above verse identifies three progressive components that are the source of our sufferings and difficulties in life. First, there is a lack of knowledge—"*they know nothing.*" Second, there is a misunderstanding or misconception of life—"*they understand nothing*" and cannot comprehend their environment. Third, there is a lack of spiritual sight—"*they walk about in darkness*"; they see nothing. The word "*darkness,*" in the original Hebrew, connotes the principle of ignorance—that men are ignorant or blind to God's principles. If you attempt to live and solve the challenges of life from a position of ignorance, then you are walking in darkness and will experience exasperation, frustration, and failure.

The result of ignorance and a lack of understanding is that "*all the foundations of the earth are shaken.*" *Foundation* implies the fundamental principles and laws that regulate the functions of the earth. In essence, when people lack knowledge and understanding of the basic, fundamental laws of God, *all of life goes off track* and ends in failure. Knowledge, wisdom, and understanding from God, then, are vital keys to understanding the right answers for your life.

Thought for the Day

When people lack knowledge of the fundamental laws of God, all of life goes off track.

Reading: Psalm 10–12; Acts 19:1–20

What Is Understanding?

Jesus Christ, the greatest Teacher of all time, said, "*He who has ears, let him hear*" (Matthew 11:15). He was separating people who simply listen to information from those who actually understand it.

Here is how I define understanding: "*Understanding is knowledge and comprehension of the original purpose and intent of a thing and of the principles by which a thing was designed to function.*" To possess understanding of something, you must know the original intent for it. First, what was in the mind of the one who made it? Second, how did the creator of a product intend for it to function?

Understanding is comprehension of the truth. Why is this important? Because nothing is truly yours until you understand it. No matter how much you sit and listen, if you don't understand a thing, it's still not yours. That's why information does not guarantee knowledge. When you understand a thing, it becomes yours. Most of our lives are exercises in misunderstanding.

If you don't understand yourself, you don't yet possess yourself. That is why people who don't know who they are imitate other people and become someone other than who they were created to be. If you don't know what you were born to be and do, then you become a victim of other people's opinions. Understanding who made you and who you are is crucial so that others do not take possession of your life. When you have understanding, you know what to do with your life.

Thought for the Day

To possess understanding of something, you must know the original intent for it.

Reading: Psalm 13–15; Acts 19:21–41

July 16

The Plans of the Lord

The plans of the Lord stand firm forever, the purposes of his heart through all generations.
—Psalm 33:11

We have acknowledged that God has purposes that He determines beforehand and then carries out. To bring this to a personal level, this includes plans for you and me. God does not do anything on a whim or without knowing the end result.

The origins of humanity are described in the book of Genesis, which means "beginning." However, the creation account that we read about in Genesis was not the real beginning. I would like to call Genesis "the end result after God finished His thought processes." When God finished deciding what He wanted to do, then He created. First, God predetermined or purposed everything. Then, He produced it.

This concept is crucial to our understanding of purpose. It means that *Genesis was not the beginning of a supernatural experiment with an unknown outcome.* Genesis was the beginning of the production of something that was sure. Therefore, in Genesis, we are looking at the start-up of the project, as I like to call it. Those who are involved in project management know that this is an important step in the process of building. When you reach the start-up phase, it means that you have all the plans drawn, all the physical resources in place, all the management resources in order, and now you're ready to begin. That's Genesis.

Thought for the Day

Genesis is both the beginning and the end result.

Reading: Psalm 16–17; Acts 20:1–16

Do You Know Where You're Headed?

I was driving along an undeveloped street near my home one day when I saw a large sign with a beautifully painted picture of a building. The sign said, Coming Soon. I sensed the Holy Spirit saying to me, "Did you see that?" I asked, "See what?" He said, "Did you see the finish?" I came back around to take another look at the painting, and the Holy Spirit continued, "If you were to see the men working on that project, digging up all the mud and muck, making big holes, and if you were to ask them what they were doing, they would say, 'We are building that.' They could tell you exactly where they were headed." I have never forgotten that lesson.

I have a question for you: Is your life similar to that? If someone were to ask you where you're going, could you answer that you're headed somewhere? Could you specify where? Are you so clear about your dream that you could paint a picture of it?

If you know where you're going, then when someone doesn't understand the reason for the mud, the muck, the water, and the hole, it doesn't matter. Everything might not look right, but you know it is part of the process. When you're in the midst of the process, your life might not look like it's becoming anything. But take careful note: there's a painting of you. God has painted it for you in His Word. Anytime you get bogged down, every time you get discouraged, you can look at that painting.

We may be able to see the outcome of God's purposes for our lives twenty years into the future or only one day ahead. Yet if we are living in God's plans for us, we have found the key to our existence.

Thought for the Day

If someone were to ask you where you're going, could you answer that you're headed somewhere?

Reading: Psalm 18–19; Acts 20:17–38

July 18

Making Up for Lost Time

I will repay ["restore to" NKJV] you for the years the locusts have eaten.
—Joel 2:25

I once spoke about purpose at a church in Baton Rouge, Louisiana. A woman came up to me after the service and said, "I'm fifty-six years old, brother. Where were you fifty-six years ago?" I asked, "What do you mean?" She replied, "You're the first person ever to come into my life and help me understand that I have a reason for living—and I can't give an account for fifty-six years right now."

Sometimes, people begin to feel the way that woman did; they're distressed because they've wasted so much time. If this is your situation, don't be discouraged. One of the wonderful things about God is that He has a way of restoring the years that the locusts have eaten. (See Joel 2:23–26.) When you go to Him, He knows how to make up for the time that you've lost.

Yet God would prefer that we follow Him and know our purpose all our lives. That is why the Word of God says very strongly to young people, *"Remember your Creator in the days of your youth"* (Ecclesiastes 12:1). The Bible is saying to us, "Remember God now—not when you've finished partying and ruining your health with drugs, alcohol, and tobacco, when you say, 'Well, I'm sick now; I'd better go find God.'" Don't wait until after you have messed up your life to remember God. *"Remember your Creator in the days of your youth."* Why? God wants you to remember the Manufacturer early so that He can set you on course for your entire life.

Thought for the Day

God knows how to make up for the time you have lost.

Reading: Psalm 20–22; Acts 21:1–17

July 19

Becoming a Whole Person

Some of you single men and women are afraid of being alone. When you hit age twenty-five, you begin to think you're past your prime, and so you say to yourselves, "I'm never going to get married. I'd better latch onto the first thing that comes along." That's the reason many people marry spouses who aren't right for them. Do you know what their problem is? They haven't learned what it means to be a whole person.

There is a difference between "being alone" and "being lonely." You can be lonely in a crowd, but you can be alone and happy as a lark. There is nothing wrong with being alone at times. The Bible tells us that it's important to be alone and quiet before the Lord. Jesus often made a point to go off by Himself in order to pray and rest. Being alone can be healthy, but loneliness is like a disease.

Adam was so occupied with his purpose of working and taking care of the garden of Eden that he didn't know he needed somebody. Yet most of us do the reverse. We don't have time for God because we're busy trying to find a mate.

Jesus talked about the attitude we should have when He said, in effect, "Don't worry about what you're going to eat, what you're going to wear, or whom you're going to marry. Seek first the kingdom of God. Become immersed in His righteousness. Then God will meet all your needs." (See Matthew 6:31–33.)

Become like Adam: get lost in the garden of God's righteousness because, when He brings you a spouse, you had better understand His ways. Adam was so busy following the command of God that, when his mate came along, he was ready, and it was the right time for him.

Thought for the Day

Be prepared for meeting your spouse by first understanding and obeying God's ways.

Reading: Psalm 23–25; Acts 21:18–40

July 20

Stop Thinking Small

Many men are not living in the purposes God has for them because they are thinking in limited terms. Let me encourage you: your dreams are not crazy; they are your lifework. Staying in a job that is not right for you is like a fish trying to be a horse. That's why you have high blood pressure. That's why there's so much stress in your life. You're doing things you weren't born to do. Stop thinking small. Move into your purpose—not only for your sake, but also for others'.

Remember, a woman was created by God to help a man, but the man has to be doing something! God's purpose for creating the female was to help the male with his purpose and assignment. When a man finds his work, a woman finds her assignment. I believe many marriages are breaking up—even in the church—because women are not helping their husbands with the work God has given them. Your wife is waiting for you to find your purpose because her assignment in life is tied to it. She was designed to help you. She may also have her own work, but for her to help you fulfill yours, you have to know your purpose.

Since God designed a female to help a male, everything He put in the female works toward that purpose. That's why a woman is such an amazing creature! She is one mean helping machine! When she shows up in your life, she has everything you need. She has insight, intuition, stamina, wisdom, counsel, the ability to carry burdens, and the capacity to incubate ideas. She can talk about your vision and protect your resources.

Men, do you understand your purpose in life? Are you thinking in limited terms—or in God's terms?

Thought for the Day

What are you doing with the dreams God has given you?

Reading: Psalm 26–28; Acts 22

July 21

The Chief Cornerstone

Consequently, you are no longer foreigners and aliens, but fellow citizens with God's people and members of God's household, built on the foundation of the apostles and prophets, with Christ Jesus himself as the chief cornerstone.
—Ephesians 2:19–20

I was traveling with a group in Israel in the area of Capernaum. We went to visit an ancient synagogue, one that Jesus was said to have taught in. Being very inquisitive, I walked around the little synagogue, and I noticed that, in back, there was a rock at the bottom of the foundation. I asked our guide, who was a Jewish rabbi, "What is that rock?" He replied, "Oh, that is the chief cornerstone."

Thinking of the verse from Ephesians, I said, "Explain that to me." The rabbi said, "They laid foundations by interlocking stones." In other words, they didn't pour concrete in those days; they used interlocking systems. Every rock was carved to fit into the rock next to it so that they locked in place. When the foundation was nearly completed, one stone had to lock into the last two stones in one corner to seal the whole thing together. That was the cornerstone. Without a cornerstone, the foundation would fall apart. To destroy a building constructed in this way, all you have to do is move the cornerstone!

If you are a male, you are God's foundation for your family, but it's an *interlocking* foundation that needs something strong to hold it secure. Jesus Christ Himself is the only hope for your continued survival and effectiveness as the foundation of your family because He is the Chief Cornerstone. "*He only is my rock and my salvation; He is my defense; I shall not be moved*" (Psalm 62:6 NKJV).

Thought for the Day

Without the Chief Cornerstone, the family's foundation will fall apart.

Reading: Psalm 29–30; Acts 23:1–15

July 22

Whose Name Is on Your Cornerstone?

See, I lay a stone in Zion, a chosen and precious cornerstone, and the one who trusts in him will never be put to shame.

—1 Peter 2:6

People all over the world are creating businesses and industries, amassing wealth, constructing houses, making ships and aircraft, and pursuing similar endeavors. They are building, building, building, but their lives are falling apart—their spouses are leaving them, their kids are on drugs, and they don't have any sense of what is really important in life. They have much wealth, but everything is coming apart because they lack a vital relationship with God and they're missing the Chief Cornerstone. Some of you reading this devotional would admit that you haven't wanted Jesus Christ in your life. Yet you need Him! He is essential to your life. He is not optional.

Today, when we dedicate a school, a church, or another building, we often put a plaque on the bottom corner of the building. That's not a real cornerstone but a ceremonial one that is based on the real, functional cornerstones of the past. Whose name goes on a cornerstone? It could be the owner of the building, or perhaps the contractor. If you go to Greece and Rome today, you can still see who built many of the ancient buildings because their names are carved in the cornerstones.

Whose name is on your cornerstone? If it's Buddha, Muhammad, Confucius, Scientology, humanism, atheism, materialism—anything besides Jesus Christ—I can tell you the future of your building. It will ultimately fall. But the Scripture assures us, "*The one who trusts in him* [Jesus] *will never be put to shame*" (1 Peter 2:6).

Thought for the Day

Jesus Christ is not optional—He is essential to your life.

Reading: Psalm 31–32; Acts 23:16–35

You and the Cornerstone

I will show you what he is like who comes to me and hears my words and puts them into practice. He is like a man building a house, who dug down deep and laid the foundation on rock. When a flood came, the torrent struck that house but could not shake it, because it was well built. But the one who hears my words and does not put them into practice is like a man who built a house on the ground without a foundation. The moment the torrent struck that house, it collapsed and its destruction was complete.

—Luke 6:47–49

Earlier, I wrote about the construction workers in London who were digging a deep foundation while building a hotel. You can't build your life on ground that shifts when it experiences too much pressure. You need to dig down deep and find the solid Rock.

When God works on a person's foundation, He uses the same principle. If you make Jesus your Cornerstone, God will build you so well that He will know you can handle the height of the building. He won't be concerned about you crumbling. If you don't know Christ as your personal Cornerstone, don't go another day without that assurance. I'm not talking about "religion" or "church." I'm talking about your reconnecting with Jesus Christ and submitting yourself to Him as the Chief Cornerstone. We have to submit to Him because, without Him, we are nothing and can do nothing. (See John 15:5.)

Surrender your life to Him today. Now is the day of salvation! "*I tell you, now is the time of God's favor, now is the day of salvation*" (2 Corinthians 6:2).

Thought for the Day

If you don't know Christ as your personal Chief Cornerstone, don't go another day without that assurance.

Reading: Psalm 33–34; Acts 24

July 24

A Temptation or a Test?

God cannot be tempted by evil, nor does he tempt anyone.
—James 1:13

The Bible assures us that God doesn't tempt us. He may test us, however. (See, for example, 2 Chronicles 32:31.) What's the difference between a test and a temptation? A test is more like the act of tempering metal.

The Greeks and Romans used tempering in the process of making swords for battle. They would put a piece of steel in the fire until it became so hot you could see into it and determine if there were any black spots in it. The black spots were areas in which the molecules were not close enough together; they were weak areas. When they discovered any spots, they would put the hot sword on a steel anvil and pound it with a steel mallet. As they struck the spots, the molecules would come together. They would keep pounding until they couldn't see any more spots. Next, they would put the sword in cold water, and the steel would harden. After that, they would put the sword back in the fire until it became hot and malleable again. They would continue this cycle—fire, beating, cold water—until they couldn't see any more spots. After a sword had gone through this process, they could be sure it would not break in the middle of a battle where a soldier's life depended on it. You never trust a sword that has not been tempered.

This process is similar to how God tests us. *Tempering means testing for weakness to insure strength.* God doesn't need the tempering process in order to see your true character. He can already see into you, and He knows your secret "spots." He knows your habits, your weaknesses, the garbage you have hidden away. The tempering is for your sake. He allows you to go through trials and tests so you can recognize what is hindering your life.

Thought for the Day

Tempering means testing for weakness to insure strength.

Reading: Psalm 35–36; Acts 25

As Strong as Our Storms

God permits storms in our lives in order to expose our weaknesses. *He* knows them, but *we* must learn what they are and allow Him to remove them because we are only as strong as the storms we survive. Every time you survive a storm, it is as if a few more "spots" have been beaten out of your life. When the spots are purged, then God can call you one of His swords. He will hold you out as an example, saying, "This man will defend my cause," or "I'm not afraid that she's going to break in the middle of the fight."

Have you ever wondered why so many "Christian celebrities" crack in the midst of trials? They haven't been in the fire long enough. They wouldn't stay under the hammer! They haven't been strengthened in the water. We're meant to dream big, but we must remember that, along the way, we will be put in the fire, beaten, and then put in cold water. Sometimes, as soon as we make it out of the water and think the test is over, God will put us back in the fire because we need to be refined further.

Think about the life of Abraham. The Lord told him, in essence, "Abraham, I want to trust you with a brand new nation I want to build. So I have to test you. Kill your only son, the son of promise, as a sacrifice to Me." Abraham had to have great faith in the midst of the test to believe that if he killed Isaac, God could raise him up again. He exercised this faith and passed the test. He obeyed to the point of sacrifice when God stopped him. God did not want him to kill Isaac, but He needed to know that Abraham would put Him before all else and trust Him to fulfill the promise in His own way and time.

Thought for the Day

We are only as strong as the storms we survive.

Reading: Psalm 37–39; Acts 26

July 26

"The Rain Came"

Everyone who hears these words of mine and puts them into practice is like a wise man who built his house on the rock. The rain came down, the streams rose, and the winds blew and beat against that house; yet it did not fall.
—Matthew 7:24–25

Jesus said, *"The rain came."* He didn't say, "The rain *might* come." Both the one who builds on rock *and* the one who builds on sand have to go through the storm.

"To everything there is a season" (Ecclesiastes 3:1 NKJV). Everything in life has a season. This means that whatever difficulties we're experiencing are not going to last. However, it also means that whatever we are enjoying now may not last, either. Many of us do not want to hear this; we think that everything is forever.

Let me remind you that even if you are in Christ Jesus, you are not immune to storms. When we look at people who are men and women of God, who are faithful in service to Him, who are praying people, or who have served others greatly, but who still find themselves in crises, we say, "This isn't supposed to happen to people like them." It doesn't matter what kind of "house" you have—the storm is coming. The issue is not really the storm. The issue is the foundation. Remember that as you hold on to the Rock, your foundation will remain sure.

I don't know what your storm is going to be. It might not be what the person next to you in church is going through. But when it comes, I want you to be able to say, "I'm going through a tough one, but my anchor is holding. I'm holding on to Jesus. It's only a season." You keep on believing.

Thought for the Day

You are not immune to storms. Are you holding on to the Rock?

Reading: Psalm 40–42; Acts 27:1–26

There Is a Season

To everything there is a season, a time for every purpose under heaven.
—Ecclesiastes 3:1 (NKJV)

One of my greatest mentors, Oral Roberts, told me, "Son, if you're going to be successful in life, expect the best and prepare for the worst."

You are not to trust in the permanence of anything on earth except for your relationship with God. Parents, friends, coworkers, pastors, church members—they're all for a season. Be prepared for the season of living without them. We must have our anchor on the Rock because the Rock has no season—He is eternal.

"The eternal God is your refuge, and underneath are the everlasting arms" (Deuteronomy 33:27). Even with those who tell you, "The Lord sent me to work with you," you can expect their departure at some point. So, when a staff member comes to me and says, "The Lord told me it's time to move on," I say, "Well, praise God, thank you for your contribution for the last twenty years. Now, what do you need to help you get where you're going?"

To everything there is a season. Suppose your business is going well. Prepare now for what you will do if your business goes through some tough times. Don't panic and say, "God has left me and the devil has taken over." No, that's just a season. Perhaps you don't like your current job. God says, "That's no problem; everything is seasonal." Think in those terms. You have to know how to handle what life brings you. You have to be an anchor that is not driven by every wind and wave.

Thought for the Day

You are not to trust in the permanence of anything on earth except for your relationship with God.

Reading: Psalm 43–45; Acts 27:27–44

July 28

Prepared for the Storm

I've lived in the Bahamas all my life, and God has used the ocean to teach me essential lessons on Christian living. Often, my friends and I have gone out on our boats early in the morning to fish, and the water is like glass as we speed over the ocean. By one o'clock in the afternoon, however, a storm may be coming, and, since we're ten miles from shore, we have to start tying everything down. The season has changed, and the boat will rock during the storm, but everyone knows what to do. We've already been trained; we've prepared for the storm.

We know to put the anchor down. We actually dive down and put that anchor under the rock. Then, we brace everything. When the storm is upon us, it's too late to do anything else; the season has come. We're beaten about by the wind and waves, but after about fifteen or twenty minutes, it passes us by. Then, it's peaceful again, and we can go back to fishing.

It will be the same with you. Once you have committed to the Rock and have prepared for the changing seasons of life, you will be able to ride out the storm and then go back to fishing. It's going to be all right, and it's going to be even better fishing because the storm will have stirred up more fish. Behind every broken experience is a wealthy experience from the Lord. There is peace in the promise that nothing earthly lasts, but the Rock is eternal.

Thought for the Day

Behind every broken experience is a wealthy experience from the Lord.

Reading: Psalm 46–48; Acts 28

An Anchor Stops Things

Men are called to protect their families and communities from the destructive currents of our modern society. Remember our definition of an anchor? It is "something that serves to hold an object firmly," and "anything that gives stability and security."

If a boat is drifting with a current, and you put the anchor down on a rock, it stops the boat from being controlled by the current. The current of our modern society is filled with so many strong, ungodly influences that the male needs to come back in the family, put his anchor on the rock of a solid, godly principle, and say, "We're not going in that direction."

Note that an anchor does not stop the current itself. The current will come, but the anchor stops the boat you are in. How many things have you stopped from happening to your son or your daughter? You see your daughter wearing certain clothes or looking a certain way, or you see your son watching something inappropriate on the Internet, and you say, "No, not in this house."

A male is an anchor, and an anchor *stops* things. You may know that your daughter and son are being taught in school that homosexuality is acceptable. As a kingdom father, you have to put the anchor down and say, "That's not from God." Many times, I had to tell my son and daughter, "That music—not in this house. That type of clothing—not in this house. This boat is anchored." They made it through the turbulent waves of those teen years. My children are upstanding young adults who don't have memories they can't enjoy.

An anchor stops things.

Thought for the Day

Men are called to protect their families and communities from the destructive currents of our modern society.

Reading: Psalm 49–50; Romans 1

July 30

Blown and Tossed by the Wind

If any of you lacks wisdom, he should ask God, who gives generously to all without finding fault, and it will be given to him. But when he asks, he must believe and not doubt, because he who doubts is like a wave of the sea, blown and tossed by the wind. That man should not think he will receive anything from the Lord; he is a double-minded man, unstable in all he does.

—James 1:5–8

You are the anchor of your family's "boat," keeping it steady in storms as you hold securely to Jesus, your Rock. Yet remember that Jesus also has given us a Compass, the Holy Spirit, to give us our bearings and direction in life. He will teach and strengthen you; He will guide your conscience and establish your convictions so you can reach shore safely. James wrote that God will give wisdom generously to everyone "*without finding fault.*" Yet we need to exercise faith when we ask, or we will be "*blown and tossed by the wind.*" Our anchor will not be secure but "*unstable.*"

Do you remember my writing earlier about the situation in which my associates and I were adrift all night in the ocean after our boat lost power? Our families called on a higher authority—the Coast Guard—to help us in our crisis. Similarly, you can call on the Holy Spirit's help. He will direct and protect you in both the calm and stormy seas of your life. Even if there is darkness all around you, He will guide you in the right direction.

> *If I say, "Surely the darkness will hide me and the light become night around me," even the darkness will not be dark to you; the night will shine like the day, for darkness is as light to you.* (Psalm 139:11–12)

Thought for the Day

The Holy Spirit will direct and protect you in both the calm and stormy seas of your life.

Reading: Psalm 51–53; Romans 2

Principles of the Male as Cornerstone/Anchor

Review these principles of the male as cornerstone/anchor and reflect on how you can apply them in your everyday life—for yourself, if you are a man, and in your relationships with men, if you are a woman.

1. The male is the foundation, but the Chief Cornerstone is Jesus Christ.
2. Without the Cornerstone, the foundation falls apart.
3. If you make Jesus your Cornerstone, God will build you so well that you will be able to handle the height of the building.
4. God allows you to go through trials and tests so you can recognize what is hindering your life.
5. Committed Christians are not immune to the storms of life.
6. As you hold on to the Rock, your foundation will remain sure.
7. We go through various seasons in life, and we need to be prepared for them by establishing our lives on the Rock.
8. Behind every broken experience is a wealthy experience from the Lord.
9. Men are called to protect their families and communities from the destructive currents of our modern society.

Built on the foundation of the apostles and prophets, with Christ Jesus himself as the chief cornerstone. (Ephesians 2:20)

Heavenly Father,
How precious is Your Son, the Chief Cornerstone, in our lives. Whether we are male or female, we know we can depend upon the Rock who is so much higher than we are. Thank You that as we go through the seasons of our lives, we know that You are the steadfast and unchanging God who loves us and provides us with the Rock of our salvation. In Jesus' name we pray, amen.

Reading: Psalm 54–56; Romans 3

August 1

Differences in Communication Styles

We have different gifts, according to the grace given us.
—Romans 12:6

Paul was writing about spiritual gifts in this verse, but the same idea applies to the different communication styles men and women display.

In His purpose and grace, God made women and men very different from each other in the way they think, act, and respond. These differences were designed to be complementary and not divisive. Adam and Eve originally lived in harmony with God, and so they were able to live in harmony with one another. They knew how to draw on each other's strengths in communication for the betterment of them both. However, when humanity turned away from God's purposes and broke relationship with Him, the lines of communication between males and females were cut or, at least, badly frayed. Thus, the differences that were originally designed for mutual support now often lead to misunderstandings and conflicts in marriage and in other relationships between men and women.

The chances are very good that you have experienced some of this misunderstanding and conflict firsthand! Handling differences of opinion and avoiding discord are universal problems in relationships. How are you to live harmoniously with a husband or wife whom you love but who processes information and responds in a manner that is different from the way that you do? Over the next two weeks, we will explore answers to this common relationship dilemma.

Thought for the Day

God made women and men very different from each other in the way they think, act, and respond.

Reading: Psalm 57–59; Romans 4

Dealing with Differences

Many women and men struggle with communication issues. How should you conduct yourself when you have been created to function differently from others with whom you live and work? How do you make yourself understood and how do you communicate effectively?

Differences in perspective and communication style can lead to misunderstandings and hurt feelings. Because of this, Colossians 3:13 is always a good guiding principle to follow: *"Bear with each other and forgive whatever grievances you may have against one another. Forgive as the Lord forgave you."*

In the next few days, seek to understand the purposes and designs of females and males that influence their communication styles. With this knowledge—and some patience and forgiveness—men and women who are seeking God's redemptive purposes for their lives can communicate effectively and happily with one another. When women and men are considerate of one another, they have the basis on which they can develop the mutual love and respect that is crucial to lasting relationships.

Also keep in mind that we will be discussing the basic natures and tendencies of females and males in communication. Of course, there will always be exceptions, for every person is unique. Yet within the variations, the general tendencies usually hold true.

Men and women must be brought into the complementary balance that was God's original purpose for them. This balance will be achieved when we understand the strengths of each communication style and learn to communicate with each other according to the style that the other party can receive and understand.

Thought for the Day

When women and men are considerate of one another, they have the basis on which they can develop mutual love and respect.

Reading: Psalm 60–62; Romans 5

August 3

A Woman Is Primarily an "Emotional Feeler"

Today, we begin to look at the female's communication style and contrast it with the male's style so that we can understand and appreciate their different perspectives.

God made the woman primarily as an "emotional feeler" and the man chiefly as a "logical thinker." When I state that a woman is an emotional feeler, I am referring to the way in which she processes the verbal and nonverbal communication she receives from the world around her. Because the woman is an incubator, she not only receives thoughts and ideas into her being, but also transforms them as she processes them in her emotional, mental, and spiritual wombs. Her communication style reflects this process. When a woman receives information, she assesses it both mentally and emotionally *at the same time.* This is what makes her distinct from the male, who generally uses these functions separately.

God's creation is remarkable. He actually designed the brains of females and males to be different. The neural pathways between the left and right hemispheres of a woman's brain (both the logical and the emotional sides) are intact. This explains what often puzzles many men: women's ability to do multiple tasks at the same time rather than having to focus on just one. The woman's brain allows her to process facts and feelings almost simultaneously. Her emotions are with her all the time she is thinking, and this influences her perspective on the world around her as well as what is communicated to her.

Thought for the Day

When a woman receives information, she assesses it both mentally and emotionally at the same time.

Reading: Psalm 63–65; Romans 6

August 4

A Man Is Chiefly a "Logical Thinker"

Yesterday, we saw that women have an awesome ability to process emotion and logic at the same time. In contrast, science has shown that there are fewer nerves connecting the two hemispheres of the male's brain, so the logical and emotional sides are not as closely connected. Because of this, a man basically needs to "shift gears" to move from his dominant logical side to his emotional side. This is why men, in general, think in terms of facts and in a linear fashion. They think like a straight line—the shortest distance between two points—which gives them the ability to see the goal (the vision) and to focus their energies on reaching it in the most straightforward and direct way.

Women, on the other hand, tend to think more like a grid than a straight line. A woman's brain is designed to pick up many details that men don't "see"—things that go beyond the mere facts, such as the personalities, motivations, and feelings of both herself and others. She can perceive, evaluate, and see relationships between things all at the same time, like x, y, and z coordinates on a grid track multiple factors at the same time.

No one person, and no one gender, can look at the world with complete perspective. Therefore, God has designed things so that when the female and the male work together in unity, they can help one another to see a more balanced picture of life. They weren't meant to understand the world and fulfill their dominion mandate in isolation from one another. For this reason, they have built-in ways of seeing the world that are of benefit to each other.

Thought for the Day

No one person, and no one gender, can look at the world with complete perspective.

Reading: Psalm 66–67; Romans 7

August 5

WHICH FILTER DO YOU USE?

God designed the woman to look at life through an emotional filter and the man to look at life through a logical filter. This does not mean that women do not use logic or that men do not have emotions. They each just have a specific way of looking at the world.

Women often have been written off as foolish and inferior by men because they are expressive and show their emotions. A woman does not need to apologize for her emotions. God made her to feel. Males have assumed that their approach is better than the females' approach rather than complementary to it. They haven't known or understood how and why the woman was created to be an emotional feeler.

The woman can help the man see aspects of life that, if overlooked or ignored, can become detours or potholes preventing him from reaching his goal or from reaching it as quickly as he might have. Her peripheral vision keeps him from being blindsided as he single-mindedly pursues his goals and objectives. On the other hand, the man's linear thinking helps the woman not to become so enmeshed in the many layers of her multidimensional thinking that she loses sight of the goal and never reaches it.

Women and men need each other in order to chart the best course in life—one that enables them to reach their common goal but also experience their journey in the fullest, wisest, and most rewarding way possible.

Thought for the Day

Women and men need each other to chart the best course in life.

Reading: Psalm 68–69; Romans 8:1–21

August 6

Feeling, Thinking, and Self-Expression

Communication between women and men comes down to *feeling, thinking*, and *self-expression*. Women and men both feel. Women and men both think. It is their manner of looking at the world and their self-expression that makes the difference. A woman's first reaction will generally be an emotional one, followed by a thinking one. A man's first reaction will be a thinking one, but he will also feel.

Let's look at a situation highlighting these different perspectives. A married couple plans a romantic evening together. The wife looks forward to an evening with her husband. She prepares the food, sets the table, arranges the flowers, and then meets him at the door when he comes home. Her husband walks in, says hello, then strides right past her without noticing that she has dressed up. He goes into the living room and says, "I'm going to have dinner in front of the TV while I watch the news." His mind is still in work mode, intent on finding out any information that may affect his work and thus his ability to provide. Because his wife doesn't understand this, she is deeply hurt at his behavior; her first reaction is to feel that he is ungrateful and inconsiderate. She approaches him angrily. Surprised, he asks, "What's the matter with you?"

At this point, she sees nothing complementary in the way he is designed! When we don't understand purpose, we begin to misinterpret motives. It is this suspicion that creates conflict. This is why understanding purpose and design is so important. Both the woman's reaction and the man's reaction are related to the way they are made. She took his apparent indifference personally, while his mind was so preoccupied with what he was thinking that he did not notice what his wife was feeling.

Thought for the Day

When we don't understand purpose, we begin to misinterpret motives.

Reading: Psalm 70–71; Romans 8:22–39

August 7

The Woman's Self-Expression

Because the woman was created to be more emotionally aware, she feels everything—from the way a person looks at her to what a person is saying or doing. A woman also can generally express her feelings and thoughts better than a man can. God designed the woman to communicate what is going on in her heart and mind. Because a man talks less than a woman does, he can sometimes give her the impression that he is not doing much thinking. Men think quite a bit; however, they often don't express their thoughts, and, when they do, they may express only the most salient points because they are interested in facts rather than details.

This is why a man can walk into the house and bypass a beautifully set table his wife has prepared without saying anything about it. The man needs help switching his focus from linear thinking about his goals and work to an appreciation of the sensory and emotional aspects of life. Then, he can notice and appreciate what his wife has done for him. The woman, on her part, needs to understand that when the man walks by her table without saying anything, it doesn't necessarily mean that he is being inconsiderate. It means that he is in a linear frame of mind because this is his natural mind-set.

A woman needs to be patient with a man and give him time to switch gears emotionally, while a man needs to learn to articulate what he appreciates and feels.

Thought for the Day

God designed the woman to communicate what is going on in her heart and mind.

Reading: Psalm 72–73; Romans 9:1–15

August 8

Do Men Really Have Emotions?

Contrary to what many women believe, men do have emotions! They just don't always express them—either because it is more difficult for them to do so or because what they are thinking, rather than what they are feeling, is at the forefront of what they are engaged in.

There are times when a woman isn't feeling what a man is thinking, and a man is not thinking what a woman is feeling. When this happens, the lack of communication between them compounds their frustration with one another. Again, when the man walks past the beautifully laid dinner table, he has to remember to express his feelings. At the same time, the woman shouldn't consider his unemotional response as being either irresponsible or inconsiderate.

The man generally bases his thoughts and actions on what is logical; he factually analyzes everything. This is both a strength and a weakness, because emotions and insights are very important to the way a person functions in the world. Therefore, the man needs someone who can balance his logic with feeling; otherwise, he'll go through life with a merely clinical outlook. He needs someone who can show him the emotional side of life, who can remind him of his need to be sensitive to others.

I appreciate God's design. He created us in such a way that males and females truly need one another.

Thought for the Day

Men don't always express their emotions—either because it is difficult for them to do so or because what they are thinking, rather than what they are feeling, is at the forefront of what they are engaged in.

Reading: Psalm 74–76; Romans 9:16–33

August 9

Are We Hearing the Same Thing?

What a woman hears, she receives as an emotional experience; what a man hears, he generally receives merely as information. They have two entirely different ways of processing language that is spoken to them.

The woman receives language in an emotional way because she is designed to absorb the world around her and to personalize it. She is designed to take in everything and incubate it. A man doesn't usually have an emotional experience with what he hears. This is why it is very important for a male to understand a female. Before a man speaks to a woman, he needs to think about what he is about to say and how he is about to say it. Because a woman receives everything as an emotional experience, a man must be sensitive about her feelings, considering his words rather than saying whatever comes to his mind.

On the other hand, a woman needs to realize that when she talks to a man, he hears it only as information. He runs on information because he's a logical thinker. When she wants to talk to a man, she has to learn to tell him what she thinks, not what she feels. Sometimes a woman will become upset at something that a man has done and will start crying. A woman needs to release her emotions, and she often expresses them through tears. However, the man says, "I'm going to leave. I'll come back when you've settled down and we can talk." To the woman, he's being cold. What he's really saying is, "I'm looking for information, and I'm not receiving any." The man doesn't want her tears because he doesn't know how to respond to them. He feels sorry that she is crying, but he wants to know what he can do to fix things. He wants information.

Thought for the Day

What a woman hears, she receives as an emotional experience; what a man hears, he generally receives as information.

Reading: Psalm 77–78; Romans 10

August 10

Women's Insight and Discernment

While Pilate was sitting on the judge's seat, his wife sent him this message: "Don't have anything to do with that innocent man, for I have suffered a great deal today in a dream because of him."

—Matthew 27:19

A woman's communication gifts include insight and discernment. Men need to be sensitive to the discernment that God gives to their wives and to other women in their lives. There is an interesting example of this truth in the incident when Pilate judged Jesus.

Pilate was carrying out his job, the administration of Roman authority over the Jews. When the chief priests brought Jesus before Pilate and accused Him of being an insurrectionist, Pilate's first inclination was to rule within the law. He saw no basis for their accusations and wanted to release Jesus. In the middle of this dispute, Pilate's wife sent a warning to him: *"Don't have anything to do with that innocent man."* In essence, she was saying, "I have a premonition about this Man. He didn't do anything wrong. Don't touch Him." She was trying to appeal to Pilate's sensibilities, warning him that he should use discretion when making his decision.

Pilate became nervous that things were getting out of hand when the religious leaders assembled an unruly crowd to demand that Jesus be crucified. He ended up being swayed by this pressure and ordering Jesus' death. He may have justified his decision by telling himself that it was logical: keeping order for Rome should take precedence over preserving the life of one innocent man. Even though Pilate knew Jesus had done nothing wrong, he had Him crucified. He would have done better to listen to the instincts of his wife.

Thought for the Day

Men need to be sensitive to the discernment that God gives to their wives and to other women for their benefit.

Reading: Psalm 79–80; Romans 11:1–18

August 11

Intuition Averts Disaster

David said to Abigail, "Praise be to the Lord, the God of Israel, who has sent you today to meet me. May you be blessed for your good judgment and for keeping me from bloodshed this day."

–1 Samuel 25:32–33

God gave females to males so that men can have balance, so that they can have the benefit of women's sensitivity and feeling. It is very easy for men to make a decision and not care what anyone thinks about it or who will be affected by it. This is why it is good for a man to have someone who can say to him, "What you are planning to do may be right, but the way you intend to go about it is wrong. Perhaps you should consider..."

The account of Abigail in 1 Samuel 25 is a good example of how a woman's discernment averted disaster for a man. Abigail combined intelligence and insight to address a deadly situation. Her husband, Nabal, had rejected David's request for food after David and his men had been honorable with him and had protected his property. Nabal wasn't using wisdom but his own form of logic and pride when he rebuffed David. David was angry at this treatment and was going to destroy Nabal and his workers. Abigail went to David and appealed to his sense of justice and righteousness before God, as well as to his compassion. Her insights and good judgment kept David from destroying her husband and his men.

Abigail is also a good example of someone who understood how to communicate with another based on knowledge of the other person's outlook. She knew what to say to David that would get his attention and resonate with his deepest convictions.

Thought for the Day

God gave females to males so that men can have balance.

Reading: Psalm 81–83; Romans 11:19–36

August 12

Women Love the Details

"Why can't you remember anything I tell you?" Well, men, how many times have you heard that question? A major aspect of the differences between the communication styles of women and men is that women don't usually forget things, whereas men generally have to be reminded over and over.

Now, a man may remember facts related to his business, but often he will forget dates, times, and events. For example, a woman may be dressing for an evening out and call to her husband, who is in another room, "You remember that we're going to your sister's birthday party tonight, don't you?" The man will have completely forgotten. He is wearing the oldest clothes he owns and holding a big bowl of popcorn, getting ready to watch the big game.

Most men don't know the reason why women remember things, and most women can't understand why men don't recall things. It has to do with their purpose and design. Men tend to think about goals and the bottom line, while women tend to remember details. These differences are complementary.

Women are generally more interested in the details, while men are usually interested in what is abstract—the principles or the philosophy related to something. This is why, after attending a wedding, for example, a woman can talk on the phone with a friend for hours discussing all the details of the event, such as the flowers, the music, what the bride wore, and what kind of food was served at the reception. When a man is asked, "How was the wedding?" he may get a blank look on his face and then simply say, "They got married."

Thought for the Day

Men tend to think about goals and the bottom line, while women tend to remember details.

Reading: Psalm 84–86; Romans 12

August 13

A Woman's Hidden Thoughts

A woman is likely to express what she feels rather than what she thinks, especially at first. For example, when a woman is under stress and wants someone to empathize with her so that she doesn't feel so alone in her difficulty, she may say something like this to her husband: "Your parents are coming for dinner tomorrow, the house is a mess, we don't have any groceries, the kids have been underfoot all day, and I just can't do it all!" Her husband, who is a thinker, will immediately try to come up with a solution for his distraught wife. "Well, what if I go buy some groceries?" "No, I have to do that tomorrow when I know what I want to cook." "Then why don't I take you and the kids out to dinner so you won't have to worry about that tonight?" "No, we can't be out late. The kids need baths, and, besides, I have to use up the leftovers." "Well, then, let me straighten things up a little." "No, I need to do that. I know where everything belongs."

By now, the man is totally exasperated because he is trying to help his wife, but she is rejecting all his suggestions. He doesn't realize that what the woman really wants is for him to take her in his arms and tell her how much she is appreciated. While she would also probably appreciate his help, she first needs emotional contact with him so that she can be emotionally stabilized. Then, the other problems won't seem as insurmountable. What she was *thinking* was that she could handle things if she received some love and affection from her husband. What she *expressed* were her overwhelming feelings of overload, which her husband interpreted as a need for him to solve her problems by taking action.

Thought for the Day

What a woman is thinking can be different from what she is saying.

Reading: Psalm 87–88; Romans 13

August 14

A Man's Hidden Feelings

Most of the time, when a man speaks to a woman, he doesn't communicate what he's *feeling*. The misunderstanding this causes contributes to problems in relationships.

It can be difficult for women to understand how very hard it is for men to express their feelings. Yet it is very important for a woman not to jump to any conclusions about a man's motivations until she discovers what he is feeling. I've counseled many couples in which the woman doesn't understand the man's nature. "He doesn't care about me. He doesn't tell me he loves me. He's indifferent." In her experience, this explanation seems true. But, all the while, the man really feels deeply. Notice that I said "feels." He feels deeply for her. The problem is that he doesn't say what he is feeling; he says what he is thinking. Note the difference: in his heart, he feels great love for her, but in his mind, this love is not always translated into specific words that he can share with her.

There are many men who are feeling emotions they find difficult to verbalize. They are hurting; they feel sad and weak inside. They feel like losers. They are depressed that they haven't been promoted for ten years and that nothing is working out with their jobs. They feel as if they have failed their wives. They feel bad, but it is hard for them to come up with the words to express these feelings.

Men have to start learning to communicate their feelings to women. They have to overcome any feelings of embarrassment they have toward feelings. To help a man do this, a woman needs to learn to create an environment that will enable him to tell her what he is feeling.

Thought for the Day

It is often hard for men to come up with words that express their feelings.

Reading: Psalm 80–90; Romans 14

August 15

A Beautiful Complement

The distinct differences between women and men are meant to be a help to them—not a hindrance or a source of pain. One way of thinking and communicating is not better than the other way, and the inherent differences between the two are not a result of the fall of humanity. The way women and men are designed is for their good. They just need to exercise patience and understanding and to value the other's contribution.

The female's emotional feeling will balance the male's logical thinking. Many women don't understand how important they are to the men in their lives. The female was created to help the man in that whatever the male lacks, the female possesses. The reverse is also true. This principle is based on God's purpose.

If women and men are not careful, they will come to conclusions about each other's motivations without knowing what the woman is really thinking or the man is really feeling. This has caused many people to think that their marriages or relationships aren't working. After a while, they say, "Forget this," and they walk away. Later on, they meet somebody else and get married, hoping things will be different this time. However, they encounter the same problems that they did in their previous relationships. They think the problem is with the other person, when the problem is often with the inability of both parties to communicate well. This cycle will continue until they learn to work through and understand the differences between women and men, why each is unique, and how God has made them to complement one another beautifully.

Thought for the Day

Men and women need to exercise patience and understanding with one another and to value each other's contributions to their relationships.

Reading: Psalm 91–93; Romans 15:1–13

August 16

Principles of Communication Styles

Review these principles of the different communication styles of men and women and reflect on how they apply to your everyday life.

1. God made women and men different in the way they think, act, and respond.
2. The woman is an emotional feeler. The man is a logical thinker.
3. The different communication styles of women and men are meant to be complementary.
4. When women and men understand the differences in their communication styles, they can learn how to use their differences for the betterment of them both.
5. A woman receives what she hears as an emotional experience. A man receives what he hears as information.
6. Women are more interested in the concrete details, while men are more interested in abstract ideas.
7. What a woman speaks is an expression of what she feels. What a man speaks is an expression of what he thinks.

Clothe yourselves with compassion, kindness, humility, gentleness and patience....Forgive as the Lord forgave you. And over all these virtues put on love, which binds them all together in perfect unity.

(Colossians 3:12–14)

Heavenly Father,
You have created us, male and female, to complement one another. Yet You know that our communication is often frustrated because of great misunderstanding. You are the Great Communicator. You speak truth to us through Your Word and Your Holy Spirit. Please teach us to speak and to listen to others with all wisdom and knowledge so that we can be used to fulfill Your plans for our lives. In Jesus' precious name we pray, amen.

Reading: Psalm 94–96; Romans 15:14–33

August 17

A Unique Leadership Position

God has given males a unique leadership influence. As the man goes, so goes the family, society, and world. I believe that if we don't remedy the male's identity crisis, our whole generation will be in trouble. There's no escaping this fact.

The answer for males in the twenty-first century is therefore to:

- define their worth based on God's purpose rather than society's roles.
- learn God's vision for their lives.
- continue to live in the truth of who they were created to be.

If males understand the purpose and responsibilities God has given them and the true design of their relationship with females, they can be free to fulfill their destiny and potential. They can be the men they were created to be.

If you are a man, you don't need to be confused about your identity and place in life, regardless of the conflicting signals society is currently sending out. You will find fresh vision and direction in rediscovering God's purposes for both males and females. Through this knowledge, men can be and do more than they ever imagined, and women can gain a new understanding and appreciation for men while enabling them to fulfill their calling.

What is a "real man"? Someone who knows the reality of who he is and lives in that reality. This knowledge starts with understanding the significance of his being created purposefully by God. Over the next few days, we will continue to explore the definition of the male as father and its implications.

Thought for the Day

Men will find fresh vision for their lives by rediscovering and living in God's purposes.

Reading: Psalm 97–99; Romans 16

August 18

God as Source

Through [Christ] *all things were made; without him nothing was made that has been made.*

—John 1:3

Earlier, we talked about the significance of the fact that the male was created as father of the human family. Recall that the word *father* in the Bible is *ab* in the Old Testament and *pater* in the New Testament, and that these words denote "source" and "progenitor." God is the Source of all substance and all life. He is the Progenitor who creates all things and then supports and upholds.

God is Father by both nature and function. He is the Father of creation. God sent forth His Word and created all that is. (See Genesis 1; Isaiah 63; Romans 1:20; John 1:3.) As the Source of all that is, God carried the seed of the universe. God the Father had everything in Him before anything was. So, He created the entire universe and brought into being all that is from nothing (*ex nihilo*). The Hebrew verb for creating is *bara*. The only proper subject for *bara* is God, for only He creates. Therefore, that which produces or creates is the source—the father.

A male needs to understand the significance of his being created purposefully by God. The highest honor God can give a man is to designate him a father. *Father* is the title or designation God uses for Himself. In fact, fatherhood is the ultimate work of the male. Fatherhood is a heavy honor and a tremendous responsibility. The father's job is to uphold and support the generation he brings forth.

Thought for the Day

As the Source, God the Father had everything in Him before anything was.

Reading: Psalm 100–102; 1 Corinthians 1

August 19

The Parable of the Loving Father

Before men can be all they were meant to be as fathers, they need to be in right relationship with the heavenly Father. Remember the parable of the prodigal son—more aptly called "the parable of the loving father"? The ambitious and ungrateful son took his good inheritance, left home, squandered his money, and ended up living in a pigpen.

If you stay away from God, He will sustain you even with "pig slop," if that's what you want. Why? You are still the son, and He is still the faithful Father. But He wants to give you so much more in life.

When the lost son came to himself, he said, *"How many of my father's hired men have food to spare, and here I am starving to death! I will set out and go back to my father"* (Luke 15:17–18). In other words, he realized that the food in his father's house, even that of the workers, was better than the food in the pigpen. When this lost son returned home, however, the father still loved him. Not only was he willing to sustain him, but he also threw him a party to celebrate his homecoming. *"But while he was still a long way off, his father saw him and was filled with compassion for him; he ran to his son, threw his arms around him and kissed him"* (v. 20).

You can decide upon the quality of life you want to live, just as the lost son did. God will feed you whatever you want to "eat." If you hang out with the pigs, you will eat pig slop. If you return home to your Father, you can live in the fullness of His grace and provision. The choice is yours.

Thought for the Day

If you return home to your Father, you can live in the fullness of His grace and provision.

Reading: Psalm 103–104; 1 Corinthians 2

Rebirthed with Everlasting Seed

God created human beings with genes, which are the source and substance of life. These genes are passed down from parent to child. Our genes determine physical characteristics, behaviors, emotional reactions, and instincts, as well as how we process our thoughts. At the core of our natural identities are our genes. When a man sows seed into the receptor (the woman) and a child is conceived, the next generation receives its identity by the genes.

Adam was the father of the human race. His genes were released into humanity. What identity did human beings inherit from Adam, the progenitor of humanity? Although God gave him life to pass along, Adam rebelled and rejected his life-giving Creator; therefore, death was passed on in Adam's seed. Adam turned away from his heavenly Father and listened to the lies of the devil, who essentially became a "stepfather" to him. "*Sin entered the world through one man, and death through sin, and in this way death came to all men, because all sinned*" (Romans 5:12).

Because Adam allowed sin to enter the world, his descendants were born with a sinful nature and with bodies that would eventually die. His son, Cain, even became a murderer. The inheritance we received from Adam was death. Since we are all Adam's offspring, we need to change fathers as soon as possible. We need to be rebirthed with everlasting seed and genes by the heavenly Father, through His Son Jesus Christ.

Thought for the Day

We need to be rebirthed with everlasting seed and genes by the heavenly Father, through His Son Jesus Christ.

Reading: Psalm 105–106; 1 Corinthians 3

WHO IS YOUR FATHER?

The LORD *God called to the man, "Where are you?" He answered, "I heard you in the garden, and I was afraid because I was naked; so I hid."*
—Genesis 3:9–10

When Adam disobeyed God, everything went wrong. Human beings experienced shame, fear, and separation from God. When the man ate the fruit, in his act of separating from the Father, all his offspring were contaminated—including Eve.

It is interesting to note that God did not call to Eve—He *"called to the man."* Women are not identified as the ones who transfer sin; men are. Remember Romans 5:12: "S*in entered the world through one man, and death through sin.*" So, the only way to get rid of Adam's seed of sin is to renounce him (the fallen nature)—and his stepfather, the devil—as your father. Only the Second Adam, Jesus, can birth new life in you and break the curse of sin and death that you inherited from your original father, Adam.

Adam did what many men still do today—he blamed Eve for his sin. (See Genesis 3:11–12.) Men are still blaming the women and mothers in our cultures for the problems we are having with our children. The truth is that the root of our problems is fatherlessness.

Men, stop blaming women. Yes, Eve was *"deceived"* (1 Timothy 2:14). Yet Adam sinned, rejected his Father, and, through his seed, became the progenitor of sin to all forthcoming generations. But Christ sows God's seed of life into all who would be born again. Renounce the father of all lies and return to the Father of light and life.

Thought for the Day

The only way to get rid of Adam's seed of sin is to renounce him (the fallen nature)—and his stepfather, the devil—and ask the Second Adam to birth new life in you.

Reading: Psalm 107–109; 1 Corinthians 4

August 22

The Identity Crisis

The greatest challenge for men today, especially young men, is that they suffer from an identity crisis. They lack the nurturing influence of a true father to give them identity. An identity doesn't come from a gang or the government. It comes from a father.

The only one who can give you your true identity as a man is a father. This fundamental principle is lacking in many of our cultures, and its absence is the source of many social problems. Most young men are running around looking for a father, and they can't find him. They're running to their friends, but to no avail. You can't find fatherhood in another peer or gang member who is also looking for a father. You cannot discover who you are by looking to someone who doesn't know who he or she is.

Do you know why being Jewish carries with it such a strong identity? Jewish tradition, particularly in family relationships, has a very real sense of the "father spirit." This sense is rooted in a ceremony called Bar Mitzvah, in which a thirteen-year-old boy goes before the men and performs some prescribed traditional rites, after which the men say to him, "Now you are a man." From that day forward, that boy takes on a different spirit. That's why Jewish communities are knitted so closely together and are so strong in business, tradition, and culture.

A man needs to be affirmed by a father in order to confirm his manhood. This is why so many young men yearn to hear their fathers say to them, "I love you, Son. You're a man now."

Thought for the Day

A man needs to be affirmed by a father in order to confirm his manhood.

Reading: Psalm 110–112; 1 Corinthians 5

August 23

Get Your Identity from God

If you haven't found a true earthly father yet, God qualifies as your Father. Hallelujah! You can come to God and say, "God, who am I?" and He'll tell you, "You're My son." *"But as many as received him* [Jesus], *to them gave he power to become the sons of God, even to them that believe on his name"* (John 1:12 KJV). If you have received Jesus, you have the power to become a child of God. Your identity then comes from Him.

Next, God the Father will say to you, "Now, mature into the image of My dear Son, Jesus Christ, and you will grow up in Him until you are a true man." Jesus the Son tells you, "You are a father." He gives you your identity as a father. The principle of fatherhood, therefore, is simple: *you provide identity.* When you receive your true identity in Christ, then you can provide true identity to others.

A male can do nothing greater than fathering—whether he is fulfilling the role of father for his children or for others in his sphere of influence. He can earn a million dollars, but if he fails to fulfill God's calling to father as God fathers, then he is a failure. He can own a huge home, manage a large stock portfolio, and have a billion-dollar estate, but if he neglects to father his family, he has failed.

A male who is physically strong but weak as a father is not a man. A male eloquent in words but silent as a father in teaching his household the Word and precepts of God is not a man. The measure of a man's success is directly related to his effectiveness as a father, for which God is the only true example and standard.

Thought for the Day

When you receive your true identity in Christ, then you can provide true identity to others.

Reading: Psalm 113–115; 1 Corinthians 6

August 24

The Head Is Responsible for the Body

As the head of the family, the father is responsible for the "body," just as Jesus, as Head of the church, is responsible for His body.

Many men love to say, "I'm the head of this house," but they forget the accountability and duty of being the head. It is vitally important to understand the spiritual function of being the head of a family. I think we can see it more clearly if we use a physical head as an analogy. First, the head contains *the brain*. If the man claims to be the father and head of the home, then he must have the mind of Christ (see 1 Corinthians 2:16), which includes the knowledge and wisdom to lead a family in the ways of God. The father has the responsibility to solve the problems the family encounters. He calculates where the family is going and seeks God's guidance to make long-term plans for it. The father is the counselor, career and financial planner, and manager of the family's resources. All those functions are in the brain.

If the father is truly the head, he becomes the visionary of the family. *The eyes* are in the head and they see what's in front of the body. The eyes are not in the back or in the stomach. If you are the head, you should have a vision for your family: insight, long-range goals, and a plan for the future. The father discerns things that are happening in the natural, as well as the supernatural, for the family. As the visionary, the father anticipates things before they happen and prepares and equips the family to face the future.

Thought for the Day

As head of the home, the father must have the mind of Christ (see 1 Corinthians 2:16), which includes the knowledge and wisdom to lead his family in the ways of God.

Reading: Psalm 116–118; 1 Corinthians 7:1–19

August 25

The Qualities of Perception, Conception, and Inception

As visionaries, fathers have *perception*, *conception*, and *inception*. *Perception* is awareness of what's going on. A father knows what's happening with his wife and children at all times. When behaviors or attitudes change, he knows it. When spiritual or physical needs arise, he is aware of them. Too often, I hear families complain, "Dad never knows or understands what's happening in our lives. He's too wrapped up in his work to notice us."

God cares about everything. Jesus was aware of everything that happened around Him, even noticing a woman in need barely touching the hem of His garment. (See Mark 5:24–34.) God the Father is aware of all things. Jeremiah prayed, "*Great are your purposes and mighty are your deeds. Your eyes are open to all the ways of men*" (Jeremiah 32:19). Like the Father, a father is aware of all that happens in his family.

Conception is the creative beginning of a process, which sets in motion a chain of events. God sets everything in motion; He is "*the God who made the world and everything in it*" (Acts 17:24). He initiates, conceives, and creates. Likewise, a father conceives the beginnings of things for his family and then becomes the source for bringing what he has conceived into reality.

Inception is the start of something new. God the Father is always doing "a new thing" in our lives. He said, "*See, I am doing a new thing! Now it springs up; do you not perceive it? I am making a way in the desert and streams in the wasteland*" (Isaiah 43:19). A father is willing to risk new things for his family.

As the head of the family, the father takes the initiative to listen to God and conceive *God's* ideas, not just what seem like good ideas.

Thought for the Day

Like the Father, a father is aware of what is happening with his wife and children and initiates godly plans for their future.

Reading: Psalm 119:1–88; 1 Corinthians 7:20–40

Are You Discerning Your Family's Needs?

A good father develops discernment for the sake of his family. Continuing with our analogy of the physical head, after the eyes, we think of the *nose.* The nose discerns. Discerning is actually related to caring—anticipating a need and meeting it. A godly father can sense what is coming against a family in the next several years. He also has a sense of what is going to happen next week. Perhaps his teenager is going through some tough changes and facing tremendous peer pressure. As the head of the household, he discerns the problem and spends time with that child to counsel, support, affirm, and advise. A godly father also senses when his wife is in need of affection or time alone. In other words, a father can detect the scent of his family, his home, his business, and his neighborhood. He discerns and prepares for the future.

God the Father prepared for our needs before the world's foundation of the world:

> *For he chose us in him before the creation of the world to be holy and blameless in his sight. In love he predestined us to be adopted as his sons through Jesus Christ....In him we have redemption through his blood, the forgiveness of sins, in accordance with the riches of God's grace that he lavished on us with all wisdom and understanding.*
>
> (Ephesians 1:4–5, 7–8)

God made preparations for Christ to die for our sins, for the gift of the Holy Spirit, and for our eternal inheritance in glory. Now, that's a real Father! God discerned our need before we were ever created. Those of us who are fathers are to do the same for our families and others within the realm of our influence.

Thought for the Day

Discerning is related to caring—anticipating a need and meeting it.

Reading: Psalm 119:89–176; 1 Corinthians 8

August 27

HEARING AND SPEAKING TO YOUR FAMILY

I love the LORD, *for he heard my voice; he heard my cry for mercy. Because he turned his ear to me, I will call on him as long as I live.*
—Psalm 116:1–2

The effective functioning of a physical head includes the *ears*. Likewise, you are a godly father if you can hear for your family. A father should always be listening to God and to his family, for God the Father always listens to us, as the psalmist wrote in the above passage. Yet I hear wives and children continually complain, "Dad never has time to listen to me." Fathers, please take time to listen.

As head of the family, here are some questions you need to ask yourself: Am I hearing the voice of God for my family? Am I picking up on what's going on in the world and preparing my family to face it? Am I hearing the true voices of my wife and children?

Many men think they are too busy to listen. Yet listening is a gift that fathers give to their families. Their listening tells their families that they care for them, while a failure to listen communicates a lack of love and caring. Because God the Father loves us, He always listens to and answers us. We fathers need to listen as our heavenly Father listens!

Finally, being the head means that the father is the *mouthpiece* for the family. The father is supposed to speak the Word of God in the home. The family should hear God's Word from the head of the family first. Everything said at church should confirm and support what has already been said at home by the father.

Thought for the Day

The father should always be listening to God and his family because the heavenly Father always listens to us!

Reading: Psalm 120–122; 1 Corinthians 9

A Helper, Not a Slave

In the family, the father is the head as a result of God's timing and creation. Yet, again, this does not mean the woman is inferior to him. The woman was created by God to be a helper, not a slave. There is a big difference between the two. The Bible refers to the Holy Spirit as a Helper. (See John 15:26; 16:7 NKJV.) Jesus said that the Holy Spirit not only would help us, but also would lead us. *"He will guide you into all truth"* (John 16:13). The Holy Spirit is the *Paraclete*, meaning the One who comes alongside to help, as well as to be a Comforter, Counselor, and Guide.

Being a helper does not mean being inferior. A helper can be a guide and a teacher. Therefore, although the male is always the responsible head in God's design, he is not the "boss." He is not the owner of the woman.

Remember that when God addresses the human race, He never addresses us as male and female; He addresses us as "man." He deals with the spirit-man within both male and female. In order to function on earth as mankind, however, males and females each exercise an aspect of leadership.

While the male is ultimately the responsible head, the female is the coleader. A good illustration of this is the relationship between Jesus and His church. Jesus is called the Head, and the church is called the body. (See Colossians 1:18.) They work in unison with one another. Christ's relationship to the church is the perfect model for us of the male-female relationship and God's purposes for the woman in her dominion leadership role.

Thought for the Day

Christ's relationship to the church is the perfect model for us of the male-female relationship.

Reading: Psalm 123–125; 1 Corinthians 10:1–18

August 29

A Father Leads His House

I cannot emphasize enough that being the head of the family does not endow the man with more worth or value. Being the head has to do with *responsibility*. Too many men confuse being the head with being the boss. A father is not the boss of his house; a father is the head. A father doesn't *rule* his house; he *leads* his house. We must understand the function of the father as leader in the home.

Let me share with you some qualities of leadership the father has in the home:

As leader, the father has a passion and desire to bring out the best in all those under his care: his wife, children, and any other family members.

A true leader does not suppress, oppress, or depress the potential and talents of others; he releases them and cultivates them.

A true leader provides an environment for growth. He does not try to inhibit family members or create an atmosphere of fear. A true leader's passion is to maximize the potential of others so they may realize their full and true abilities.

In a very true sense, a father who is a genuine leader does exactly what God said to do from the beginning–he cultivates. To cultivate means to create an orderly environment that brings out the best in a thing, to culture it. As a leader, the father develops, expands, instigates, motivates, inspires, encourages, and exhorts. All those functions enrich the soil in which others grow.

Thought for the Day

A father doesn't rule his house; he leads his house.

Reading: Psalm 126–128; 1 Corinthians 10:19–33

August 30

Leaders Are Servants

Men, the fact that you are the head of the family does not make you superior, better, or greater than your wives. It means you have first responsibility and accountability to God for the family. Remember, being the head is not a value statement about worth or intrinsic value.

> *Your attitude should be the same as that of Christ Jesus: who, being in very nature God, did not consider equality with God something to be grasped, but made himself nothing, taking the very nature of a servant, being made in human likeness.* (Philippians 2:5–7)

As Head of the church, Jesus humbled Himself as a servant. Heads and leaders are first and foremost servants like Christ. It is impossible to assume a position of leadership without first serving. Jesus said,

> *You know that those who are regarded as rulers of the Gentiles lord it over them, and their high officials exercise authority over them. Not so with you. Instead, whoever wants to become great among you must be your servant, and whoever wants to be first must be slave of all. For even the Son of Man did not come to be served, but to serve, and to give his life as a ransom for many.* (Mark 10:42–45)

A father can never say that being the head or leader makes him the greatest. He must always look to serve in leadership, as Jesus did.

> *Now that I, your Lord and Teacher, have washed your feet, you also should wash one another's feet. I have set you an example that you should do as I have done for you.* (John 13:14–15)

Thought for the Day

It is impossible to assume a position of leadership without first serving.

Reading: Psalm 129–131; 1 Corinthians 11:1–16

August 31

Principles of Leadership

Today, review these principles of the male's leadership and reflect on how they apply to your everyday life—for yourself, if you are a man, and in your relationships with men, if you are a woman.

1. Fathers must have the mind of Christ (see 1 Corinthians 2:16), which includes the knowledge and wisdom to lead a family in the ways of God.
2. As the visionary, the father anticipates things before they happen and prepares and equips the family to face the future. Fathers have perception, conception, and inception.
3. Fathers discern and address the ongoing needs of their families.
4. Listening is a gift that fathers give to their families. When men listen, their listening tells their families that they care for them.
5. A father speaks the Word of God in his home.
6. A father doesn't dominate or control his house. He develops the potential of everyone in his house through his leadership.
7. Heads and leaders are first and foremost servants like Christ. It is impossible to assume a position of leadership without first serving.

Even the Son of Man did not come to be served, but to serve, and to give his life as a ransom for many. (Mark 10:45)

Heavenly Father,
You have made the spirit of the Father so very important in our lives. That spirit of love and protection has been passed from You to the males in our world. We pray that men would look at this position as one of honor and responsibility. Please show them that with God all things are possible, and that You will provide them with all that they need to fulfill this role. In Jesus' name, amen.

Reading: Psalm 132–134; 1 Corinthians 11:17–34

What's Love Got to Do with It?

He [the Bridegroom] *has taken me to the banquet hall, and his banner over me is love.*

—Song of Songs 2:4

Marital love is the binding of one spouse to another. Sex is a physical sign of a spiritual act—the giving of oneself completely to another and for another. Today, people are looking for sex without love, love without marriage, and marriage without responsibility. The world's idea of sex is shallow and distorted. The world says, "Make love." God says, "Love." We have confused sex with love. It's one thing to know how to make love to someone; it's quite another to actually love someone. "Let's make love" refers to a performance. It means to go do something. "Making love" is merely a technical experience, whereas loving is a spiritual act.

Love is the desire to please another, the total giving of oneself to another, not the taking of something. Marriage is for love, not just sex. Its foundation should be love. There are many ways to express love and physical affection; sex is just one of them. People can find complete fulfillment in one another without having the technical experience that our culture glorifies so much because their relationship goes beyond the bedroom. To me, that's a real relationship. *Sex was given by God to help express love, not to create it.*

We need real men and women in our communities—people of the Word who know what true love is. No one can understand the deep meaning of Jesus and the church better than a married couple that has a good sexual relationship. It can be a model of Christ's love for His bride, the church, if we follow God's original plan for sexuality.

Thought for the Day

People are looking for sex without love, love without marriage, and marriage without responsibility.

Reading: Psalm 135–136; 1 Corinthians 12

September 2

Sex Is God's Idea

How do we know that sex is a good thing? Genesis 1:31 says, "*God saw all that he had made, and it was very good.*" God created man and woman and their sexual nature. Therefore, He said that sex is "*very good.*"

God is not negative about sex. He *created* it. (See Genesis 1:28.) Sex is God's idea, not man's idea. It is such a beautiful expression of love and giving that only God could have thought of it. Men and women were designed as sexual beings. Every baby is born as a sexual creature with the potential to have a sexual relationship as an adult. God is negative only about the *misuse* of sex because it harms the people He created to have a fulfilling relationship with the opposite sex. Second, we must realize that the Bible itself is very open about the subject of sexuality. The main theme of the book of Song of Songs is sexual love. It is the story of a young bridegroom and his bride and their love and desire for one another.

Why did God create sex? The primary reason is that unity is a central aspect of God's nature and purposes. In the Bible, the sexual union of marriage is used as a metaphor to describe the intimacy between Christ and the church. Christ as the Bridegroom and the church as the bride gives us an idea of the preciousness with which God views sex. He views it as a symbol of His oneness with His beloved humanity, who have been created in His image and redeemed through His love.

Thought for the Day

God is negative only about the *misuse* of sex because it harms the people He created to have a fulfilling relationship with the opposite sex.

Reading: Psalm 137–139; 1 Corinthians 13

September 3

Understanding the Sexual Nature

How can a young man [or woman] *keep his way pure?*
By living according to your word.
—Psalm 119:9

Unfortunately, sexuality is often extremely misunderstood—not only in the secular world, but also in the church. I am deeply concerned about the damage this lack of understanding about sex has done—and is doing—to people's lives. It has led to confusion and broken relationships between men and women. It has prevented males from living up to their full potential as men and husbands. It has destroyed marriages—and lives. My prayer is that men and women will find wholeness in God as they understand His purpose and plan for human sexuality.

How did you first learn about sexuality? When I've asked men in my seminars how they were introduced to the concept of sex, they've listed various sources, such as friends or peers, movies and television, biology books, pornographic magazines or videos, and sexual experimentation during youth.

Unfortunately, most of us were introduced to sex through one of these avenues. No one ever says he learned about sex from his parents or from the Bible. Something is very wrong with how we are learning about sexuality. Note that, in the above list, not one of these sources is qualified to provide accurate information. This is why our society is filled with people who have distorted and unrealistic expectations about sexuality.

Thought for the Day

People's misunderstanding about human sexuality has led to confusion and broken relationships between men and women.

Reading: Psalm 140–142; 1 Corinthians 14:1–20

September 4

Ignorance about Sexuality

Some of you are suffering right now from the consequences of uninformed or unwise sexual activity. How a person first learned about sex determines, to a great degree, how he engages in it.

When we receive our information about sex from one or more of the sources mentioned yesterday and then pass along this information to others, we perpetuate cultural ignorance about sexuality. This is what has been happening in many of our societies. Much of what we have learned about sex has been acquired in an unwholesome context, and it is filled with misinformation. Men and women lack positive, informed teaching on the subject of sexuality.

Much of the blame for this lack of teaching falls on the church and the home. In general, the message we've heard from our churches and families is that sex is unholy or dirty and should not be discussed. Young people get the idea that parents and children aren't supposed to talk about sex, because their own parents don't discuss it with them. They are prevented from expressing their sexual questions in the context of a loving home or church community, so they seek information from other sources. When we neglect to teach our children God's truth about sex, then we abandon them to the culture for their information.

No one has a right to shape your child's concept and attitudes about sex, except you. Make sure that a questionable sex education class or *Playboy* magazine isn't your child's teacher. Train your child in the way he or she should go. Then, when a friend or teacher starts to say something erroneous about sex, your child can dismiss it with the knowledge, "That isn't what my parents told me. I know that isn't the truth."

Thought for the Day

When we neglect to teach our children God's truth about sex, then we abandon them to the culture for their information.

Reading: Psalm 143–145; 1 Corinthians 14:21–40

September 5

Created for Pleasure, not Remorse

In Deuteronomy, we find a remarkable statement: "*If a man has recently married, he must not be sent to war or have any other duty laid on him. For one year he is to be free to stay at home and bring happiness to the wife he has married*" (Deuteronomy 24:5).

Imagine—God wanted young married couples to enjoy sex so much that He issued a decree to insure that it was provided for. The very thing we think God opposes, He actually promoted. A newly married man was to have no other responsibilities during his first year of marriage but to bring his wife happiness.

Note that it doesn't say the husband is to bring happiness to himself, but to his wife. Lust focuses on itself, but true love focuses on the other person. God was saying to the husband, "Your desire in marriage should be to make your wife happy." Now, when you make your wife happy, guess who wins? You both do. When you give, you receive.

God established marriage so the sexual relationship can be full of pleasure, not repercussions and remorse. God is not against sex. He's against the violation of the sexual boundaries He's established for our own good. God's laws are for our protection, not our restriction. His boundaries have been established for our preservation, not our irritation. We think God doesn't want us to have any fun. In reality, He is trying to protect us. Whenever we break a law or violate a principle of God, we invite spiritual death and suffering.

Thought for the Day

God created sex for pleasure, not repercussions and remorse.

Reading: Psalm 146–147; 1 Corinthians 15:1–28

September 6

A Protective Boundary

May your fountain be blessed, and may you rejoice in the wife of your youth....Why be captivated, my son, by an adulteress? Why embrace the bosom of another man's wife?
—Proverbs 5:18, 20

The boundary God has given us to enjoy sex safely is the marriage covenant. Sex must be engaged in only in the context of marriage—a solemn, lifelong commitment between two people before God.

The Scripture says that a man is to *"bring happiness to the wife he has married"* (Deuteronomy 24:5). It doesn't say to move in with somebody for a year and try things out. There are no provisionary covenants. Solomon said, *"May you rejoice in the wife of your youth....May her breasts satisfy you always, may you ever be captivated by her love"* (Proverbs 5:18–19). This passage is a reference to sex. Enjoy *"the wife of your youth"*—not someone else. There is a vacuum in the male that needs to be filled by the female. And God says, "Make sure your wife is the one who fills that vacuum."

The Scripture says, *"For this reason a man will leave his father and mother and be united to his wife, and they will become one flesh"* (Genesis 2:24). *"For this reason."* For what reason should a man leave? To *"be united."* To whom? *"To his wife."* The minute that law is violated, we begin to reap the repercussions. Verse 24 says, *"And they will become one flesh."* The boundary that God has established for the one-flesh experience is the husband and wife relationship.

Thought for the Day

The primary boundary God has given us to enjoy sex safely is the marriage covenant.

Reading: Psalm 148–150; 1 Corinthians 15:29–58

September 7

Made for God

The body is not meant for sexual immorality, but for the Lord, and the Lord for the body.
—1 Corinthians 6:13

The Scripture doesn't say the body is not meant for sex. It simply says the body is not meant for sexual *immorality*. This is one of God's sexual laws, which He gives us for our good. Something negative happens in a man or woman's body when he or she has an immoral sexual experience. If the body was not created for it, then something goes wrong when it is subjected to it. This is why people often feel guilty after such a sexual experience, whether they admit it or not.

What has happened? Their bodies were not made for immorality. Somehow the knowledge that they broke the law of God is translated into chemicals in their bodies, and they feel bad. Science has proven that there are a few things our bodies are not built to handle. One of them is guilt. Our bodies have no hormone, enzyme, or chemical to handle guilt. Only the blood of Jesus can free us from guilt.

"The body is not meant for sexual immorality, but for the Lord." What is your body made for? It is made for God. It was created to be used in the context that God has already established. God placed specific boundaries on sexual behavior—the marriage covenant—and we can have all the fun we want within that context. We won't experience these negative repercussions if we stay within God's plan.

Thought for the Day

"The body is not meant for sexual immorality, but for the Lord."

Reading: Proverbs 1–2; 1 Corinthians 16

September 8

Flee from Sexual Immorality!

Do you not know that he who unites himself with a prostitute is one with her in body? For it is said, "The two will become one flesh." But he who unites himself with the Lord is one with him in spirit. Flee from sexual immorality.
—1 Corinthians 6:16–18

In the Greek, the word translated "*flee*" means "Run away. Shun. Escape." In other words, *avoid it like the plague.* How do we respond to plagues? We get as far away from them as we can! We insulate ourselves from them.

"*All other sins a man commits are outside his body, but he who sins sexually sins against his own body*" (v. 18). Paul was saying, "If you steal, it is outside the body. If you fight, it is outside the body." You don't become one with a person when you slap that person. But when a man has sex with a woman, he can't separate himself from her. Remember that sexual intercourse is a covenant. Some people can't understand why couples who sleep together and then break off their relationship have trouble going their separate ways. It is because the separation causes real trauma in their souls. This is a serious matter. That's why relationships outside God's plan can be so dangerous.

Your body belongs to God twice. He didn't just create you; He also redeemed you, and the price was high—the life of His Son Jesus. How can you honor God with your body? First, by waiting until you're married to engage in sex; second, by having sex only with your husband or wife. You are God's temple. You lift up your hands to worship God; you can use those same hands to caress your spouse. Both acts are holy in His sight.

Thought for the Day

You can you honor God with your body by waiting until you're married to engage in sex and by having sex only with your husband or wife.

Reading: Proverbs 3–5; 2 Corinthians 1

September 9

Self-Control Is Essential

The male was designed to be a leader, a teacher, a cultivator, and a protector. Therefore, he is wired always to be ready to act. If attack comes in the middle of the night, he has to be prepared. If attack comes at midday, he can't be caught off guard. If problems arise at sunset, a leader has to be a leader. Because God designed the male to be ready, he is in a state of readiness in all the various aspects of his life, including his sexuality. His sexual energy never stops. It may pause, but it never really stops.

Many women interpret this aspect of the male as something unnatural. Yet because it is his nature always to be prepared, his body has been designed in that way, as well. Therefore, it's not unnatural for a man to be sexually ready at all times. The man needs to realize that being ready doesn't always mean taking action.

Paul wrote, "*Encourage the young men to be self-controlled*" (Titus 2:6). Self-control is a recurring theme in Paul's writings. He knew that sex can control men. When you're always ready, you must be able to exercise self-control. A man's need for sex is one of the strongest needs imaginable. Many men don't understand this drive themselves. Yet it is an aspect of the makeup of a man that gives him great fulfillment.

Some men believe that whenever they experience sexual desire, they have to find someone with whom to release it. They even pay to try to meet this need, yet they still aren't satisfied. They don't understand that God made them ready because of the leadership purpose He's given them. Therefore, their energy should be channeled into positive leadership.

Thought for the Day

Because God designed the male to be a leader, he is in a state of readiness in all the various aspects of his life, including his sexuality.

Reading: Proverbs 6–7; 2 Corinthians 2

September 10

A Balance of Needs

Yesterday, we talked about how some men are too aggressive in their sexual energy, and their wives think of them as thoughtless or insensitive. On the other hand, there is a sense in which some women neglect their husbands' sexual needs because they claim they are too busy serving God.

Paul told us that this type of situation is a recipe for disaster. He said that whenever a husband and wife forgo sexual relations in order to serve God, they should do so only by mutual consent and only for a short period of time.

> *The husband should fulfill his marital duty to his wife, and likewise the wife to her husband. The wife's body does not belong to her alone but also to her husband. In the same way, the husband's body does not belong to him alone but also to his wife. Do not deprive each other except by mutual consent and for a time, so that you may devote yourselves to prayer. Then come together again so that Satan will not tempt you because of your lack of self-control.* (1 Corinthians 7:3–5)

This passage means that if you are going to pray and fast or go on a missions trip, you should get the consent of your spouse before you abstain from sexual relations. Sex was part of God's original design for humanity, and it is a holy thing between a husband and a wife. The Bible says that the wife's body belongs both to herself and to her husband, and the husband's body belongs both to himself and to his wife. There is to be a balance between having one's needs fulfilled and showing consideration for the other person's needs.

Thought for the Day

The wife's body belongs both to herself and to her husband, and the husband's body belongs both to himself and to his wife.

Reading: Proverbs 8–9; 2 Corinthians 3

Principles of Sexuality

Today, review these principles of sexuality and reflect on how they apply to your life.

1. Most of us have learned about sexuality from faulty sources instead of from God's Word.
2. God designed men and women as sexual beings. He created sex and said that it is *"very good."* (See Genesis 1:31.)
3. God is negative only about the misuse of sex. He wants us to avoid repercussions and remorse.
4. The body is not meant for immorality. This is one of God's sexual laws, which He has given us for our good.
5. The Bible uses sexual union in marriage as a metaphor for the intimacy and unity of Christ and His bride, the church.
6. God wants us to enjoy sex so much that He has told us what its safe boundary is: the marriage covenant, a solemn, lifelong commitment between two people before God.
7. Sex is a physical sign of a spiritual act—the giving of oneself completely to another and for another.

Heavenly Father,
When You created us, You considered every aspect of our lives, including our sexuality. In Your wisdom, You created male and female with the ability to express love and experience pleasure through the sexual act in marriage. My prayer is that men and women will find wholeness in You as they understand Your purpose and plan for human sexuality. Please help them to heed Your commands to engage in sexual union only within the boundary of the marriage covenant. Help Your church and individual families to communicate this message to our young people so they may resist the immorality of the world around us and live according to Your good plan. In Jesus' name, amen.

Reading: Proverbs 10–12; 2 Corinthians 4

September 12

Cultivate Your Family

The LORD *God took the man, and put him into the garden of Eden to dress it and to keep it.*
–Genesis 2:15 (KJV)

God's instruction to Adam referred to discipline and order. To "*dress*" means to cultivate, and to cultivate means to train. We have seen that a father is given the responsibility by God the Father to train and equip everything under his care, including his family. To clarify this assignment, let us look at the difference between cultivation and growth.

When plants grow without cultivation, they are essentially weeds. Cultivated plants form a garden. Trees that grow without cultivation and order are a forest. Cultivated trees are a grove. Without cultivation, there is no order and no systematic development. But when there is planned development and training, we see discipline and cultivation taking place.

Genesis 2:5 reveals that cultivation is part of God the Father's plan for humanity. "*And no shrub of the field had yet appeared on the earth and no plant of the field had yet sprung up, for the* LORD *God had not sent rain on the earth and there was no man to work* [*"cultivate"* NASB] *the ground.*" Adam's job description included cultivating the ground given to him for sustenance. God placed man in the garden and gave him instructions to work, train, and keep the earth; He did not want wild, unrestrained, and disorganized growth. God the Father has an orderly, disciplined, and purposeful plan for everything.

Thought for the Day

When there is planned development and training, we see discipline and cultivation taking place.

Reading: Proverbs 13–15; 2 Corinthians 5

September 13

Nurture Her Potential

While men have a special responsibility for cultivating their wives, they often have unrealistic ideas about women, so they can end up neglecting or hurting them. Most of us men are walking around with specific pictures in our minds of who we want our wives to be, and, when they don't meet our expectations, we tend to blame them. At one point, God showed me that I had this attitude toward my wife, and He had to correct me.

Here's the way a man often thinks: he is a certain type of man, so he wants a certain type of woman. He has ideas such as these: "I am a musician, so I want her to sing." "I'm a banker, so I want her to know about finance." "I am slim, so I want her to be slim." "I want her to be smart." "I want a woman who dresses well." "I like long hair on a woman." Now, there isn't anything wrong with desiring these things. However, I want to tell you something: *the "perfect" woman you are looking for does not exist.*

It is your job to cultivate your wife so that she can be all that *God* created her to be. You are to help her to blossom and grow into God's woman, not tear her down because she doesn't meet your specifications. In addition, you can help your wife become all that you saw in her when you first met her, and which you now think is missing. You need to nurture all the potential she has. This is not to be done in a controlling way, but in a loving and giving way, which is the nature of Christ. Think about it: what pressures are present in her life that are keeping her from being all that she desires and needs to be?

Thought for the Day

It is your job to cultivate your wife so that she can be all that God created her to be.

Reading: Proverbs 16–18; 2 Corinthians 6

September 14

What Are You Cultivating?

If you are a man, God has created and designed you to cultivate anything you desire, including your family. So, whenever a man receives a woman as a wife, he is given the opportunity to exercise his ability to cultivate. A man should pray and ask God to show him how to cultivate his wife. He is to water her, prune her, and give her sunlight. He is to add nutrients to her life until she blossoms into the woman she is meant to be.

Now, God designed the male to be able to cultivate and produce a beautiful tree. Therefore, if the tree looks like an old bush after twelve years, it is not the tree's fault. Similarly, it is usually not the woman's fault if she is not what she needs to be. The cultivator was not putting in the right nutrients and the right water. A wife should be flourishing under her husband's loving care. Men, don't go looking for someone else whom you believe is more like what you want your wife to be. You are the cultivator—cultivate your wife.

Let me say a word here to the young, unmarried men: what are *you* cultivating? When a young lady comes into your presence, she should leave a better person than she was before she came. She may try to come on too strong. Yet when she leaves, she should walk away a lady. If someone asks her, "What happened to you?" she should be able to say, "I met a man who told me he wouldn't sleep with me or degrade me because he respects me." Cultivate these young ladies. Don't drag them down, and don't let them drag you down. A young woman shouldn't leave your presence pregnant. She should leave with her dignity and her virginity. Give these young women some good soil. That's being a real man.

Thought for the Day

A man should pray and ask God to show him how to cultivate his wife.

Reading: Proverbs 19–21; 2 Corinthians 7

September 15

Lead Your Family to the Father

Part of Adam's job description from God was to cultivate the earth. When Eve came along, followed eventually by the children, Adam, as a father, was to make certain they did not grow "wild."

The world believes children need to "sow wild oats" as they grow up, but that is in direct contradiction to God's plan of cultivation and discipline. Today, we have boys throwing their seed—their sperm—all over the place because we are not cultivating, training, and disciplining them.

Consider the example of Abraham. God said,

> *Abraham will surely become a great and powerful nation, and all nations on earth will be blessed through him. For I have chosen him, so that he will direct his children and his household after him to keep the way of the* Lord *by doing what is right and just, so that the* Lord *will bring about for Abraham what he has promised him.*
>
> (Genesis 18:18–19)

Abraham received favor from God because he cultivated his household in God's commandments. He even cultivated his servant. He did not allow anyone to work in his household without being trained and disciplined in the ways of God. He made certain that even his servants obeyed God's standards and followed his example. Abraham did not want a pagan working for him. Everyone in his household followed father Abraham, and Abraham followed God the Father.

The principle is this: A father follows the example of the heavenly Father and teaches his offspring to follow him. A godly father leads everyone following him to the Father.

Thought for the Day

Abraham received favor from God because he cultivated his household in God's commandments.

Reading: Proverbs 22–24; 2 Corinthians 8

September 16

Love Your Children by Teaching Them

Abraham made sure that his household learned God's standards and followed his example. It's impossible to teach something you haven't learned yourself. This is one of the reasons a father needs to read and study the Word of God. He must know the commands of God so he can teach them to his children. Let's look again at what God said about Abraham, whom He called His friend (see Isaiah 41:8):

> *Abraham will surely become a great and powerful nation, and all nations on earth will be blessed through him. For I have chosen him, so that he will direct his children and his household after him to keep the way of the LORD by doing what is right and just, so that the LORD will bring about for Abraham what he has promised him.*
>
> (Genesis 18:18–19)

God made a promise to Abraham and said the fulfillment of the promise was connected to Abraham's teaching his family the Word of God. There's a relationship between the two. God is holding up some fathers' blessings because they don't love their children enough to teach them the Word.

When fathers teach their children the commands of God, their children will learn that fathers who know the Word are worth listening to. Proverbs 1:8–9 says, *"Listen, my son, to your father's instruction and do not forsake your mother's teaching. They will be a garland to grace your head and a chain to adorn your neck."* A garland was a crown or wreath given to athletes who won a race. When children receive godly instructions from their fathers, they can win the race that ends in eternal life.

Thought for the Day

It's impossible to teach something you haven't learned yourself.

Reading: Proverbs 25–26; 2 Corinthians 9

September 17

The Father Instructs and the Mother Commands

My son, hear the instruction of thy father, and forsake not the law of thy mother.
—Proverbs 1:8 (KJV)

There is a difference between an instruction and a command or law. Instruction is the giving of original information for direction and function. A command or law is a repetition and enforcement of instruction. In a family context, an instruction is the truth or principle that a father has learned from the heavenly Father. He imparts that instruction to his wife. As a mother, she repeats as a command what she has heard. When I was growing up, that sounded something like this in our house: "Myles, your father said to wash the dishes. Paul, your father said to clean the floor." Dad gave the instruction, and Mom issued the command. She repeated and enforced the instruction of my father.

I asked no questions and gave no excuses, because I knew that behind my mother's command were my father's power and authority. When she said, "Wash the dishes," I didn't hear her, I heard my father! I knew that if I disobeyed her command, I also would be disobeying my father, even though he was not physically present at that moment.

Because men have been given such a clear responsibility to teach, some men believe that they are more intelligent than women. If this were a matter of intelligence, many women would blow us away! Being a teacher doesn't mean that you are more intelligent—it simply means that your purpose is to communicate God's Word and will to your family.

Thought for the Day

Being a teacher means that your purpose is to communicate God's Word and will.

Reading: Proverbs 27–29; 2 Corinthians 10

September 18

No Other Source but God

In the garden of Eden, Eve received instructions from a source other than God or her husband. Men, we need to teach our wives and children not to receive instructions from any source other than God's Word. This is a very important principle: In today's culture, if our children can learn to compare the information they receive in books, magazines, and other media to God's truth, then they can go anywhere and face anything and still know the truth.

I encountered many diverse and spurious philosophies in college, but my father had already taught me the truth rooted in God's Word. That truth became the standard by which I measured everything. If Eve had compared what the serpent said to what Adam had already told her, she would have known immediately that the serpent was lying. Instead, she accepted the serpent's lie without checking it against the truth. She received instruction from a source other than the Father and, consequently, she was deceived.

The godly father should always emphasize to his family that what he has learned is from his heavenly Father. Such a father desires that this be said of him: "*As long as he lived, they* [his family and descendants] *did not fail to follow the Lord, the God of their fathers*" (2 Chronicles 34:33).

As a father teaching my children, I am serving not my earthly father but the God of my spiritual fathers—Abraham, Isaac, Jacob, Joseph, Moses, David, and the prophets. I am serving the Father of my Lord Jesus Christ.

Thought for the Day

Men, we need to teach our wives and children not to receive instructions from any source other than God's Word.

Reading: Proverbs 30–31; 2 Corinthians 11:1–15

Take Teaching to the Next Level

What is biblical discipline? Discipline is not punishment. Discipline takes teaching to the next level. It is one thing to teach a child, but correction and further instruction help to shape a child's character. Discipline, therefore, is training.

"Train a child in the way he should go, and when he is old he will not turn from it" (Proverbs 22:6). Notice the application of this principle in Ephesians 6:4: *"Fathers, do not exasperate your children; instead, bring them up in the training and instruction of the Lord."* Again, I want to emphasize that discipline is not punishment rendered by an irate or enraged parent. Paul clearly warned, *"Fathers, do not embitter your children, or they will become discouraged"* (Colossians 3:21). Fathers have a way of provoking their children by impatience or harshness. The above verses encourage fathers, "Don't provoke but train. Don't provoke but instruct."

A father's primary responsibility is to be like the heavenly Father and to do what He does. God does not point one way and then go another. A true father never says, "Do what I say but not what I do." Instead, a godly father with integrity can say unashamedly to his wife and children, "Live the way I live, and you will be like the Father." This is what the apostle Paul said to the believers in the Corinthian church, who were his spiritual offspring: *"Even though you have ten thousand guardians in Christ, you do not have many fathers, for in Christ Jesus I became your father through the gospel. Therefore I urge you to imitate me"* (1 Corinthians 4:15–16).

Likewise, a father becomes in Christ what he wants his wife and children to become.

Thought for the Day

It is one thing to teach a child, but correction and further instruction help to shape a child's character.

Reading: Ecclesiastes 1–3; 2 Corinthians 11:16–33

September 20

Training by Example

"My son, do not make light of the Lord's discipline, and do not lose heart when he rebukes you, because the Lord disciplines those he loves, and he punishes everyone he accepts as a son." Endure hardship as discipline; God is treating you as sons. For what son is not disciplined by his father? If you are not disciplined (and everyone undergoes discipline), then you are illegitimate children and not true sons. Moreover, we have all had human fathers who disciplined us and we respected them for it.

—Hebrews 12:5–9

Yesterday, we saw that a man must become in Christ what he wants his wife and children to become. Let us continue to look at what it means for fathers to be examples to their families. The word *discipline* comes from the word *disciple*, which refers to one who learns by following. So, fathers train and disciple their children by giving them a worthy example to follow. Their children learn by imitation. That is exactly what Jesus had His disciples do. He told them, "Follow Me!" (See, for example, Matthew 4:19.)

A concrete example of this concept is a train. We call an entire line of railroad cars on a track a "train." Yet *train* comes from a word meaning "to draw" or "to drag." Technically, only the engine is the train because everything else attached to the engine is a follower. The principle that governs a train is similar to the principle God wants us to implement in our families. A father is never supposed to just point his wife or children in a direction. He is the engine, and he should be able to say, "Hook up to me. Follow me. Imitate my example, and then you'll be going in the right direction."

Thought for the Day

Fathers train and disciple their children by giving them a worthy example to follow.

Reading: Ecclesiastes 4–6; 2 Corinthians 12

September 21

Live What You Teach

Be careful, and watch yourselves closely so that you do not forget the things your eyes have seen or let them slip from your heart as long as you live. Teach them to your children and to their children after them.
—Deuteronomy 4:9

God is saying to men, "Don't let My ways out of your sight. Make sure you understand and obey them first." Then, "*teach them to your children and to their children after them.*" Why? Because you are supposed to be the teacher.

Don't just tell your children, "Do this" or "Don't do that." Show them. Watch your life and make sure you keep the Word of God. Some men say one thing but do another. For example, they may tell their children to be honest but then call off work when they're not sick. Some fathers tell their children, "Tobacco is bad for you"; meanwhile, they're puffing away on a cigarette. Children see this and think, *To be a grown-up, you have to smoke.* Adults reinforce this idea by their actions. God tells us not to do this to our children. People don't seem to understand that you cannot teach something if you're not being a model of it yourself. A good teacher is one who teaches by example.

Where, again, does the father get his original instruction and information so he can teach it? From God the Father and His Word. Even if a father has not been fathered by a godly man, he can return to our heavenly Father, be saved, and learn God's ways. He can receive godly instruction from his pastor and righteous men in the church who know and love the Word of God. And, of course, as a born-again believer, a father (as well as a mother) has the Holy Spirit within him, teaching him everything that the Son hears from the Father. (See John 16:5–15.)

Thought for the Day

God is saying to men, "Don't let My ways out of your sight."

Reading: Ecclesiastes 7–9; 2 Corinthians 13

September 22

TRAIN UNDER VARIOUS CONDITIONS

A father disciples his children by letting them see how he functions under different conditions. A disciple is a follower who learns by observation. Disciples in the past always left home because learning was *living* life, not just talking about it. The father not only teaches in the home, but he also takes his children out into the world with him so that they can observe how he handles various situations in a godly way.

It is impossible to be effective as a long-distance father. A father cannot father children he is not with or train children who are not by his side. You cannot disciple successfully on the telephone or via e-mail. Not being present in his children's lives makes a man a biological supplier of sperm, not a father. A father trains a child by having the child observe what he does, says, and decides in the real world.

Fathers need to disciple their households by letting their families observe them in the following ways: reading and applying the Word of God; praying and interceding; making right decisions based on the absolute truths of God's Word; living out the example of Christ while working in the real world; sharing the gospel with others; openly worshiping and praising God the Father; treating their wives with honor and dignity; honoring others above themselves; being reconcilers between races and economic classes; and loving their enemies.

Thought for the Day

A father trains a child by having the child observe what the father does, says, and decides.

Reading: Ecclesiastes 10–12; Galatians 1

September 23

A Good Inheritance

Solomon said, "*A good man leaves an inheritance for his children's children*" (Proverbs 13:22). I like that concept. A good man doesn't think about the past; he thinks about the future. Moreover, a good man doesn't leave an inheritance of just money and land. That's not the only inheritance Solomon was talking about. He was talking about a strong heritage—something to stand on, and something to lean on throughout life.

I was recently speaking about this topic in Barbados, and a young man said to me, "But you don't understand the history of the Afro-Caribbean man. I inherited my granddaddy and great-granddaddy's legacy, you know." I said, "Hold it right there. Whenever a negative history predicts your future, your present is in trouble. Don't come and tell me that you have to repeat your history. What we are about is *creating* history. We need to create a new history for all our children's children." Then, I told him, "It doesn't matter who your grandfather was. The important issue is what your *grandchildren* are going to say about you."

Maybe when you were growing up, your father left when things got tough, and you think you need to do the same thing now that you have a family. Let me tell you: if you leave your child, you'll teach him the same thing your father taught you. It doesn't stop; it causes a perpetual cycle of destruction. We have to stop this cycle by getting back to God's Manual and getting on course again.

Thought for the Day

A good man leaves his children a strong heritage—something to stand on, and something to lean on throughout life.

Reading: Song of Songs 1–3; Galatians 2

September 24

WHAT DO YOU CALL YOUR CHILDREN?

Do not be deceived: God cannot be mocked. A man reaps what he sows. The one who sows to please his sinful nature, from that nature will reap destruction; the one who sows to please the Spirit, from the Spirit will reap eternal life.
—Galatians 6:7–8

A wife and children will bear good fruit when the father sows into them the fruit of the Spirit. In contrast, we see the results of sowing the works of the flesh. Fathers who sow abuse reap abuse. Fathers who sow addiction frequently have addicted wives and children. Fathers who sow divorce reap broken families. But fathers who sow the seed of the Spirit's fruit reap love, joy, peace, patience, kindness, goodness, faithfulness, gentleness, and self-control. (See Galatians 5:22–23.)

Fathers are to teach only the truth they hear from God the Father. As the perfect example of a teacher, Jesus asserted, "*When you have lifted up the Son of Man, then you will know that I am the one I claim to be and that I do nothing on my own but speak just what the Father has taught me*" (John 8:28). All that the Son taught came from His Father, the Source. What a powerful force a father is in his family when his wife and children know that whenever he acts or speaks, he has heard from God.

The godly father doesn't react in anger toward his children by calling them names like *fool*, *idiot*, or *stupid*. Why not? Because the Father never calls him those names. The godly father calls his children saints, holy ones, priests, and sons of the Most High God. The father declares to his wife and children the image of God in Christ Jesus.

Thought for the Day

Fathers who sow the seed of the Spirit's fruit reap love, joy, peace, patience, kindness, goodness, faithfulness, gentleness, and self-control.

Reading: Song of Songs 4–5; Galatians 3

September 25

Perfect Love

The church is described in the Bible as a "she," a bride, a woman. It is given a feminine designation. As Eve was presented to Adam in perfection, Christ says that He will present to Himself *"a radiant church... holy and blameless"* (Ephesians 5:27). Jesus told His bride, "I love you." Then, He said to men, "Husbands, love your wives as I love My wife." How does Christ show love to the church? He cleanses her by His Word (see verse 26), just as Adam was supposed to have done for Eve.

Adam's job was to protect Eve and to make sure that she was kept continually cleansed by communicating God's Word to her. Adam's failure was that he, in a sense, abandoned Eve, and that is why she was vulnerable to Satan's enticements. Then, when Eve went to Adam after having disobeyed God's Word, instead of correcting her, he joined with her in disobedience.

Jesus, however, is the perfect Man. He told his wife, *"Never will I leave you; never will I forsake you"* (Hebrews 13:5). This is what makes the difference. Satan cannot overcome the church because Christ will never leave her, and He will always guide her into all truth. (See John 16:13.) His love for His bride is perfect; He understands fully what is best for her. He's maintaining His perfect vigil over her. He is the Perfect Adam.

Men, what kind of love are you showing your wives?

Thought for the Day

Christ keeps the church by His Word. Likewise, men are to help their wives keep spiritually cleansed by communicating God's Word to them.

Reading: Song of Songs 6–8; Galatians 4

September 26

Ruling by Delegated Authority

A woman is designed to rule by delegated authority. My father gave my mother directions for our family, just as Christ does with His bride, the church. Jesus gave believers instructions, and then He left to return to the heavenly Father:

> *All authority in heaven and on earth has been given to me. Therefore go and make disciples of all nations, baptizing them in the name of the Father and of the Son and of the Holy Spirit, and teaching them to obey everything I have commanded you.* (Matthew 28:18–20)

We remain in the world with Jesus' instructions and the Holy Spirit. We are supposed to go out to disciple the nations, possess the land, and take back what the devil has stolen. We have the authority of the Father to do so. When we command, lives change because the authority of the Father is in us through His Holy Spirit.

It is tragic that in many homes today, the mother cannot invoke the name of her child's father with authority. In fact, many curse the father's name. Why? Because fathers have abandoned their responsibility to be teachers of the Word of God in their homes.

We have seen that one of Satan's primary strategies is to remove fathers from the home. Satan attacks fathers to keep them from being the teachers to their families. He wants the home to be in rebellion against both the earthly father and heavenly Father. If Satan can remove the father, the family will lack authority. If there is no authority, there is anarchy and chaos. When there is anarchy and chaos, any number of undesirable things can happen—kids join gangs, get involved in drugs, and run with bad company—all because there is no authority in the home.

Thought for the Day

When we command, lives change because the authority of the Father is in us through His Holy Spirit.

Reading: Isaiah 1–2; Galatians 5

September 27

The Nature of Submission

[Jesus], *being in very nature God, did not consider equality with God something to be grasped, but made himself nothing, taking the very nature of a servant, being made in human likeness. And being found in appearance as a man, he humbled himself and became obedient to death—even death on a cross!*
—Philippians 2:6–8

There is an evil spirit abroad in the world today promoting the idea that nobody needs to be in submission to anybody else. Yet Jesus Himself gave us our model of authority and submission when He submitted to His Father. Even though Jesus is equal to God, He submitted Himself to the Father and to the Father's plan. The prophet Isaiah talked about this when he said, in essence, "You aren't going to believe this report. A Son will be born, and His name shall be called Wonderful Counselor, the Mighty God." (See Isaiah 9:6.)

We might ask, "But Isaiah, you just said, '*For unto us a Child is born, unto us a Son is given*' (v. 6 NKJV). What do you mean that this Child, this Son, will be called Mighty God? How can He be God and Son?" Isaiah's answer would be, "He is God, but He took on the position of Man and Servant for the sake of your redemption."

Purpose necessitated the position. God's purpose was redemption. The Godhead said, "Somebody has to go down and submit to Us in order to bring about the salvation of mankind." So Jesus, the Word of God, who is God Himself, said, "I'll go. I know I am an equal in the Godhead, but for the purpose of redemption, I will be made in the likeness of man and will submit." Similarly, a woman isn't any less than her husband; however, for God's purposes, it is her position to submit. (See Ephesians 5:22–23.)

Thought for the Day

Jesus Himself gave us our model of authority and submission when He submitted to His Father.

Reading: Isaiah 3–4; Galatians 6

September 28

Submission Activates Heaven

A man ought not to cover his head, since he is the image and glory of God; but the woman is the glory of man.
—1 Corinthians 11:7

In the above verse, Paul was saying that once the man is covered with Christ, his marriage is under authority. However, the woman then needs the man to cover her. First Corinthians 11:9–10 says, *"Neither was man created for woman, but woman for man. For this reason, and because of the angels, the woman ought to have a sign of authority on her head."*

If you are a female, and you want to do a work for God, all of heaven is ready to work for you. God says, "All right, we'll do spiritual work, but how are your relationships in the natural realm? What is your relationship with your husband, your family members, the members of your church?" Any woman who says, "I don't need the church; I can do this by myself," isn't going to find any angels supporting her. The angels are looking for your authority. They will ask, "Whom are you under? How can you expect us to help you under God's authority when you yourself aren't under anybody?" Submission activates heaven.

Now, if Christ submitted to the Father, who do we think we are? You may be independent, famous, a fantastic businessperson, and doing very well. However, if you aren't going to submit to anyone, heaven won't trust you. Don't believe that you can run off and do God's work without being in submission. Don't ever run away from a ministry and do your own work because somebody there made you upset. The angels are watching. You may actually remove God's protective covering from yourself when you move out from under your authority. This spiritual principle applies to both males and females.

Thought for the Day

If you won't submit to anyone, heaven won't trust you.

Reading: Isaiah 5–6; Ephesians 1

September 29

Are You a Qualified Authority?

Do you know a major reason why marriages, relationships, and society aren't working? It is because people are refusing to accept their positions. What if the tires on your car decided they wanted to take on the role of the steering wheel? The whole car wouldn't be able to move. This is the stalemate that our society is in. Everybody wants the same position. Nobody wants to trust anybody else.

God created the spirit-man and placed him within the male and the female. Then He subjected the male to Christ Jesus and the female to the male. If we do not understand our positions, we will function in ignorance, and the results will be pain and destruction. People perish because of a lack of knowledge. (See Proverbs 29:18 KJV.)

Men, you have no right to have your wife submit to you if you don't submit to anybody else. You are exercising illegal authority if you are demanding submission without being submitted. As a matter of fact, you can't really discipline your children if you're not disciplined yourself.

The male needs to be under authority before he is able to exercise it properly. It's impossible for you to say you are the head of a home when you aren't submitted to anybody else. The head of Christ is God, and the head of man is Christ, and the head of woman is man. (See 1 Corinthians 11:3.) Any man who is out from under Christ is not really a qualified authority.

Thought for the Day

Men, you have no right to have your wife submit to you if you don't submit to anybody else.

Reading: Isaiah 7–8; Ephesians 2

September 30

The Woman's Source and Provider

A woman's ultimate Source and Provider is God, and she can always turn to Him. But God has designed things so that the female can receive earthly provision through the male. "*Man did not come from woman, but woman from man*" (1 Corinthians 11:8) means that the man is responsible for the woman because she came from man. This is God's original plan.

Now, if a man starts thinking that this is *his* plan, rather than God's, his responsibility for the woman will turn into domination over her. We have to understand that the female's provision by the male is God's design, or we will misuse and abuse it.

The man is responsible for providing because of his position in the relationship of things. There is a parallel to this in the spiritual realm. Spiritually, we are to go to God for what we need. Jesus has told us, "Remain in Me and I will remain in you. If you are separated from Me, you can't do anything. I am the Vine; you are the branches, which receive nourishment from the Vine." (See John 15:4–5.)

God says that the woman should remain connected to her source. She should be able to go to the man to get answers. If you are a married woman, and you have a question, ask your husband. If he doesn't have the answer, then go to the next man who is in godly authority. This also applies to a woman who is not married. The man could be your father, your pastor, or your big brother in the Lord, as long as it is someone who represents God as source and provider. That person should be able to give you guidance. The woman is always supposed to be able to go to her source to receive whatever she needs.

Thought for the Day

A woman's ultimate Source and Provider is God, and she can always turn to Him.

Reading: Isaiah 9–10; Ephesians 3

October 1

THE PROVERBS 31 WOMAN

A wife of noble character who can find? She is worth far more than rubies. Her husband has full confidence in her and lacks nothing of value.
—Proverbs 31:10–11

Our overview of males and females and their relationships would not be complete without a look at the woman who is considered the epitome of both womanhood and power: the woman of Proverbs 31.

Some women don't even like to read this chapter of the Bible because they are overwhelmed by all the things this woman is apparently able to do! "Well, if I had a staff of servants like she had, I could do all those things, too!" they exclaim. Yet when we consider our exploration of God's purposes for the woman from creation to redemption, and when we think about how the woman has been set free to fulfill His purposes, Proverbs 31 gives us tremendous perspective on what a woman is meant to be. Let us not become overwhelmed when reading about what this woman *does* and miss out on the central message of *who she is.*

One theme that Proverbs 31 communicates is this: The woman is a doer. She is a multitasker. She is responsible for taking care of her husband, children, home, job, talents, church commitments, charitable work, and sometimes elderly parents. She is a helper *and* she is a leader. She receives seed into her physical, emotional, psychological, and spiritual wombs, incubates it, and then uses it to build and transform the world around her.

Thought for the Day

Let us not become overwhelmed when reading about what the Proverbs 31 woman *does* and miss out on the central message of *who she is.*

Reading: Isaiah 11–13; Ephesians 4

October 2

A Woman Who Honors God

Charm is deceptive, and beauty is fleeting; but a woman who fears the L*ORD is to be praised.*
—Proverbs 31:30

Even while a woman is fulfilling all her vital purposes in her home and in the world, she must always remember that *a woman's first place is in God.* Proverbs 31 reminds her, "Don't neglect your relationship with God, and don't forget to develop His character in your inner being as you go about your extremely busy life."

It is much too easy to begin to overlook God when you are taking care of so many other people and responsibilities. Remember, the woman was created to be loved by God and to have fellowship with Him as a spirit-being made in His image. She was meant to reflect His character and likeness, to represent His true nature. God created the woman to have His moral characteristics within her inner being. She is to resemble Him not only as a spirit, but also in these qualities. She was designed to act and function as God does, in love and grace. Therefore, Proverbs 31 is saying, "While you are doing what God has called and gifted you to do, don't forget the importance of His character in your life." That is why it speaks of the "*wife of noble character*" (v. 10).

Women need to realize that having a relationship with the Lord and developing His character in their lives form an essential foundation that will strengthen and sustain them in all their activities and accomplishments. With continual refreshing from the Lord, they can purposefully engage in their many responsibilities and fulfill the exciting purposes God has for them.

Thought for the Day

It is much too easy to begin to overlook God when you are taking care of so many other people and responsibilities.

Reading: Isaiah 14–16; Ephesians 5

October 3

It Is for Freedom

It is for freedom that Christ has set us free. Stand firm, then, and do not let yourselves be burdened again by a yoke of slavery.
—Galatians 5:1

In some ways, a woman may derive her self-esteem from her activities almost as much as a man derives his self-image from his work. She wants to feel that she is *valued* for the contribution she is making to her family and community. Yet because she is an emotional feeler, she places this need in the context of her relationships and emotions, and so it is not as easily recognized for what it is.

Christ has freed the woman and made her an equal partner with the man so that she can fulfill His purposes for her and develop all the gifts that He has given her. He has freed her from the effects of sin and from the oppression that says she is inferior to men. However, now that she has been set free, she has to guard against oppressing *herself.* How might she oppress herself? By *doing* at the expense of *being.*

The world tells us to prove our worth by what we accomplish. The Bible tells us to accept our worth in the One who loves us. You don't have to justify your worth by how much you are doing for others or how many activities you are engaged in. Remember the story of Martha and Mary when Jesus first visited their home? Although Martha was busy preparing a meal for Jesus, He quietly reminded her that Mary had made the better choice by simply sitting at His feet to hear His words of life. (See Luke 10:38–42.)

Thought for the Day

The world tells us to prove our worth by what we accomplish. The Bible tells us to accept our worth in the One who loves us.

Reading: Isaiah 17–19; Ephesians 6:1–9

October 4

Finding Her Identity

I have been crucified with Christ and I no longer live, but Christ lives in me. The life I live in the body, I live by faith in the Son of God, who loved me and gave himself for me.

—Galatians 2:20

Why do police investigators check for fingerprints at crime scenes? Because they are looking for identity. All of us have fingerprints that no one before us ever had and no one after us ever will have. This distinction is an indication of how God created all of us to be different. Yet, we often still look for our identities in other people or things.

There is a tremendous pull by the culture for women to seek identity in all the wrong places. A woman's true identity is not in her appearance, her clothes, her wealth, her job, or even her husband and children. Regardless of what culture and society may say, the highest worth and dignity were given to the female by God in creation. Remember that the woman was created to be loved by God and to have fellowship with Him forever.

A woman first needs to find her identity in who she is in Christ—God's beloved child. It is only as she does this that she can be fulfilled and carry out His plans for her. When a woman submits to God, Christ will work in her and through her by His Spirit. In this way, she will be enabled to fulfill all the purposes He has for her—but in His strength, not her own. "*We have not received the spirit of the world but the Spirit who is from God, that we may understand what God has freely given us*" (1 Corinthians 2:12).

Thought for the Day

A woman needs to find her identity in Christ.

Reading: Isaiah 20–22; Ephesians 6:10–24

October 5

"You Surpass Them All"

Many women do noble things, but you surpass them all.
—Proverbs 31:29

The woman of Proverbs 31 is not just a busy woman; she is a woman who knows her purpose in God. Let's look at some reasons why this is so:

- She knows that she is to trust God and draw her strength from Him so that she will not be paralyzed by anxiety; her family and others with whom she is in relationship will be able to put their confidence in her; they will know she has their best interests in mind (vv. 11–15).
- She knows that God values her abilities and intelligence, and so she is free to pursue opportunities and make plans for expanding her realm of influence (vv. 16–18, 24).
- She knows that God is her ultimate Source and that He desires to bless her, so she sets about her work with energy and anticipation. She has a good attitude and doesn't complain (v. 17).
- Since God has blessed her, she desires to be a blessing to others, and she reaches out to those less fortunate than she (v. 20).
- Because she knows that her worth comes from her position in God, she treats herself with respect (v. 25).
- She has immersed herself in God's Word in order to know His ways; therefore, she is able to give godly wisdom and instruction to others (v. 26).
- Because she has come to know the God of all encouragement, she is an encouragement to her husband, children, friends, and coworkers, and she invests herself in their lives (v. 28).

Thought for the Day

The woman of Proverbs 31 is not just a busy woman; she is a woman who knows her purpose in God.

Reading: Isaiah 23–25; Philippians 1

October 6

Principles of "The Proverbs 31 Woman"

Today, review these principles of "The Proverbs 31 Woman" and reflect on how they apply to your everyday life—directly for yourself, if you are a woman, and in your relationships with women, if you are a man.

1. A woman of noble character is hard to find; the husband of such a woman *"lacks nothing of value"* (Proverbs 31:11).
2. Women should not become so overwhelmed by what the Proverbs 31 woman *does* that they miss the message of who *she is.*
3. The woman is a doer. She is a multitasker.
4. The woman is a helper *and* a leader. She is responsible for taking care of her husband, children, home, job, talents, church commitments, charitable work, and sometimes elderly parents.
5. A woman must always remember that *her first place is in God.*
6. The Bible tells women that they must accept their worth not in what they do but in the One who loves them.
7. A woman needs to find her identity in who she is in Christ—God's beloved child.
8. The woman of Proverbs 31 is not just a busy woman; she is a woman who knows her purpose in God.

Heavenly Father,
The noble woman in Proverbs 31 works very diligently. In everything she does, she encourages her family and she pleases her God. We pray that we would not see a superwoman to envy, but rather a gifted woman who is simply surrendered to the will of God in her life. As we each surrender to Your will and purposes, may we be used by You as You see fit. And may we always find the time to sit at Your feet and worship You before we take on all the busy projects in our lives. In Jesus' mighty name we pray, amen.

Reading: Isaiah 26–27; Philippians 2

October 7

When I Consider the Heavens

When I consider your heavens, the work of your fingers, the moon and the stars, which you have set in place, what is man that you are mindful of him, the son of man that you care for him?

—Psalm 8:3–4

With all the magnificence of the universe, it is mankind that is at the center of God's thoughts. The wonder of this idea struck King David one day. David asked God, in effect, "Why are You thinking only about us?" Although Psalm 8 doesn't give us God's answer, I think His reply would be, "Every time you see the moon and the stars, and everything else I've created, I want you to know that it all exists because of you."

When my wife and I were expecting our first child, we had the nursery fixed up before the baby arrived. I remember standing and looking at the whole thing the day it was finished. We had thoroughly cleaned the room. We had the new crib, pillow, sheets, powder, baby oil, diapers, baby food, and everything else all ready. We had little pictures on the walls. There was no baby, but everything the baby would need and use was ready. Then we stepped back, looked at the room, and said, "This is good." What were we doing? Preparing. That's exactly what God was doing in Genesis 1 when He made the world in preparation for the creation of mankind.

When God finished creating the world, He called everything good. I believe He said this because everything was ready. It was after God called the physical world good that He said, "*Let us make man*" (Genesis 1:26).

Thought for the Day

With all of the magnificence of the universe, it is mankind that is at the center of God's thoughts.

Reading: Isaiah 28–29; Philippians 3

October 8

Humanity's Redeemer

And I will put enmity between you and the woman, and between your offspring and hers; [the Redeemer] *will crush your head, and you will strike his heel.*
—Genesis 3:15

Is humanity doomed to live in the effects of the fall? Has God's purpose been lost forever? No. His purpose has never changed. His original design still stands. As we have seen, in the very hour when humanity rejected God's purpose, God promised a Redeemer who would save men and women from their fallen state and all its ramifications. The Redeemer would restore the relationship and partnership of males and females. Jesus Christ is that Redeemer; because of Him, men and women can return to God's original design for them! Purpose, peace, and potential can return to humanity. In Luke 1:68, Zechariah joyously announced the fulfillment of the promise in Genesis 3:15: *"Praise be to the Lord, the God of Israel, because he has come and has redeemed his people,"*

A return to God's plan, however, means a return to God Himself. It means coming back to God through the Redeemer, yielding your life to Him, and asking Him to fill you with His Holy Spirit so that you will be able to live in His original plan for you. When you do this, God will do an amazing thing. He will cause the human spirit within you—which is dead as a result of the fall—to come alive again, so that you will be able to reflect His character and His ways. As you return to God and continually yield your spirit to God's Spirit, you will be able to fulfill the purposes for which you were created.

Thought for the Day

The Redeemer, Jesus Christ, brought purpose, peace, and potential back to humanity.

Reading: Isaiah 30–31; Philippians 4

October 9

Jesus Is the Author of Salvation

Christ Jesus is the *"author of eternal salvation"* (Hebrews 5:9 KJV) and the *"author and finisher of our faith"* (Hebrews 12:2 KJV). The *"author of eternal salvation"*—what does that mean? Jesus initiated, generated, produced, upholds, and sustains the salvation of all mankind. He is the sole Source of our redemption.

If you want to come to God, therefore, Jesus is the ultimate Source. Despite the works of Muhammad, Buddha, and Confucius, you can't go to any of those men for salvation because, according to Scripture, they didn't generate, create, or author mankind's redemption. Jesus is the Generator of salvation; it germinated with Him and it is completed in Him. He is both the Author and Finisher of our faith.

I'm so glad He's not just the Author, but also the Finisher. Many men are merely authors of babies; they don't finish as fathers. Jesus is the Finisher of your faith. He didn't just start your faith; He'll see it to the end until it is complete. (See Philippians 1:6.) He will cause you to grow up to the full stature and measure of His purpose for you, so that you look just like Him. (See 2 Corinthians 3:18; Ephesians 4:13.)

Jesus provides the "gene" for the new generation of man. He is the Source of seed for salvation. In Isaiah's description of the Messiah, he concluded with the titles Wonderful Counselor, Mighty God, *Everlasting Father,* and Prince of Peace. (See Isaiah 9:6.) In this verse, the Son is also referred to as the Father because He produced a new generation of human beings; He produced the *"new man"* (Ephesians 2:15).

Thought for the Day

Jesus is the Author and the Finisher of our faith.

Reading: Isaiah 32–33; Colossians 1

October 10

Right Relationships

When you have a right relationship with God, you can have right relationships with other people. The reverse is also true: *"Therefore, if you are offering your gift at the altar and there remember that your brother has something against you, leave your gift there in front of the altar. First go and be reconciled to your brother"* (Matthew 5:23–24).

A right relationship with God is dependent on right relationships with other people. This truth brings the matter of reconciled relationships between men and women down to where it hurts, doesn't it? We must understand clearly what God's Word says so that we have no excuse for failing to mend our broken relationships.

Can you imagine husbands stopping in the middle of Sunday morning worship and stepping outside with their wives to make things right with them? If that were to happen, we'd have a brand new church and society. Yet I find that people often try the easy route when they have been in conflict with others. They go to God and say, "God, please forgive Mary," "God, tell Mary that I forgive her," or "God, I ask You to change Mary." They don't want to go to the person directly. We love to hide behind God so we don't have to accept the responsibility of face-to-face relationships. Our reluctance to deal honestly and directly with others is the reason why there are so many problems in relationships, even in the body of Christ.

I honor my wife and do right by her, not only because I love her, but also for the sake of my relationship with God. *"Husbands,...be considerate as you live with your wives...so that nothing will hinder your prayers"* (1 Peter 3:7). Jesus said that my relationship with God is even more important than my relationship with my wife—and yet God made my relationship with Him contingent on my relationship with her.

Thought for the Day

We hide behind God so we don't have to accept the responsibility of face-to-face relationships.

Reading: Isaiah 34–36; Colossians 2

October 11

The Importance of Forgiveness

For if you forgive men when they sin against you, your heavenly Father will also forgive you. But if you do not forgive men their sins, your Father will not forgive your sins.
—Matthew 6:14–15

Whatever you ask for in prayer, believe that you have received it, and it will be yours. And when you stand praying, if you hold anything against anyone, forgive him, so that your Father in heaven may forgive you your sins.
—Mark 11:24–25

Jesus talked a great deal about the importance of forgiveness in our relationships. He said that if you do not forgive someone who has something against you, or whom you have something against, then the Father will not forgive you and will not hear you. Jesus was saying that relationships with other people are even more important than worship, because you cannot worship except in the context of your relationships.

It doesn't matter how serious and sincere you are about God. It doesn't matter how filled you are with the Holy Spirit or how much Scripture you've learned. God is not overly impressed by your ability to communicate with Him, by your ability to articulate your worship, prayer, or praise. His reception of your worship—whether it is through your giving, your praise, your administration of the kingdom of God, or your ministry of the gifts of the Spirit—is contingent upon your relationships with others, especially your spouse. So, if you give God a thousand dollars, whether or not God receives it depends on whether or not you are in right relationship with others. God's acceptance of even your tithes is contingent upon your relationships with other people, not on how much you give Him.

Thought for the Day

You cannot worship except in the context of your relationships.

Reading: Isaiah 37–38; Colossians 3

October 12

Increase Your Investment

A real man looks out for the needs of others and helps them to grow. Some men concentrate on only their own fruit, their own accomplishments. They are just bettering themselves. That's called selfishness. They don't have fruitful wives or children because they've neglected to care for them.

Every part of society should be developing if we have real men in our presence. Too often, we have destroyers instead of developers. They are tearing down our homes, spraying graffiti on our buildings, stealing, and shooting. Men need to come back to their purpose and stop using their strength for the wrong reasons.

A male has been designed to do his work in such a way that he is able to make it into more than it was originally. In the parable of the talents, the man traveling out of the country entrusted the first servant with five talents, the second with two, and the third with one. It is implied that the man said to them, "Now, when I come back, I don't want to see just the money I gave you. I want to see an increase in my investment." When the man returned and found that the servant with the one talent had done nothing to increase his master's money, he called the servant "*wicked*" and "*lazy*" (Matthew 25:26).

If a man is still working at what he was working at ten years ago and hasn't improved it at all, there's something wrong. Men are designed by God to be cultivators who don't just sit on good ideas but implement them, who don't complain about others but see their potential and help them reach it. Ask God to start working out the ideas He has put within you.

Thought for the Day

Men are designed by God to be cultivators who don't just sit on good ideas but implement them.

Reading: Isaiah 39–40; Colossians 4

Developing Your Family

God the Father carefully provides for the development of His people. To develop means "to cause to grow gradually and continually in fuller, larger, and better ways." Consider what Paul wrote about our heavenly Father:

> *I planted the seed, Apollos watered it, but God made it grow. So neither he who plants nor he who waters is anything, but only God, who makes things grow. The man who plants and the man who waters have one purpose, and each will be rewarded according to his own labor. For we are God's fellow workers; you are God's field, God's building.* (1 Corinthians 3:6–9)

The human father is likewise to develop the people God has placed under his care. To understand the father as developer, we return to the garden of Eden and remember God's instructions to Adam to "*dress it*" and "*keep it*" (Genesis 2:15 KJV). In dressing and keeping the garden, Adam had to plan for the orderly growth of both plant and animal life. Developing for order and cultivation started when Adam named the animals. (See verses 19–20.)

Inherent in God's purpose is His plan. The heavenly Father, as Developer, planned the garden and also planned what would be in it. He structured streams to come up from the earth in order to water the garden. He provided food for Adam and Eve, had a plan concerning what they could and could not eat, and gave specific usage instructions to Adam.

Fathers must not leave their family members to wander in a spiritual and moral desert. The godly father who develops his family has a plan for their growth—physically, intellectually, emotionally, and spiritually.

Thought for the Day

To develop means to cause to grow gradually and continually in fuller, larger, and better ways.

Reading: Isaiah 41–42; 1 Thessalonians 1

October 14

The Developer Always Has a Plan

Yesterday, we focused on the principle that inherent in God's purpose is His plan. *Planning* is the first step in development. Before a developer starts constructing a housing division or shopping complex, he makes a building plan. He presents the plan to the appropriate governmental officials in order to obtain the required permits to build. The plan includes what will be constructed, as well as how it will be used. Structure and usage are essential to a plan.

Preparing or *planting* the ground is the second feature of development. Once there is a plan, the developer begins the necessary groundwork for building. Earthmovers come in and drainage is provided. The land is prepared to accept the building–first a foundation and then a framework. Likewise, a sower prepares the soil and sows the seed in planning for a harvest.

The next step is *protecting*. Every developer protects his construction site. He may construct a tall fence with barbed wire to keep out intruders. He may hire security guards. In a similar way, the farmer who develops a crop uses whatever means of protection his crop needs to guard against insects, diseases, and vandals. He tends the crop by pulling weeds and providing adequate irrigation.

The Scriptures show how God the Developer protected man in the garden. He warned him not to eat from the Tree of Knowledge of Good and Evil and gave him instructions on what to do in the garden. (See Genesis 2:15–17.) He also walked with Adam and Eve in the cool of the evening. (See Genesis 3:8.) Keeping in fellowship with God was protection for them. God plans, prepares, and protects His people, and this is what He calls fathers to do for their families.

Thought for the Day

In what ways are you planning for, preparing, and protecting your family?

Reading: Isaiah 43–44; 1 Thessalonians 2

October 15

Light Produces Light

After planning, preparing, and protecting, it is time for *producing.* Once a building is finished, the developer uses his shopping complex, houses, or commercial building to produce income. The farmer who grows a crop doesn't just leave it in the field. He harvests it because he has produced fruits or vegetables that can be sold and used. Likewise, the Father develops us to be productive in His plan and purpose. Jesus addressed this issue of development very specifically: "*This is to my Father's glory, that you bear much fruit, showing yourselves to be my disciples*" (John 15:8).

A father walks each step with his family as he prepares and equips them in the ways of God. He plants the seed of God's Word in their hearts. He protects them with prayer, as well as with his presence and provision for their lives. As a godly father walks with his family, he is an example of holiness for them. He expects the best from them in producing good fruit, which gives glory to the Father. He develops his offspring to glow with the glory of God. A father expects his family to be the light of the world, the salt of the earth, and witnesses for Christ in the world.

Light produces light. The light of Christ in a father's life sets his family ablaze for Christ. The prayer of every godly father is that his children will become flames of fire, blazing with the Father's Spirit and shining as stars. "*Those who are wise will shine like the brightness of the heavens, and those who lead many to righteousness, like the stars for ever and ever*" (Daniel 12:3).

Thought for the Day

The light of Christ in a father's life sets his family ablaze for Christ.

Reading: Isaiah 45–46; 1 Thessalonians 3

October 16

Growing into Christ's Image

If anyone is in Christ, he is a new creation; the old has gone, the new has come!
—2 Corinthians 5:17

A godly father is constantly developing his family members to grow in God's limitless potential, to be their best through His strength, and to accept others as they are growing in Christ. He stretches his wife and children to achieve their utmost for His highest.

The objective of development is permanent growth. The father cultivates his relationship with his wife and children so that they will grow beyond themselves and into the believers God purposed them to be. The powerful message of 2 Corinthians 5:17 is that new creations in Christ are continually having old things—sin, bad habits, ignorance, and strongholds—pass away, while all areas of life are becoming new.

Fathers understand that God's children are always becoming! We are developing and growing into Christ's image. We are being changed "*from glory to glory*" (2 Corinthians 3:18 KJV). Fathers put a badge on their family members, including themselves, which reads, "Please be patient. God isn't finished with me yet!"

Fathers develop fathers. A father grows in fatherhood by leaning on the heavenly Father. A man learns how to father from a father. The goal of fathering is to develop men who can father and women who can mother under the covering of a godly husband. So when your son starts to make decisions as good as or better than you have been making, you can affirm to him that he is now a father while continuing to encourage him as he grows in fatherhood. Jesus promised that when we are in the Father and the Father is in us, just as the Father is in Him, then we will do greater works than He did. (See John 14:12.)

Thought for the Day

Fathers understand that God's children are always becoming!

Reading: Isaiah 47–49; 1 Thessalonians 4

October 17

Creating an Environment for Growth

A man is to provide an encouraging environment for his family that supports their development. The father disciples his offspring by providing an example of the Father. A father who is like the heavenly Father encourages discovery and learning as parts of the developmental process. He promotes steady, consistent, and progressive growth in his family. Let me share with you some environmental qualities of a father who develops his offspring:

Encouragement: The father edifies his offspring. "*Therefore encourage one another and build each other up, just as in fact you are doing*" (1 Thessalonians 5:11). Fathers never tear down the esteem of a family member. Paul wrote to the Corinthians that God gave him power to edify, not destroy. "*Our prayer is for your perfection. This is why I write these things when I am absent, that when I come I may not have to be harsh in my use of authority—the authority the Lord gave me for building you up, not for tearing you down*" (2 Corinthians 13:9–10). Such is the power that God gives fathers—to build up their families, not pull them down.

Positive feedback: Instead of criticism, a father like the Father gives constructive correction. He develops his wife and children by building on their strengths and focusing on what they can do well instead of condemning them for their weaknesses. In fact, the father bears the weaknesses of his family. (See Romans 15:1.) He covers—not exposes—their vulnerability, and he protects them from attack with his own prayers and instructions.

Thought for the Day

A father who is like the heavenly Father encourages discovery and learning as parts of the developmental process.

Reading: Isaiah 50–52; 1 Thessalonians 5

October 18

Opportunity to Try

Parents must understand that some of the most significant learning experiences in life result from failure. Children can learn from their failures if a father uses them for teaching instead of judgment and punishment. This is how a father develops an atmosphere of acceptance for his family. He will not reject them just because they tried and failed. He accepts his family "for better or worse," just as Christ has accepted him. *"Accept one another, then, just as Christ accepted you, in order to bring praise to God"* (Romans 15:7). Development creates an environment that is conducive to others encountering learning experiences under the guidance of a father's godly wisdom.

A father does not make comparisons. He understands that the only standard for life is Jesus Christ. He never compares his wife or children to others, thinking that, by making a comparison, he will force improvement. For instance, a father never says to his children, "Why can't you be more like So-and-so? They are such good kids and never cause their parents any trouble. They make such good grades in school; why can't you?" He never says to his wife, "Why can't you dress and look like So-and-so? She is such a good cook and helpmate. Why can't you be more like her?"

Such comments by a father come from the father of lies. Satan desires that we compare ourselves and our families to others so that he can divide us and conjure up strife. Paul warned against false comparison. (See 2 Corinthians 10:12.) Fathers are not to show favoritism, just as the heavenly Father does not show favoritism. (See Acts 10:34.) Instead, they should develop an atmosphere in the family of mutual love, respect, honor, and caring for one another.

Thought for the Day

Parents must understand that some of the most significant learning experiences in life result from failure.

Reading: Isaiah 53–55; 2 Thessalonians 1

October 19

Principles of the Father as Developer

Today, review these principles of the father as developer of his family and reflect on how you can apply them in your everyday life—directly for yourself, if you are a man, and in your relationships with men, if you are a woman.

1. As developers, fathers plan, prepare, plant, protect, and produce that which God has placed in their care.
2. The godly father who develops his family has a plan for their systematic growth—physically, intellectually, emotionally, and spiritually.
3. A godly father is an example of holiness for his family and develops them to be the light of the world, the salt of the earth, and witnesses for Christ.
4. The objective of development is permanent growth. A godly father provides encouragement, positive feedback, and an opportunity to try and fail, and he does not make comparisons.
5. Development creates an environment that is conducive to others encountering learning experiences under the guidance of a father's godly wisdom.
6. A husband and father stretches his wife and children to achieve their utmost for God's highest. He cultivates his relationship with his family members so they can grow beyond themselves and be the believers God purposed them to be.
7. Fathers develop fathers. A man grows in fatherhood by leaning on God the Father. A man learns how to father from a father.

Heavenly Father,
We have been created to be developers, and You are a God who allows us to grow and develop in an environment of love, encouragement, and correction. Help earthly fathers to learn to create this same environment in their families and in the communities in which they live. In Jesus' name, amen.

Reading: Isaiah 56–58; 2 Thessalonians 2

October 20

A Father Cares

The father is not only one who develops his family members, but also one who cares deeply for them. In many ways, the functions of caring and developing go hand in hand. The father's role of caring is rooted, once again, in Genesis 2:15: *"The* LORD *God took the man, and put him in the garden of Eden to dress* [*"cultivate"* NASB] *it and to keep it"* (KJV). The word *"dress"* means to cultivate, and the word *"keep"* means to care for. To care is to pay close attention to needs and also to meet those needs. In fact, caring goes far beyond our normal thoughts of serving, encouraging, and ministering to those around us.

Again, the word *care* means to anticipate a need and meet it. In other words, to care means that you calculate the next need of a person before he or she is aware of it. You make provisions before he or she even senses the need. I believe that is the kind of caring that Psalm 8:4 describes: *"What is man that you are mindful of him, the son of man that you care for him?"* To be mindful of someone means to have one's mind filled with thoughts about that person. God the Father has filled His thoughts with us. He anticipates and thinks about what we will need before we even need it.

> *So do not worry, saying, "What shall we eat?" or "What shall we drink?" or "What shall we wear?" For the pagans run after all these things, and your heavenly Father knows that you need them. But seek first his kingdom and his righteousness, and all these things will be given to you as well.* (Matthew 6:31–33)

Thought for the Day

To care means to calculate the next need of a person and make provisions for it before he or she even senses the need.

Reading: Isaiah 59–61; 2 Thessalonians 3

October 21

Setting the Right Priorities

On what are you spending most of your time? A father who is like God the Father cares by spending his time and energy anticipating what his wife and children need next. This is a beautiful picture of a father. No matter what he is doing, he is thinking about what his daughter will need the next day, what his son will need the next week, or what his wife will need the next year. He's thinking daily about caring for his family.

Our work-driven cultures try to force men to think continually about what the company needs, so that they have no time to think about anyone else's needs. Men no longer work to live, but live to work. Even at home, a man's mind is often drifting off to work and either solving problems or thinking of new projects. Or, the father comes home so tired from working that he dozes off in front of the television. Meanwhile, he neglects his family because he is too tired or busy to think about their needs.

Fathers must set the right priorities. A father who cares like the heavenly Father thinks of his wife and children before his job. A father should see his job as a gift from God that enables him to care adequately for his wife and children. The job is a means to an end, *never the end itself.*

Men who are wrapped up in their careers and running after the corporate world have their motivation and priorities out of place. They have taken their work—a gift from God that He intended to help them support their families—and made it an idol. They end up caring more about the gift than the family for which it was given or the God who gave it.

Thought for the Day

A father who cares like the heavenly Father thinks of his wife and children before his job.

Reading: Isaiah 62–64; 1 Timothy 1

October 22

The Church's True Husband

Many people look to the pastor as a model father. Yet, today, pastors have a growing divorce rate. Why? Many could be properly classified as "workaholics." Often, pastors' wives feel helpless trying to turn their husbands' hearts back toward home. Many pastors seem to care for everyone else before their families. To defend their workaholism, pastors may say to their wives, "This is my calling. I'm doing this for the Lord." Unable to compete with God, their family members desperately try to get their needs met in other ways. The church then becomes a "mistress" to the pastor, who leaves his wife and family to suffer without him.

Laypeople also need to take this caution to heart, for they often are a major cause of these pastors' problems. They expect the pastor to be Christ and not simply the pastor. The man of God can never take the place of Christ caring for His bride. As a pastor, I am not married to my church; I'm married to my wife. The "woman" that I oversee—the assembly of believers—is not my wife; she's Christ's wife. Ultimately, who meets the church's emotional needs? Not I. Who meets her physical needs? Not I. Who meets her spiritual needs? Not I. Christ meets all the needs of His wife, the church. Only Christ is omnipresent, omniscient, and omnipotent—not the pastor.

The answer to this problem is found in Ephesians 5, where Paul laid down the principles concerning Christ and His bride, and the husband and his wife. *"Husbands, love your wives, just as Christ loved the church and gave himself up for her"* (v. 25). Pastors, as well as laymen, are to love their wives as Christ loves the church.

Thought for the Day

Pastors, as well as laymen, are to love their wives
as Christ loves the church.

Reading: Isaiah 65–66; 1 Timothy 2

October 23

Be the Person God Created

On television, I once saw a picture of a little child with a caption that read, "Missing." The Lord spoke to me and said, "I have many children who are missing." Some of you may be missing. You are present in the world but missing in regard to fulfilling the specific purposes for which you were created. God is saying to you, "I want you to stop trying to be like someone else and be who you are."

Remember that Paul said, "*Follow my example, as I follow the example of Christ*" (1 Corinthians 11:1). In other words, he was saying, "When I look like Christ, imitate me." The only thing we see in other people that we are to imitate is the life of Christ.

God has special plans for you, if you will be who He created you to be. He has given you your personality and gifts for a specific reason. "*For we are God's workmanship, created in Christ Jesus to do good works, which God prepared in advance for us to do*" (Ephesians 2:10).

God made you unique because of the purpose He had in mind for you. The same thing is true for everyone else. We run into trouble when we try to change people into what we are. This often happens when people get married. After the honeymoon, people start to try to make their spouses think and behave as they do. People spend years trying to change their mates. But God made males and females different because of what they were designed to do. That means your wife is the way she is because of why she is. Your husband is the way he is because of why he is. No one can alter God's purposes.

Thought for the Day

The only thing we see in other people that we are to imitate is the life of Christ.

Reading: Jeremiah 1–2; 1 Timothy 3

October 24

Out of God's Presence

If a man is not living in the presence of God, he might be moving, but he is not really functioning. You can't fully trust the perspective of a man who doesn't know God. You cannot even totally trust the perspective of one who is just beginning to get to know God, because he's still getting used to the Presence. Outside the presence of God, people can be like dangerous, uncontrolled beasts. The first chapter of Romans explains that when people reject or are ignorant of the purposes of God, they end up continually abusing themselves. They abuse their bodies, their minds, their relationships, and their talents.

It is only by being continually in God's presence that our minds and hearts can be renewed. We need to learn to walk *"in step with the Spirit"* (Galatians 5:25) rather than in step with our own ideas about life. As the prophet Jeremiah said, *"The heart is deceitful above all things and beyond cure. Who can understand it?"* (Jeremiah 17:9).

The problem with many of us men is that we think we don't need God, when, in fact, He's the first thing we need. I'm amazed when I observe men trying to make it without God. They may appear to be making it, but they aren't. They're not fulfilling their true purpose. Often, the "making it" is just an external face they put on to keep people from seeing the way things really are. If you knew what was truly going on in their lives, you'd know they weren't making it.

We should never doubt our need for God. Do you recall the first thing God gave the male? He didn't give him a woman, a job, or even a command; He gave him His presence.

Thought for the Day

It is only by being continually in God's presence that our hearts and minds can be renewed.

Reading: Jeremiah 3–5; 1 Timothy 4

October 25

Images of Leadership

When you see the word *leadership*, whose face pops into your mind? Who is your idea of a strong leader?

Most of us have developed our images of leaders from the wrong sources. We have looked to athletes, musicians, movie stars, and politicians as our role models. Yet the majority of these famous men and women don't know what a true leader is. If you don't believe me, ask them where their children are; ask them where their wives and husbands are; ask them how their home lives are. Many of the world's wealthiest, most famous, most prestigious people can't keep their homes together.

We have looked to status and personal accomplishment as the measure of leadership rather than to God's standards. God is concerned with people who have a vision from Him and who can support, sustain, and nurture their families and others in pursuit of God and His purposes.

Some men want to run away from the responsibility of leadership. They look at it as too much of a burden. They let their wives run everything. Others want to pursue their own selfish interests without worrying about the needs of others. Certain men don't think they deserve to be leaders. They think you have to be rich, successful, or highly educated in order to lead.

Let me make something very clear: if you are a male, you were born to lead. God made the male first because He wanted him to be responsible. A male doesn't decide to lead or not to lead. He has his position by virtue of his purpose; it is inherent. In God's plan, that is not a debatable issue.

Thought for the Day

We have looked to status and personal accomplishment as the measure of leadership rather than to God's standards.

Reading: Jeremiah 6–8; 1 Timothy 5

October 26

Advancing God's Family Business

When Jesus knew that His earthly ministry was coming to an end, He talked to His disciples about their role in advancing the "family business" on earth: *"I no longer call you servants, because a servant does not know his master's business. Instead, I have called you friends, for everything that I learned from my Father I have made known to you"* (John 15:15).

What was Jesus' reason for calling His disciples His friends? He said, in effect, "The servant doesn't know what the boss is doing. I call you friends because I have told you everything the Father has revealed to Me."

Think about how large and prosperous God's business is. It is so big that God says He can supply all your needs. (See Philippians 4:19.) In this context, I don't think that He is referring to your smaller needs, such as a house, a car, clothes, or food. Remember, Jesus told us that God knows these needs even before we ask. (See Matthew 6:31–32.) Therefore, God must be talking about further investment for the purpose of expanding the company business. He is saying, in essence, "The company has so much collateral that My children never have to worry about materials for further investment."

I believe that if we will get busy spreading the influence of God's company and building His interests, our access to His resources will be opened up. (See Matthew 6:33.) God created mankind to be His offspring and to work in His business, and He has all the resources we need to fulfill this purpose.

Thought for the Day

If we will get busy spreading the influence of God's company and building His interests, our access to His resources will be opened up.

Reading: Jeremiah 9–11; 1 Timothy 6

Teach Your Children and Grandchildren

In Deuteronomy, Moses gave instructions from God to the heads of the households about teaching their families God's ways:

> *Be careful, and watch yourselves closely so that you do not forget the things your eyes have seen or let them slip from your heart as long as you live. Teach them to your children and to their children after them.* (Deuteronomy 4:9)

God is very concerned that parents teach their children about Him. He isn't saying here to send your children to church, Sunday school, or vacation Bible club. He's saying to teach them yourself. These other activities are good, but if what they teach is not reinforced in the home, children can get the impression their parents don't think the Bible is important. Parents don't realize the negative impact this attitude can have on their families.

"*Teach them to your children and to their children after them.*" I want to say a word here to grandparents. When your daughter or son sends that little boy or girl to you, what does the child go back home with? Some kids learn things from their grandparents that are disgraceful. Parents find their little children coming back home cursing or telling foul stories, and they wonder where they are hearing them. They're getting them from Grandpa and Grandma! Your children's children should get the Word from you. When your children send their kids to you, those kids should go back home knowing more about God.

Timothy received a strong spiritual heritage from both his mother and his grandmother. Paul wrote, "*I have been reminded of your sincere faith, which first lived in your grandmother Lois and in your mother Eunice and, I am persuaded, now lives in you also*" (2 Timothy 1:5).

Thought for the Day

God is very concerned that parents teach their children about Him.

Reading: Jeremiah 12–14; 2 Timothy 1

October 28

What Do You Talk About?

These commandments that I give you today are to be upon your hearts. Impress them on your children. Talk about them when you sit at home and when you walk along the road, when you lie down and when you get up. Tie them as symbols on your hands and bind them on your foreheads. Write them on the doorframes of your houses and on your gates.

—Deuteronomy 6:6–9

Reflecting on the above Scripture passage, let's look at two specific ways in which God told Moses parents are to talk to their children about His commandments.

"*Talk about them when you sit at home.*" What do your children hear in your house? What do they hear when you sit down to eat? Some scandal reported in the newspaper? The latest movie? What do you discuss? Do you talk about the goodness of the Lord? When you sit around your house during your leisure time, what do you do? Do you spend time teaching your children the Word? Do you have family devotions?

"*Talk about them...when you walk along the road.*" What do you talk about when you drive your children to school or go on trips? Do you yell at other drivers or listen to less-than-edifying radio shows? What example do you set for your children when you're out in public? Do you talk about others behind their backs? Or do you live out God's Word in a natural, everyday way?

Some men never talk about God outside the church. It hurts to see men ashamed of the gospel of Jesus Christ. They think they're supposed to be cool, so cool they can't talk about Jesus. God says, "A real man whom I respect is a man who won't just have devotions at home, but will walk out into the world and talk about Me along the road of life."

Thought for the Day

Do you live out God's Word in a natural, everyday way?

Reading: Jeremiah 15–17; 2 Timothy 2

Fortify Your Children through the Word

Yesterday, we looked at the first two of God's instructions from Deuteronomy 6 about how we are to talk to children about His commandments. Today, let's examine the last two "talking points":

"Talk about them...when you lie down" (Deuteronomy 6:7). Before you say good night to your children or tuck them into bed, what words do you leave them with? The assurance of God's presence and peace during the night? An encouraging psalm? Or do you wave them off to bed while you finish working on something?

In fact, what do you think about before you drift off to sleep? Do you know that the last thing you think about at night is usually the first thing you think about when you wake up? Sometimes you dream about it. It amazes me that people deliberately think about the worst things. Some of you read the worst kind of books before you go to bed. Then you wonder why your spirit is disturbed.

"Talk about them...when you get up" (v. 7). When you wake up in the morning, you will more likely think about the Word of God if you have meditated on it before going to bed. And you will start ministering as you talk about it with your family.

How do you usually greet your children in the morning? With a quiet reminder of God's love and strength for the day? With what spiritual armor do you send them off to school? It's a difficult world for children to grow up in today, and they need God's Word to fortify them for daily living.

Thought for the Day

Children need the Word of God to fortify them for daily living.

Reading: Jeremiah 18–19; 2 Timothy 3

October 30

The Means of Gaining Wisdom

My son, if you accept my words and store up my commands within you, turning your ear to wisdom and applying your heart to understanding, and if you call out for insight and cry aloud for understanding, and if you look for it as for silver and search for it as for hidden treasure, then you will understand the fear of the Lord *and find the knowledge of God. For the* Lord *gives wisdom, and from his mouth come knowledge and understanding.*

—Proverbs 2:1–6

In the above passage, Solomon spoke of the wisdom to be gained from godly instruction. Ephesians 6:4 says, "*Fathers,...bring them* [your children] *up in the training and instruction of the Lord.*" We have seen that many fathers leave this responsibility solely to the mothers. This becomes especially difficult for women when the children reach a certain age at which they don't want to submit to authority. Men need to set a strong spiritual example for their children, especially at that particular time in their lives.

There is a popular idea today that every person should take total responsibility for himself or herself, no matter how young that person is. What the world is saying is that children should be allowed to bring themselves up. This idea is foolish. Children are children; grown-ups are grown-ups. Sometimes adults *act* like children. But children are definitely not adults, and they shouldn't be treated as if they were. Parents have a responsibility before God to raise their children and instruct them in the ways of the Lord. God does not leave the care and upbringing of your children to themselves or to society. He leaves it to you.

Thought for the Day

God does not leave the care and upbringing of your children to themselves or to society. You have a responsibility to raise your children in the Lord.

Reading: Jeremiah 20–21; 2 Timothy 4

October 31

God's Word Everywhere in Our Lives

In Deuteronomy 6, after the Lord said we are to talk about His commandments with our children, He continued, *"Tie them as symbols on your hands and bind them on your foreheads. Write them on the doorframes of your houses and on your gates"* (vv. 8–9).

The point God was making is that whatever your hands find to do, make sure it is in accordance with His Word. Whatever is in your thoughts, make sure it's the Word of God. *"The doorframes"*—I like that. The doorposts in Moses' day were two major posts that held up the frame of the house. Anyone who came through those doorposts came into your home. This means that all of your house should be held up by the Word of God, and that you are supposed to check who comes into your house to make sure they pass through the Word of God.

God is saying to fathers, and to young men who aspire to be good fathers, "Get the Word in you. Plaster your whole life with the Word." If anybody wants access to your life or your home, he or she is to come through the Word of God. If any woman wants to marry you, tell her straight, "If you don't know God and His Word, I don't care how cute you look or how much you can give me—forget it."

I would love for God to raise up men who wouldn't compromise, who wouldn't marry a woman who's not a woman of God. Sometimes we don't have any standards. We must have standards and values again. Our values come from what we believe. They create our morals and affect our behavior. If we believe the Word of God, that's our value system.

Thought for the Day

If anybody wants access to your life or your home, he or she is to come through the Word of God.

Reading: Jeremiah 22–23; Titus 1

November 1

God Sent a Woman

I brought you up from the land of Egypt, I redeemed you from the house of bondage; and I sent before you Moses, Aaron, and Miriam.
—Micah 6:4 (NKJV)

Women should take the above verse to heart and remember it for the rest of their lives. God was saying, "I sent you three leaders." We always talk about Moses, the representative and administrative leader. We also talk about Aaron, the high priest and spiritual leader. But God mentioned another leader that many people are uncomfortable reading about. He said, "I also sent Miriam to lead you."

God *sent* a woman to lead. This fact contradicts many of the attitudes that men have had for years about women in leadership. When God purposefully appointed Miriam to be a leader to His people, He endorsed the idea that it is valid for a woman to be in leadership. It is noteworthy that God did not send Miriam to lead because no men were available at the time. Rather, He sent her to lead *alongside* the men. He put her in a team of leaders. Since God acknowledged Miriam in the same list or category with Moses, we don't have to question whether God intended women to be leaders. "*I sent before you Moses, Aaron, and Miriam.*"

The Sinai leadership team included a director, a priest, and a woman. The director was Moses, the executive leader; the priest was Aaron, the spiritual leader. Yet right in the middle of the executive leader and the spiritual leader, a woman was needed in order to bring balance to both of them.

Thought for the Day

God sent a woman to lead.

Reading: Jeremiah 24–26; Titus 2

A Woman's Leadership Role

Miriam's influential role as a leader over Israel looks *back* to God's purposes for the woman that He established when He created humanity and *ahead* to Christ's redemptive purposes for the woman in salvation. God intended women to be leaders from the creation of the world, and He confirmed His continued commitment to this intention through the ministry of His Son Jesus Christ. This is the basis on which we will look at the woman's role in leadership.

Throughout our exploration of God's purposes for men and women and male-female relationships, we have seen the following:

- Women and men (as man) are spiritually equal before God and equally as important to Him.
- Women and men (as man) were given the dominion mandate.
- Males and females (man's "houses") have distinct purposes and designs.
- The complementary roles and abilities of males and females bring balance, strength, and help to one another as they fulfill God's purposes.

In light of these principles, the question many people have been asking, "Should women be in leadership?" becomes an entirely different question. Instead of asking *if* women should be in leadership, we should be asking *how* they are to exercise their leadership, given their purpose and design. Over the next week, we will explore how the woman's purpose and design shape her leadership role.

Thought for the Day

God intended women to be leaders from the creation of the world, and He confirmed His continued commitment to this intention through the ministry of His Son Jesus Christ.

Reading: Jeremiah 27–29; Titus 3

November 3

Designed to Lead

God created man in his own image, in the image of God he created him; male and female he created them. God blessed them and said to them, "Be fruitful and increase in number; fill the earth and subdue it. Rule ["*have dominion*" KJV] *over the fish of the sea and the birds of the air and over every living creature that moves on the ground."*

—Genesis 1:27–28

Consider once more that the creation account reveals that the dominion mandate was given to man, both male and female. It is God's purpose that the woman, as well as the man, be fruitful and multiply, replenish, subdue, and have dominion over the earth. To have dominion means to govern, rule, control, manage, lead, or administrate. *Dominion* is a powerful word. God loves leadership and had it in mind when He created the earth. When God told man to have dominion, He was telling man who he is. Man (male and female) is a leader who is to cultivate the earth.

There is no incidence of subjection, submission, or oppression of women in the first and second chapters of Genesis. In God's perfect will, there is no such arrangement. The woman and the man were both equal, blessed, subduing, ruling, and having dominion, and God said, "This is very good." Any other arrangement than this was the result of the fall. This means that anything that God said about the male-female relationship after Genesis 2 is a repair program.

Since God's purpose for man was leadership, He designed male and female with the built-in potential and ability to be a leader. The leadership spirit is in every person. However, the ways in which males and females *execute* dominion are different based on their distinct designs.

Thought for the Day

God designed both male and female with the built-in potential and ability to be a leader; the leadership spirit is in every person.

Reading: Jeremiah 30–31; Philemon

November 4

The Influence-Power of Women

Both the man and the woman were created to lead, but their leadership functions are determined by their specific dominion assignments. God designed the woman not only for relationship with Himself, but also to help fulfill His purposes in His great plan for humanity. Therefore, women are designed by God to execute an assignment that can be fulfilled only by women.

God designed the male to be a leader by position and the female to be a leader by influence. Thus, the man has *position-power* and the woman has *influence-power.* There is a difference between these two forms of leadership. A perfect example of this distinction was Queen Esther's position in relation to King Xerxes. The king had position-power. Yet because of Esther's godly heart and her great beauty, she had influence-power with the king and was able to convince him of Haman's evil plans against the Jewish people. (See Esther 4–5.)

When God designed the female, He obviously had influence in mind. A woman is a receiver. God designed her to receive from the male and to incubate what she receives so that it can grow and develop. A woman is built to influence. Her wombs—whether physical, emotional, mental, or spiritual—have a tremendous influence on what they receive by providing a nurturing and transforming environment. There is much truth in William Ross Wallace's famous quote: "The hand that rocks the cradle is the hand that rules the world."

Position-power and influence-power are not mutually exclusive; they are meant to be exercised together in dominion.

Thought for the Day

The man has *position-power*, and the woman has *influence-power.*

Reading: Jeremiah 32–33; Hebrews 1

November 5

Distinct Leadership Functions

Power and influence are equal but different. A woman and a man are equal in leadership. The difference is in their leadership functions.

There are two important aspects of position-power. First, position-power generally comes with a title, such as king, governor, or pastor. Second, position-power is usually executed through commands, whether verbal or written. It is the authority that goes with the position—and underlies the commands—that is the nature of the man's power.

Influence-power manifests itself in a very different way. First, a woman may have a title, but she doesn't need a title in order to lead. She leads by influence. This is why women usually run the households. Men call themselves "the head of the house," but the women run the homes. Second, a woman doesn't need to talk in order to run things. She leads just by her influence. My father used to run our household with his mouth. He would say, "Clean the kitchen"; "Take the garbage out"; "Take your feet off that chair." However, my mother would just *look* at me, and my feet would be down off that chair. The woman doesn't need to say a word; she just looks, and people respond. This is a powerful influence. Some men assume that because certain women are quiet or don't bark out orders, they are weak. They do not understand influence-power.

Influence-power may be more subtle and quiet than position-power, but it has a potent effect. Satan understood this influence. The fall of man resulted from the serpent's interference with influence leadership.

Thought for the Day

Influence-power may be more subtle and quiet than position-power, but it has a potent effect.

Reading: Jeremiah 34–36; Hebrews 2

November 6

Restored to Leadership

Husbands, in the same way be considerate as you live with your wives, and treat them with respect as...heirs with you of the gracious gift of life.

—1 Peter 3:7

Influence-power is a tremendous gift from God that was intended to be used by women for the good of themselves, their families, their communities, their nations, the world, and the kingdom of God. Yet women have to realize its potential for evil as well as for good. Even redeemed women have to be careful to discipline their influence-power.

We need to remember that, even though the woman's influence-power has the potential to harm, it was God who originally gave her this leadership gift when He created her. The *influence* is not the result of the fall; the *corruption* of the influence is. God desires that the woman be restored to her full leadership role and use this influence for His good purposes. God indicated that this was His plan even at the time of the fall. All of the declarations that God gave Eve and Adam in Genesis 3 are God's response to the fall. He said that in the end, He was going to restore what He had established in the beginning. How? Through the redemption of Jesus Christ and the coming of the Holy Spirit.

When the Holy Spirit comes back into a woman's life, God's plan for her reverts to what it was originally. Women are joint and equal heirs of salvation with men. This means that when a woman receives salvation in Jesus Christ, she becomes equal in rulership again.

Thought for the Day

God desires that the woman be restored to her full leadership role and use her influence-power for His good purposes.

Reading: Jeremiah 37–39; Hebrews 3

November 7

What about Paul?

There is neither Jew nor Greek, slave nor free, male nor female, for you are all one in Christ Jesus.
—Galatians 3:28

When Paul wrote the above statement to the Galatians, he was talking about the spirit-man residing in both males and females whom Christ has redeemed. Therefore, in the body of Christ, in the Spirit, you're dealing with *man,* where there is no difference in gender. In other letters, such as those to Corinth and Ephesus, Paul addressed problems in which people's cultural heritages were making it difficult for them to adjust to their new Christian faith. For example, he told the Corinthians, "*Women should remain silent in the churches. They are not allowed to speak, but must be in submission, as the Law says*" (1 Corinthians 14:34).

This passage has been terribly misunderstood and has been used as a general rule in order to keep women down, to subjugate and oppress them. Many people don't realize that, in the same letter, Paul gave instructions to women who pray or prophesy in the church. (See 1 Corinthians 11:5.) Obviously, they needed to speak in order to do that. Therefore, I believe that Paul's instructions to the Corinthians had to do with keeping order in the churches when the people's carnality or cultural backgrounds were creating confusion and discord. God is a God of order. Based on Paul's other writings, as well as additional passages and biblical principles from both the Old and New Testaments, these few instructions of Paul's should not be considered the sole or final word on the matter.

Thought for the Day

In the body of Christ, in the Spirit, you're dealing with *man,* where there is no difference in gender.

Reading: Jeremiah 40–42; Hebrews 4

November 8

Culture or Christ?

What is more important, culture or Christ? Did Jesus ever command a woman to be silent? Did Jesus ever stop a woman from preaching? As a matter of fact, the woman at the well began preaching after Jesus set her free, and then she became an evangelist.

Sometimes, we make Paul's statement in 1 Corinthians 14:34, "*Women should remain silent in the churches,*" more important than Jesus' own revelation of God's purposes. *Please do not misunderstand what I am saying. It is all God's Word.* Yet I truly believe that Paul was dealing with specific cultural issues; Christ was dealing with principles. Culture should not be confused with principles. Jesus elevated, promoted, and restored women to their original dignity. Moreover, Paul himself affirmed the female's equality with the male in Christ.

Even before Jesus died on the cross, He affirmed women in His earthly ministry in a way that was revolutionary to fallen man but was right in line with God's purposes for man in creation. This was a striking illustration of His respect for women and their value to Him, their Creator and Redeemer.

Therefore, it is not only the male, but also the female, who can be a leader. Their leadership styles do not cancel each other out; it is the *combination* of position-power and influence-power that enables man to exercise dominion over the world, and which will bring the kingdom of God on earth. The devil is in trouble when the two types of power come together in unity of purpose.

Thought for the Day

Jesus elevated, promoted, and restored women to their original dignity.

Reading: Jeremiah 43–45; Hebrews 5

November 9

A Trusted Leader

All authority in heaven and on earth has been given to me. Therefore go and make disciples of all nations.
—Matthew 28:18–19

When Jesus was about to ascend to heaven, He told His followers, in effect, "I have to return to My Father, but I want to influence the world for My kingdom. I am the King and I am the Word; therefore, I exercise position-power. To influence the world, I need a wife, a partner, who has influence-power."

Christ left the earth in the hands of a "woman," the church. Being a member of the body of Christ means not only receiving salvation, but also helping the Lord in His purpose of winning the world to Himself. This is why He gave the church the responsibility of going into the world as a witness for Him. Christ sees her as a perfect leader, and He shows this by the fact that He has entrusted the Word of God to her.

Now, the implication is that the female is a trusted leader, just as the male is. The church is not the servant of Jesus, just as the female is not the servant of the male; she is his partner. Jesus said to His disciples, "*I no longer call you servants....Instead, I have called you friends, for everything that I learned from my Father I have made known to you*" (John 15:15).

Jesus also told the church, in effect, "You will be seated *with* Me in heavenly places." (See Ephesians 2:6.) He did not say, "You will be seated *below* Me." Since Christ is the King, the church is His queen. We need to see God's intent for the female in this portrayal of Christ and the church. She is not meant to sit below the male but to be his partner in leadership, in dominion.

Thought for the Day

We need to see God's leadership intent for the female in the Scriptures' portrayal of Christ and the church.

Reading: Jeremiah 46–47; Hebrews 6

November 10

Principles of Female Leadership

Today, review these principles of female leadership and reflect on how you can apply them in your everyday life—for yourself, if you are a woman, and in your relationships with women, if you are a man.

1. God endorsed women in leadership when He purposefully sent a woman (Miriam) to be a leader to His people.
2. Instead of asking *if* women should be in leadership, we should be asking *how* they are to exercise it, given their purpose and design.
3. The spirit-man in every male and female is a leader.
4. The execution of dominion is different for males and females based on their purpose and design. The male exercises position-power and the female exercises influence-power.
5. Power and influence are equal but different. A woman and a man are equal in leadership. The distinction is in their leadership functions.
6. Jesus affirmed women in His earthly ministry in a way that was revolutionary to fallen man but was right in line with God's purposes for humanity in creation.
7. Through redemption, Christ restored the woman to full partnership with the man.
8. Paul's writings on women reflect two contexts: a woman's equality with a man based on their redemption in Christ and a cultural context.
9. The female is a trusted leader, just as the male is.

Heavenly Father,
You have created us male and female according to Your perfect plan. You have also restored us in Christ to Your original plan for creation. Open the eyes of Your sons and daughters to Your true purposes for their dominion rule. Show them how Your plan for male and female leadership should work in a practical way. May men see their need for women to rule beside them as You have determined since creation. In Jesus' name we pray, amen.

Reading: Jeremiah 48–49; Hebrews 7

November 11

The Choice of Submission

Wives, submit to your husbands as to the Lord. For the husband is the head of the wife as Christ is the head of the church.
—Ephesians 5:22–23

Let us return to the topic of submission in light of what we have been learning about a woman's leadership role. The definition of *submit* is to "willfully give your will to another." Submission has nothing to do with force or pressure. *It is an act of the will.* To submit is the *choice* of the person who is submitting, not the command of one who wants to be submitted to. Put another way, you cannot submit unless you want to, and no one can make you submit if you don't want to.

Many men's distorted understanding of strength can be seen in the way they view the concept of submission. Any man who has to force a woman to submit does not deserve to be submitted to. He is no longer worthy of submission; he has become a slave driver.

Do you know what makes a slave a slave? Force and fear. These elements are dominating too many homes. The Bible says, "*Perfect love drives out fear*" (1 John 4:18). This means that if a man has to make a woman afraid of him in order to force her to do something he wants her to do, then he doesn't know what love is.

I've never heard of Jesus slapping one of His children. I've never heard of Jesus screaming or swearing at His people. No matter what we do to Jesus, He is ready to forgive us. This is how husbands need to treat their wives.

Thought for the Day

Submission has nothing to do with force.
It is an act of the will.

Reading: Jeremiah 50; Hebrews 8

November 12

Overwhelming Love

I have loved you with an everlasting love; I have drawn you with loving-kindness.
—Jeremiah 31:3

I believe that about half of us men do not deserve our wives' submission! Jesus said to His church—His bride—"*Never will I leave you; never will I forsake you*" (Hebrews 13:5). Yet some men stay out all night, then come home and expect their wives to cook for them. They forsake their wives and their children spiritually, emotionally, and even financially—and they still want submission. That's a sin, men. You don't deserve submission. Submission is not dependent on what you say. It is dependent on how you live.

Do you believe in the Lord Jesus Christ as your personal Savior? All right, then. Before you were saved, did Jesus ever come to you and hold you up against the wall by your collar and say, "If you don't believe in Me, I'll send you straight to Hades?" He didn't do that. As a matter of fact, He probably waited a long time for you. When you were involved in all your foolish living, He didn't force you to accept Him. He didn't break down your door. He is very polite. He quietly convicts people. He doesn't pressure us. He just shows us His love. As we see in Jeremiah 31:3, God loves His people and draws them to Himself with loving-kindness.

So, one day, you realized, *This love is overwhelming,* and you accepted His love. You desired to follow Jesus. One of the things I love about Jesus is that He calls us to follow Him. He doesn't drag us; He leads and we follow. This is the same overwhelming love that men should show their wives.

Thought for the Day

In their relationships with their wives, men should imitate God, who loves His people and draws them to Himself with loving-kindness.

Reading: Jeremiah 51–52; Hebrews 9

November 13

"Follow Me"

"Come, follow me," Jesus said.
—Matthew 4:19

"Follow me," [Jesus] *told him, and Matthew got up and followed him.*
—Matthew 9:9

Have you ever been on a guided tour of a cavern? The guide takes you down through dark tunnels, and you follow him. You submit to his authority because He knows the way through the tunnels. Of course, you can turn around anytime and go back, but you would probably walk into some walls and stub your toes and scrape your knees because you are not familiar with the cavern. However, the point is that you can turn around if you want to.

That is what Jesus is trying to tell us. He doesn't force us to submit to Him. All He ever says to His disciples is, "Follow Me." This is exactly what husbands are supposed to be able to say to their wives: "Honey, follow me." Following is what submission is really about.

Do you know why we keep following Jesus? It is because He knows where He's going, He knows how to get there, He's the only way there, and we like where He's going. Even more than that, His love draws us to Him. Why do we love Him? It is not because He threatens us with a big hammer, saying, "If you sin, I'll kill you." Instead, He says, "If you sin, I am faithful and just to forgive you." (See 1 John 1:9.) Isn't it wonderful to follow Him? Every time you slip, He picks you up and brushes you off. Husbands, with the help of the Holy Spirit, you can love your wives as Christ loves the church.

Thought for the Day

We submit to Jesus because of His love, and we love Him in return.

Reading: Lamentations 1–2; Hebrews 10:1–18

November 14

EARN HER RESPECT

We love because he first loved us.
—1 John 4:19

Do you show contempt for the riches of his kindness, tolerance and patience, not realizing that God's kindness leads you toward repentance?
—Romans 2:4

Let me be direct: Men, don't quote Scripture to a woman unless you are behaving like Jesus does. When you start acting like Jesus, you won't have to demand that your wife submit. When you start loving her like Jesus loves her, when you start forgiving her like Jesus forgives her, when you start blessing her like Jesus blesses her, when you start caring for her and listening to her like Jesus does, she will do anything for you—because she wants a man like Jesus in the house.

God is saying to men, "Don't you dare demand respect. Don't you dare order submission. Earn it." Remember that Jesus never once commanded anybody to follow Him. Never. He always asked, because He knew who He was and where He was going. He didn't need to demand allegiance to give Himself a sense of importance.

Jesus said, "If you love Me, you'll keep My commandments." (See John 14:15.) Our keeping of His commandments is based on our loving Him. That's the pattern we're to follow in the marriage relationship—and, really, in all relationships between males and females. If a male wants to be a true leader, he must learn who he is in God and become someone who earns respect—someone who loves, guides, and inspires rather than who forces others to do what he wants.

Thought for the Day

Become the kind of person who earns respect.

Reading: Lamentations 3–5; Hebrews 10:19–39

November 15

False Submission

Dealing with submission in a situation where a woman has an unbelieving husband can be difficult, but the Bible gives us guidelines for what to do under these circumstances. First Corinthians 7 says that if a woman holds to the standards of the Word of God, and her unbelieving husband agrees to stay with her, *"let her not leave him"* (v. 13 KJV). However, if he cannot live with her convictions, the Scripture says, *"Let him depart"* (v. 15 KJV). In other words, if he can't live with her commitment to the Lord, the Bible tells her, "Let him go." You don't compromise your faith, even for your spouse.

Some women have a false view of submission. They allow their husbands to beat them half to death because they think that is being submissive. I have counseled many women who think this way. They come to my office badly battered, and ask, "What am I supposed to do?" I say, "Remove yourself from the premises." "But the Bible says to submit." "Yes, but not to a beating. You are to submit to the Lord. Until you see the Lord in the house, leave. You are not to be foolish enough just to sit there and let your life be put in jeopardy."

There is nothing in the Bible that says a woman should agree to do something that's against God's Word or allow herself to suffer abuse. First Peter 2:19–20 says that if you suffer for the sake of the gospel, that is true suffering. But if you suffer for the sake of your own sin and folly, that is not to your credit. It's foolish for you to let somebody beat you black and blue and then turn around and say, "It's all for Jesus." That is not submission.

Thought for the Day

There is nothing in the Bible that says a woman should allow herself to suffer abuse.

Reading: Ezekiel 1–2; Hebrews 11:1–19

Submit to One Another

A man...is the image and glory of God; but the woman is the glory of man. For man did not come from woman, but woman from man.
—1 Corinthians 11:7–8

Is the above statement about woman coming from man true? Sure. God caused the man to go into a deep sleep and drew the woman out of him.

The passage continues: "*Neither was man created for woman, but woman for man*" (v. 9). Is this statement true? Yes. God said, "*I will make a helper suitable for him*" (Genesis 2:18). Paul wrote, "*For this reason* [purpose], *and because of the angels, the woman ought to have a sign of authority on her head*" (1 Corinthians 11:10). The Scripture says, "*For this reason....*" In other words, this is God's order in creation, and so men and women should live in that order.

Yet here's what most people forget: men and women are created to be *inter*dependent. "*In the Lord, however, woman is not independent of man, nor is man independent of woman*" (v. 11). God is saying, in effect, "Men and women need one another. They need each other to be complete."

"*For as woman came from man, so also man is born of woman*" (v. 12). I like that statement. Men need women to give birth to them, but women need men to enable them to conceive. This is definitely not an inferiority-superiority situation. It has to do with complementary purposes. Ephesians 5, which talks about wives submitting to their husbands, also says, "*Submit to one another out of reverence for Christ*" (v. 21). There has to be a mutual submitting to one another if God's purposes are to be carried out on the earth.

Thought for the Day

Men and women are created to be interdependent.

Reading: Ezekiel 3–4; Hebrews 11:20–40

November 17

An Equal Partner

So the man gave names to all the livestock, the birds of the air and all the beasts of the field. But for Adam no suitable helper was found.
—Genesis 2:20

Genesis tells us that God presented every animal to the man (see Genesis 2:19), but none was suitable for him. There was no one to whom he could relate, no one who could help him in his proprietorship of the earth. So, God said, in essence, "It's not good for man to be alone in one body." It is impossible for love to love alone. Thus, God created the woman. Remember, the primary purpose of the female was to receive love from the male, just as God's major purpose for creating the spirit-man was to have a relationship of love with mankind.

"*It is not good for the man to be alone. I will make a helper suitable for him*" (v. 18). I don't think that men can read or hear this Scripture often enough. You might not think that a man who has a close relationship with God; who understands his role as foundation; who has been given the vision; and who can lead, teach, cultivate, provide, and protect needs anyone else. Yet even a man who knows and lives in his purpose is not complete, according to God. The male needs a companion, someone to be his helper—not as a subordinate or a sidekick, but as an equal partner with a complementary purpose. This is as true for single men as it is for married men. Men need women as fellow workers and colleagues in this world if they are to fulfill their purpose in life.

Thought for the Day

Even a man who knows and lives in his purpose
is not complete in himself.

Reading: Ezekiel 5–7; Hebrews 12

November 18

Special and Specific Responsibilities

If men and women would realize the following truths, we would go a long way toward restoring both harmonious relationships between males and females and God's plan for humanity:

- Dominion is not the same thing as domination.
- Dominion is to be exercised over the world, not over other people.
- Submission is something earned rather than demanded.
- Men and women are equal but different.
- Men and women need one another.

I am convinced that there can be no true dominion over the earth unless God's original design is intact. It is crucial for us to understand the principle that the way we are designed is due to our purpose for existence. Males and females each have been called to special and specific responsibilities in God's kingdom purposes.

Again, some people have problems with this concept because they believe that being different implies being inferior or superior to others. Different does not imply inferiority or superiority; it simply means different. A woman is not less than a man because she is a woman, and a man is not more than a woman because he is a man. Their differences are necessary because of their purposes. The only way to fix our confused society is to get back to God's plan. Purpose, not varying societal expecations, determines position.

Thought for the Day

There can be no true dominion over the earth unless God's original design for men and women is intact.

Reading: Ezekiel 8–10; Hebrews 13

November 19

A Global Identity Problem

Confusion over personal identity is a global problem. I have traveled to many nations, and I have concluded that most of the world is suffering from what I call the "consequences of ignorance of purpose." In every nation, in every community, no matter what language the citizens speak or what color their skin is, people are experiencing a common dilemma. They are suffering the debilitating effects of a misconception of purpose. They don't understand who they really are, and, therefore, they aren't living up to their full potential in life. In fact, they are destroying their own and others' potential.

Why are many social ills caused by men? The problem is not a biological one of maleness but a spiritual one of identity. There is no way that we can have a safe and productive world as long as humanity, as a whole, doesn't know its reason for existence—and as long as men, in particular, don't have a clear idea of their identity. The world's crisis of identity, therefore, is not just a distressing problem. It is also a powerful opportunity for helping others to find their true purpose.

God is calling men not only to understand and live in the fullness of their identity in Christ, but also to help others to come into the same understanding. This is what I call "the spirit of a father." In the next several days, we will explore the nature and responsibility of this father spirit.

Thought for the Day

The world's crisis of identity is a powerful opportunity for helping others find their true purpose in God.

Reading: Ezekiel 11–13; James 1

November 20

The Spirit of a Father

The spirit of a father is the awareness that everyone around a father is his responsibility. As we have studied in Genesis, the woman and the family came out of the man. So, every woman and child that a father meets are his responsibility if they are fatherless.

Godly fathers must become fathers of their communities and nations. There are many women whose husbands are not functioning in their lives as source and sustainer. There are many children who have only a biological father, not a true one. Christian fathers need to take responsibility by praying for these families and supporting them in other ways so that they may be restored to their heavenly Father's plan for their lives.

There are also women and children who have lost husbands and fathers to divorce or death. James wrote, "*Religion that God our Father accepts as pure and faultless is this: to look after orphans and widows in their distress and to keep oneself from being polluted by the world*" (James 1:27). The fatherless should be fathered by Christian men who can step in the gap, sustaining and cultivating them.

Matthew 25 includes a parable in which Jesus reveals that those who truly follow Him will father those who are imprisoned, hungry, naked, thirsty, sick, and strangers. Men, inasmuch as we father the least of these, we minister to the Lord Himself. (See verses 40, 45.)

David declared, "*A father to the fatherless, a defender of widows, is God in his holy dwelling. God sets the lonely in families*" (Psalm 68:5–6). What is the family into which God places the fatherless? It is *His* family, the church. We are to go wherever the fatherless are found and become fathers and families to them.

Thought for the Day

Godly fathers must become fathers of their communities and nations.

Reading: Ezekiel 14–15; James 2

November 21

Fathering the Fatherless

How do we heal the many men, women, and children who never had fathers like the heavenly Father? Godly fathers must go out and father them. Recall once more the prophecy for our day in Malachi 4:6: *"He will turn the hearts of the fathers to their children, and the hearts of the children to their fathers; or else I* [God] *will come and strike the land with a curse."* When godly fathers fail to father the fatherless in a society, a curse comes upon that land. Scripture never mentions returning the hearts of the children back to the mothers because our greatest problem is a father problem.

Men, we must incorporate the scriptural functions of fatherhood into our lives so that we will finally understand and fulfill our true priority, position, and role as males. God the Father is our Source. Masses of men must return to God the Father so that the children's hearts may be turned to their fathers and to God. We need men of the Spirit to be responsible as progenitors and providers for the future generations, and men who are fathers to be willing to sustain their offspring.

As a father—like *the* Father—remember that each child you meet is your responsibility. You are to support and pray for that child's father or be a godly father to the child if he or she is fatherless. Every woman you meet is your responsibility and should be treated with dignity and respect. Every elderly person you meet is your responsibility. God has equipped you through His Spirit, His Word, and your fellow believers to handle these responsibilities for Him.

Thought for the Day

We need men of the Spirit to be responsible as progenitors and providers for the future generations, and men who are fathers to be willing to sustain their offspring.

Reading: Ezekiel 16–17; James 3

November 22

Turning the Children's Hearts

Salvation is the result of a Man—Jesus, the Second Adam—providing the orphaned children of humanity with the way to return to their Father and their original identity in Him. Remember, Adam voluntarily left his Father. The mission of Jesus was to return fatherless humanity back to God and to restore earthly family relationships to the way He intended.

Malachi prophesied that the fathers' hearts would begin to turn toward their children when a prophet came to prepare the way for the Messiah. That prophet was John the Baptist. When the angel Gabriel appeared to John's father, Zechariah, telling him about John's forthcoming birth, he quoted from the Malachi passage we read yesterday:

> *Many of the people of Israel will he bring back to the Lord their God. And he will go on before the Lord, in the spirit and power of Elijah, to* ***turn the hearts of the fathers to their children*** *and the disobedient to the wisdom of the righteous—to make ready a people prepared for the Lord.* (Luke 1:16–17)

The people needed to return to their Creator and Father. John the Baptist was preparing them for what they desperately needed—One who could lead them back to the heavenly Father. The problem of fatherlessness that started with Adam still affects us to this day. Jesus came to eliminate the pain and devastation of fatherlessness. Brothers, our nations could be healed if every man became a responsible father through Christ.

Thought for the Day

Jesus provided the orphaned children of humanity with the way to return to their Father and their original identity in Him.

Reading: Ezekiel 18–19; James 4

November 23

Jesus and His Father

My Father, who has given them [My disciples] *to me, is greater than all; no one can snatch them out of my Father's hand. I and the Father are one.*
—John 10:29–30

Jesus spoke of His Father more than anyone else. He expressed and emphatically confessed His need for, dependency on, and submission to His Father at every opportunity. He never hesitated to give credit to His Father for any activity or success, thereby confirming the sustaining work of God in His life. He saw His Father as the Source, Resource, and Purpose for His entire life.

Whenever Jesus was questioned about His identity, His work, His purpose, His heritage, His power, His authority, His family, His message, His philosophy, His theology, His legitimacy, or His destiny, He referred to "My Father."

How many men do you know today who speak of their fathers in such a way? Of course, Jesus was referring to God Himself, the perfect Father. Yet, how many men give their fathers credit for any of their activities and successes? On the contrary, most men today consider it "less manly" to give credit to another because it is perceived as a weakness. What a stark contrast to the attitude of the ultimate Man, Jesus Christ! His perception of, and relationship with, His Father should serve as the standard by which we measure the effectiveness and success of true fatherhood.

> *I do nothing on my own but speak just what the Father has taught me. The one who sent me is with me; he has not left me alone, for I always do what pleases him.* (John 8:28–29)

Thought for the Day

Jesus emphatically confessed His need for, dependency on, and submission to His Father at every opportunity.

Reading: Ezekiel 20–21; James 5

November 24

Counterfeit Fathers

Jesus declared, *"If God were your Father, you would love me, for I came from God and now am here. I have not come on my own; but he sent me"* (John 8:42). Jesus was addressing those who did not believe in Him. The root of their unbelief was that they did not know the heavenly Father. If you don't know the Father, you cannot know His Son. Unbelief is caused by fatherlessness.

Similarly, wayward children, in effect, have no father. They have no respect for their elders and cannot submit to authority. Children need to learn about God the Father through fathers who teach them about Him and His ways.

I thank God for my earthly father. He made certain that his children respected their elders. He taught me about authority. My father generated in me the knowledge of what submission, authority, and respect are all about. He was the source of my understanding about fathers because he knew God the Father.

Unfortunately, many children today do not have a father in the home. They don't have the benefit of a father to create within them the respect they need for other authority figures. Instead, they curse people on the streets, talk back to their teachers, and utterly disrespect their elders. Without godly fathers creating in us a knowledge, respect, and fear of God, we are destined to be spiritual orphans. By not knowing our real Father—and not having our identity in Him—we inevitably substitute a fraud and counterfeit.

Thought for the Day

If you don't know the Father, you cannot know His Son.

Reading: Ezekiel 22–23; 1 Peter 1

November 25

A New Identity

Jesus knew that the Jews of His day had become fatherless in regard to their relationship with God. They thought that Abraham was their father, failing to recognize that the God and Father of Abraham was their Source. They had lost a sense of their true identity. The Jews, as a race of people, did not start with father Abraham. It was God, Abraham's Father, who called them into being. Like them, we need to change fathers. We have lost our original Father God, and we follow a stepfather, the devil, with contaminated blood and genes filled with evil and ignorance.

Jesus spoke to the religious leaders who questioned His identity and integrity,

> *You belong to your father, the devil, and you want to carry out your father's desire. He was a murderer from the beginning, not holding to the truth, for there is no truth in him. When he lies, he speaks his native language, for he is a liar and the father of lies.* (John 8:44)

Jesus wanted God's rebellious children to turn their hearts back to the Father and away from Satan. Everything He did was to get us back to the Father. After Jesus returned to heaven, He sent the Holy Spirit to live within those who had been restored to their relationship with the Father. Through faith in Jesus, God has provided a way for us to be set free from our stepfather and born anew into His family. Paul wrote that we are "new creations" in Christ Jesus. (See 2 Corinthians 5:17.) That new creation includes a new Father and a new identity.

Thought for the Day

Through Jesus' redemption, we have a new Father and a new identity.

Reading: Ezekiel 24–26; 1 Peter 2

November 26

Knowing God the Father

And he will he called Wonderful Counselor, Mighty God, Everlasting Father, Prince of Peace.
—Isaiah 9:6

Since Jesus is the Everlasting Father, as well as the Son, His fatherhood requires us to be submitted and obedient to His every word, because all that He says and commands comes straight from the Father. In this way, we are transformed by the Holy Spirit into the likeness of Jesus Christ. (See 2 Corinthians 3:18.) In His likeness is the perfect image of what it means to be both a child of the heavenly Father and a father to our own offspring, so that their hearts will be turned to the Father.

Remember these key principles for knowing God the Father:

- As the Source, God the Father had everything in Him before anything was. Everything that exists was in God.
- God is the Progenitor. He upholds and supports all that He created.
- Sin is the result of the first man—Adam—turning his back on his Father.
- Salvation is the result of a Man—Jesus, the Second Adam—providing us with the way to return to the Father.
- Fathers are progenitors. They birth generations after them that are like themselves and their forefathers. When a man is fathered by God, he produces godly fathers.
- Fathers are the source of instruction, information, and knowledge about God the Source.

We learn how God disciplines, teaches, instructs, and acts through earthly fathers who emulate the Father.

Thought for the Day

Jesus is the perfect image of what it means to be both a child of the heavenly Father and a father to our own offspring.

Reading: Ezekiel 27–29; 1 Peter 3

November 27

Fishers of Men

The primary mission of the church is to be "fishers of men." (See Matthew 4:19; Mark 1:17.) In doing so, the church calls men back to their original Father, and they are restored to the Father by salvation through the Son. When men return to the Father, they can be sustained and nurtured by their Source and then become the sustainers they are called to be for their families.

Remember, when humanity fell, God never asked the woman where she was, but the man. *"The Lord God called to the man, 'Where are you?'"* (Genesis 3:9). In other words, Adam was out of position. The foundation had been shaken and destroyed. The whole of creation was unbalanced. God fathered Adam so that he could father and sustain Eve. Without fathers, marriages, families, communities, and nations lie in shambles. A nation can be sustained, nurtured, and protected only when men are fathers like the Father.

Isaiah prophesied what would happen when men abandoned true fatherhood and the foundations of the culture shattered. *"Youths oppress my people, women rule over them. O my people, your guides lead you astray; they turn you from the path"* (Isaiah 3:12). When women *exclusively* rule, the nation, community, or household is in trouble.

Isaiah 3:12 describes a society or nation much like those in the world today in which women chase after men, men rule like mad children, and boys—not men—become leaders. In such cultures, immorality and satanic oppression will be rampant. If an enemy wanted to destroy a nation, a community, or a family, whom would the enemy attack? The father is a primary target of Satan's attack! When fathers move out of their place as sustainers, nurturers, and protectors, the foundations are destroyed and society crumbles.

Thought for the Day

The primary mission of the church is to be "fishers of men."

Reading: Ezekiel 30–32; 1 Peter 4

November 28

An Unshakable Foundation

It is time for churches to go after men and lead them back to the Father through Jesus Christ. When men get back to Christ, they return to their rightful position in creation as fathers like the Father. Only then can men bring healing to the brokenness and sustain their marriages, families, communities, and nations.

Men who live like the heavenly Father are the unshakable foundation God purposed from the beginning. In Christ, men return to their Source—God the Father—and then become sustainers, nurturers, and protectors.

Fathering like the heavenly Father encompasses these principles:

- In His foreknowledge, God spoke creation into being in order to sustain those created in His image.
- God wanted everyone to have one source, so He put the initial seed for their existence in one body—Adam's.
- The foundation for the whole human family is the male. Everything to sustain women should come from their fathers or their husbands (who are also their "fathers").
- A father, like God, sustains, nourishes, and protects what comes out of him as the source.
- Fatherhood is the foundation of the family, the church, and the culture.

The Spirit of the Sovereign LORD is on me, because the LORD has anointed me to preach good news to the poor. He has sent me to bind up the brokenhearted, to proclaim freedom for the captives and release from darkness for the prisoners....They will rebuild the ancient ruins and restore the places long devastated; they will renew the ruined cities that have been devastated for generations. (Isaiah 61:1, 4)

Thought for the Day

Men who live like the heavenly Father are the unshakable foundation God purposed from the beginning.

Reading: Ezekiel 33–34; 1 Peter 5

November 29

Too Tough to Worship?

Some men have been restored to their heavenly Father through Christ, but they have the idea that they're too tough to worship Him, as if it isn't manly. Let me ask you: Who wrote the book in the Bible that's filled with worship and praise? It was a man who killed a lion and a bear with his bare hands. He killed a ten-foot giant with a rock.

Anyone can sit down in a pew and fold his arms. It takes a giant-slayer like David to write things like, "*O Lord, our Lord, how majestic is your name in all the earth! You have set your glory above the heavens*" (Psalm 8:1), and "*I will extol the Lord at all times; his praise will always be on my lips. My soul will boast in the Lord*" (Psalm 34:1–2). I love to worship more than anything else. I've led worship in our church for years. I've written books on it. Worship is the most important thing in my life because it protects the rest of my life and gives glory to God.

Psalm 150:6 says, "*Let everything that has breath praise the Lord.*" Yet, when they do go to church, many men feel ashamed to lift their hands to the God who made them. Satan doesn't want you ever to feel comfortable worshipping God, because when you worship Him, you attract His presence. When you become ashamed of public worship, you are an embarrassment to God's assignment for you as a man. On Sunday, you should be the first one at church, sitting up front, because you are the worship leader of your family—not your wife, sisters, or daughters. The first thing that makes you a man is your capacity to enter Eden—the presence of your God.

Thought for the Day

"Let everything that has breath praise the Lord."

Reading: Ezekiel 35–36; 2 Peter 1

November 30

A Beneficial Union

"Everything is permissible for me"—but not everything is beneficial.
—1 Corinthians 6:12

We have seen that when a man gets into God's presence, when he falls in love with God's presence, he begins to function as he was meant to. Women, when a man wants to marry you, do not ask him if he loves you; ask him if he loves God. If his love for God is not his first priority, then he is a poor prospect for a fulfilling, lasting relationship.

Refuse to form relationships with plastic men who melt when the heat and pressures of life get turned up high. Find someone who is real. Until you find a man who knows that God the Father is his Source and Sustainer, you must lean on Jesus. He will husband you until you find a man who can be a godly husband and father.

Some single people become nervous and depressed that they're getting older, and so they marry the first person who comes along. They are permitted to marry. They are of age. It is permissible—but will it be beneficial to them? The criteria for marriage is not merely being old enough, but also whether or not it will be beneficial. If you don't have a clear understanding of the purpose of marriage, it's not going to benefit you. If your spouse doesn't have a clear understanding of who he or she is in Christ and who males and females were created to be, it will not be beneficial for you.

Follow God's purpose and you will avoid heartache and regret in your relationships because His purpose is the key to your fulfillment.

Thought for the Day

Women, when a man wants to marry you, do not ask him if he loves you; ask him if he loves God.

Reading: Ezekiel 37–39; 2 Peter 2

December 1

The Blessing of Differences

As we have seen throughout this year, males and females perceive the world in very distinct ways, and they react differently to people and circumstances. However, they complement one another perfectly, bringing balance to each other's lives. What one fails to see, the other perceives. Where one is weak, the other is strong.

No one person, and no one gender, can look at the world with complete perspective. Therefore, God has designed things so that when men and women live and work together in harmony, His purposes are accomplished on the earth and both male and female can have a wiser and richer experience of life. *"Two are better than one, because they have a good return for their work: if one falls down, his friend can help him up"* (Ecclesiastes 4:9–10).

Needs are a built-in component to men and women because of the way they are designed. However, when we focus only on our own needs, and when we refuse to be content unless they are met immediately, we bring conflict and unhappiness into our relationships. We stop seeing one another as gifts from God and start resenting one another.

If you want to be blessed, don't focus on your needs; rather, discover what the other person's needs are and seek to fulfill them. This approach will become a double blessing, because consistently meeting the needs of another person will often cause that person to want to fulfill yours. Whenever you are not receiving what you need in a relationship, evaluate whether you have been trying to meet the other person's needs first. Giving to others by satisfying their needs—not demanding to have our own needs satisfied—will bring true fulfillment.

Thought for the Day

When we focus on only our own needs, and when we refuse to be content unless they are met immediately, we bring conflict and unhappiness into our relationships.

Reading: Ezekiel 40–41; 2 Peter 3

December 2

Fulfillment in Life and Relationships

In this devotional, I have emphasized the vital truth that God's purpose determines design in creation. My desire is that this truth would permeate your thinking about the relationship between females and males, because it is such a fundamental principle and is crucial to understanding their differences. In this final month of the year, therefore, we will summarize several major differences between men and women based on their distinct designs, such as the following:

- Women tend to takes things to heart; men tend to take things impersonally.
- Women are like computers. Their minds keep processing in the background until a problem is solved. Men are like filing cabinets. They take problems, put them in the file, and close the drawer.
- A woman's home is an extension of her personality; a man's job is an extension of his personality.
- Women tend to be guilt-prone; men tend to be resentful.
- Women are constantly changing; men level off and stay the same.
- Women tend to become involved with things more easily and more quickly; men tend to stand back and evaluate.

Considering these differences, in addition to the others we've discussed throughout this year, we shouldn't wonder why men and women have misunderstandings and conflicts in their relationships! Yet we need to keep in mind that the above differences are related to the specific designs of women and men. Again, males and females must understand that fulfillment in life and in relationships can come only when they work together to address one another's needs.

Thought for the Day

Fulfillment in life and in relationships can come only when males and females work together to address one another's needs.

Reading: Ezekiel 42–44; 1 John 1

Giving and Receiving

Males and females were created both similarly and differently in order to fulfill God's purposes. Just as God drew mankind from Himself, creating humans as spiritual beings, He drew the woman out of the man and made her a physical being. This parallel in creation illustrates the oneness and mutual love that God and man, and male and female, were created to have.

The male is essentially a "giver." He is designed to give to the woman. Built into the man's desire to work and provide is his need to give. God designed the male to gain satisfaction from both working and providing. When he's able to do these two things, he's a happy man. If you want to undermine a man's nature, then provide for him instead of letting him provide.

The woman is essentially a "receiver." If you look at the way the female body is made, she is a receiver from A to Z. She receives seed into her physical, emotional, psychological, and spiritual wombs, incubates it, and makes it something greater than she was originally given. Her receiving complements the male's giving. The woman is of the same essence as the man because the receiver has to be like the giver. However, in order for the woman to be the receiver, she also has to be different from the man.

These differences are complementary in nature and are designed so that the male and female can fulfill one another's emotional and physical needs while they are spiritually nourished by God and His love—and so that, together, they can fulfill their mandate to have dominion over the world.

Thought for the Day

Men and women were created with complementary designs that reflect their individual roles in fulfilling the larger purposes for which they were created.

Reading: Ezekiel 45–46; 1 John 2

December 4

Woman Made for Man

Neither was man created for woman, but woman for man.
—1 Corinthians 11:9

Have you noticed the mystery in this statement? The man was not made for the woman; the woman was made for the man. This means that the woman was made for whatever the man has. All of his money—she was made for it. All of his vision—she was made for it. All of his dreams—she was made to help bring them to pass. All of his hopes—she was made to help see that they become reality.

> *For you created my inmost being; you knit me together in my mother's womb. I praise you because I am fearfully and wonderfully made; your works are wonderful, I know that full well.* (Psalm 139:13–14)

A woman's mind is an awesome machine. God gave the woman a way of thinking that is amazing. If you take a little thought, a little idea, and drop it into a woman's mind, you'll never get that simple idea back—you'll get a fully developed plan.

Do you know why many men turn the running of the home over to their wives? A woman can take a mortgage that's overdue or a business that's falling apart and say, "You sit down; let me handle this." She knows how to get a man through these things. She can dig him out of a hole. The sad thing is that when some men get out of the hole, they proceed to walk over their wives. The unique qualities and contributions of women must be valued by men. Men, I pray that during this year, you have developed a great appreciation for the women in your life and the gifts God has given them.

Thought for the Day

A woman's mind is an awesome, God-created machine.

Reading: Ezekiel 47–48; 1 John 3

December 5

The Essence of the Matter

In the Lord, however, woman is not independent of man, nor is man independent of woman. For as woman came from man, so also man is born of woman. But everything comes from God.
–1 Corinthians 11:11–12

Everything comes full circle. After all that Paul had said up to this point—that woman came from man and was created for man—he then placed both male and female in the same spiritual position.

My wife and I are equal before the Lord. She can go before the Lord and get the same spiritual help that I get. She doesn't need to go through me, her husband. That is why, if you are a single mother, your spirit can go to God and do business with Him. You don't need to get permission from a man to go to God; you have a spirit-man within. *The essence of the matter is this:* in the spiritual realm, there is no difference between men and women, but in the physical realm, there has to be the proper relationship of submission.

Once, I was speaking to a woman who is in management at an insurance company. She told me, "You know, at work, I'm the boss. Yet when I walk through the door into my home, I'm a wife." That's a smart woman. Of course, you can be the boss at work. But when you get home, you're a wife, and your husband is your head, or authority. That means you can't treat your husband like one of your employees at the office. An altogether different authority takes over. Yet a husband has to understand that he is supposed to be in the Lord when he's in the home, and that he himself is under God's authority.

Thought for the Day

In the spiritual realm, there is no difference between men and women, but in the physical realm, there has to be the proper relationship of submission.

Reading: Daniel 1–2; 1 John 4

December 6

Need for Respect/Need for Love

Each one of you [husbands] *also must love his wife as he loves himself, and the wife must respect her husband.*
—Ephesians 5:33

As we have discovered this year, a man doesn't just desire respect; it is one of his primary needs. It is part of his nature as leader, protector, and provider. The need for respect is at the core of his self-esteem, and it affects every other area of his life. More than anyone else, a wife can meet her husband's need for admiration and respect by understanding his value and achievements. She needs to remind him of his capabilities and help him to maintain his self-confidence. She should be proud of her husband, not out of duty, but as an expression of sincere admiration for the man with whom she has chosen to share her life.

God created the female so the male would have someone with whom to share earthly love. To love means to cherish and to care for. Because she was created for the purpose of receiving love, a woman doesn't just desire love; she truly requires it. As much as a man needs to *know* that he is respected, a woman needs to *feel* that she is loved. A woman wants to feel that she is important and special to her husband. When a man spends time with a woman, it makes her feel cherished because she knows she comes first in his life. She feels cared for when he goes out of his way to make sure she has everything she needs.

Thought for the Day

The need for respect lies at the core of a man's self-esteem, while receiving love is a woman's greatest need.

Reading: Daniel 3–4; 1 John 5

December 7

Need for Recreation/Need for Conversation

A man's competitive nature leads to his need for recreational companionship, his need to be involved in challenging activities. Although he likes to win, he also desires to share these experiences with others. Nothing blesses a man more than when a woman is involved in his favorite recreation. If a wife participates in what her husband enjoys doing and lets him tell her all about it, she can strengthen her relationship with him. He will feel good that she is involved in his interests. When a couple shares important aspects of their lives with one another, they build understanding, companionship, and intimacy in their marriage.

A woman has a need for conversation. Yet, because males have a leadership mind-set, sometimes their conversations with their wives amount to instructions rather than a give-and-take dialogue. A woman desires to have a man talk *with* her, not *at* her.

Some men don't realize that a woman has a need to express herself and therefore has much within her that she wants to share. A man can fulfill a woman's need for intimate conversation by continually making a point to communicate with her. To truly meet her need, he should talk with her at the *feeling* level and not just the knowledge and information level. She needs him to listen to her attitudes about the events of her day with sensitivity, interest, and concern, resisting the impulse to offer quick solutions. Instead, he should offer his full attention and understanding.

Thought for the Day

A male needs to share his interests, and a female needs conversation: these related needs can be a wonderful bridge of communication between men and women.

Reading: Daniel 5–7; 2 John

Need for Sex/Need for Affection

It is important for a woman to be sensitive to her husband's need for sex. Sometimes, a woman sees a man's sexual energy as animalistic and thoughtless. If his approach is too abrupt or too aggressive, she may tell him to leave her alone. There are also times when she is not ready for sexual relations because of her cycle, so she will put him off. In these situations, the man may interpret her refusals as disinterest or disrespect, instead of recognizing the underlying reasons behind them.

While one of the male's primary needs is sex, one of the female's primary needs is affection. The woman's natural focus is on the sensory, intuitive, and emotional realms of life, and this is why she has a corresponding need for affection. She needs an atmosphere of affection in order to feel loved and fulfilled.

Men and women need to understand that affection creates the environment for sexual union in marriage, while sex is the event. Affection is the environment in which to grow a wonderful marriage. Giving affection to a woman means appealing to that which makes her an emotional being. Sometimes a woman just wants her husband to sit with her, hold her hand, and talk with her. Her need can also be met by plenty of hugs and kisses; a steady flow of words, cards, and flowers; common courtesies; and meaningful gifts that show that the man is thinking of her—that he esteems her and values her presence in his life.

The Bible says that husbands and wives are to fulfill one another's sexual needs. (See 1 Corinthians 7:3–5.) It also says that a husband is to be sensitive to his wife's overall needs, treating her with kindness and respect. Men and women must balance having their own needs fulfilled with showing consideration for one another.

Thought for the Day

Men and women must balance having their own needs fulfilled with showing consideration for one another.

Reading: Daniel 8–10; 3 John

December 9

Different Approaches to Life

Over the months, we have looked at many examples that illustrate the remarkable difference in how men and women approach and react to life. While some people may question this, I believe that the male is naturally a "logical thinker," whereas the female is naturally an "emotional feeler."

Fewer nerves connect the two hemispheres of the male's brain compared to a woman's brain, so that the logical and emotional sides are not as closely related as they are for women. Because of this, a male basically needs to "shift gears" to move from his dominant, logical side to his emotional side. This is why men often think in a linear fashion—like a straight line, the shortest distance between two points—which gives them the ability to see to the goal and focus their energies on reaching it.

Because men think linearly, they often dismiss women as emotional or illogical. They don't understand how women are made and the perspective they provide on life. Unlike the male brain, the neural pathways between the left and right hemispheres of a woman's brain (both the logical and the emotional sides) are intact. This is why women are able to do multiple tasks at the same time rather than focusing on just one. A woman tends to think more like a grid than a straight line. Recall that she can perceive, analyze, evaluate, and see relationships between things all at the same time, like x, y, and z coordinates on a grid track a multiple of factors at the same time.

Instead of dismissing each other as "unfeeling" or "emotional," men and woman need to appreciate their unique perspectives, which can greatly benefit one another.

Thought for the Day

The next time you are tempted to label members of the opposite sex as "unfeeling" or "too emotional," stop and appreciate their unique outlook, which brings balance and perspective to your life.

Reading: Daniel 11–12; Jude

December 10

Differences in Speaking/Listening

When a male speaks, it is generally an expression of what he is *thinking*. When a female speaks, it is usually an expression of what she is *feeling*. As we have seen, they are communicating two completely different types of information. Women often don't understand how very hard it is for men to express their feelings. It's very important for a woman not to come to any firm conclusions about a man's motivation for what he's saying until she discovers what he's feeling.

In contrast, a woman doesn't always tell a man what she's thinking. If she becomes emotional, he needs to be patient and work through her emotions to find out what she's thinking. Sometimes, he has to dig deep to find out what is actually on her mind because what a woman is thinking may be different from what she is saying.

As a "logical thinker," a man will hear a verbal communication and conclude that it is useful or worthless, true or untrue, logical or illogical. It is all facts and information to him. However, because a woman is an "emotional feeler," she evaluates both the verbal and nonverbal communication she receives and perceives from the world around her. When a woman receives information, she assesses it both mentally and emotionally at the same time, while the male generally uses these functions separately.

Once men and women understand their differences, however, they can exercise patience and endeavor to come to the heart of the matter. Both men and women will experience great satisfaction when they are truly listened to and appreciated.

Thought for the Day

A man says what he thinks. A woman says what she feels.

Reading: Hosea 1–4; Revelation 1

December 11

Differences in Problem Solving

Men and women's distinct approaches to problem solving often cause them to react differently to life's difficulties or to conflicts in interpersonal relationships.

Men generally are like filing cabinets: they make decisions quickly and "file" them away in their minds. Or, they put a problem in a mental "to do" folder and go on to other things. They reopen the folder only when they feel ready to deal with it. In contrast, women generally are like computers. Their minds keep working things through until a problem is solved.

Men tend to be resentful about problems, and it's harder for them to see past their anger. They might just "file away" their problems and ignore them for awhile. On the other hand, women are guilt-prone; therefore, they often feel responsible for these situations, whether they have caused them or not. Even if they are angry, they will look within to see what they could have done differently or how they can resolve the situation.

Men and women can eliminate much frustration in their relationships by understanding each other's problem-solving strengths and using them to benefit one another. For instance, a woman can assist a man in resolving a problem with a coworker by talking through the difficulty with him and helping him to recognize the motivations and feelings involved. A man can help a woman reach a decision more quickly by acknowledging her feelings about a situation but also clearly outlining for her the facts and options involved. Taking into consideration both intuitive and factual information will help men and women to make better decisions.

Thought for the Day

Different approaches to problem solving often are the reason men and women will react differently to life's difficulties or conflicts in interpersonal relationships.

Reading: Hosea 5–8; Revelation 2

Differences in Realizing Goals

When it comes to material things, such as a job task, a building project, or financial planning, men want to know the details of how to get there. They like to know what steps they must take to achieve a task. In contrast, women tend to look at overall goals. They think about what they want to accomplish rather than focusing on a step-by-step outline of what needs to be done. While a man will sit down and write out a list of points, a woman might just start doing something to make sure it gets done.

However, when it comes to spiritual or intangible things, the opposite is generally true: males look at overall goals, while females want to know how to get there. These tendencies are why men usually remember the gist of a matter, while women often remember the details and overlook the gist. Men are interested in the principle, the abstract, the philosophy. They see the general direction they need to go in spiritually, and they head toward it. As long as they know what they believe, they don't always see the need for activities designed to help them arrive at their goal. However, women like to be involved in the process. They will attend prayer meetings and Bible studies, read Christian books, and participate more in the life of the church because it will help them grow spiritually.

Men and women can bring balance to one another in both material and spiritual things by helping each other to keep visions and goals clearly in mind while identifying the steps that are necessary to accomplish them effectively.

Thought for the Day

When it comes to spiritual things, males look at overall goals, while females want to know how to get there. Men see the general direction they need to go in, while women like to be involved in the process.

Reading: Hosea 9–11; Revelation 3

December 13

Differences in Personality and Self-Perception

A man's job is an extension of his personality, whereas a woman's home is an extension of hers. This difference can cause much conflict in relationships. A woman may want her husband to spend time with her at home, but he can enjoy working twelve hours a day away from the home because he's cultivating something that is a reflection of who he is. Remember, when a man loses his job, it can be devastating to his self-esteem because he considers his job to be almost synonymous with himself.

A woman places high value on her physical surroundings and on creating a home. Men don't understand why women become upset when they track sawdust in the living room after it has just been vacuumed. Men are not trying to be inconsiderate; they just don't think in the same terms that women do. When the beauty and order of the home are disturbed, it can be unsettling for a woman.

Another aspect of the differences in male and female personality is that men's personalities are fairly consistent, while women are continually changing. Women seek personal growth and development more than men do. They like to redecorate the home, discover new skills, or gain a new outlook. Men are often satisfied to follow the same routines, think in the same patterns, and wear the same suits—for twenty years!

Understanding these differences in personality traits is essential because they involve sensitive areas of our lives, such as what we value and how we perceive ourselves. Men and women can use their knowledge of these distinctions to build up each another's self-esteem and to give each other latitude when they view life differently.

Thought for the Day

Men's personalities are fairly consistent, while women are continually changing.

Reading: Hosea 12–14; Revelation 4

December 14

Differences in Ideas of Security and Comfort

Because men put a strong emphasis on their jobs and are not as emotionally connected to their physical surroundings, they have a tendency to be nomadic as they look for new career opportunities. Conversely, many women have a great need for security and roots. While a move due to a new job seems like an adventure for a man and signals progress in his career, it can be stressful and difficult for his wife, who may have to leave family and friends behind for an uncertain future. Women will also change geographic locations for jobs; however, married women are less willing to make a move to advance their own jobs than they are for their husbands' jobs. They are less inclined to want to disrupt the lives of their families, especially when they have children.

On the other hand, when it comes to encountering something new, men tend to stand back and evaluate at first. Women are more ready to accept new experiences, and they participate in them more easily.

Matters involving security and comfort can require great understanding on the part of a spouse. They reflect issues such as fulfillment, trustworthiness, fear, and feelings of instability. When men or women want to make job changes or embark on something new, they should be aware of the possible reactions of their spouses and show kindness and patience as they work through these potential changes to their lives.

Thought for the Day

Matters involving security and comfort can require great understanding on the part of a spouse because they reflect issues such as fulfillment, trustworthiness, fear, and feelings of instability.

Reading: Joel; Revelation 5

December 15

Fulfilling One Another's Needs

All Scripture is God-breathed and is useful for teaching, rebuking, correcting and training in righteousness, so that the man of God may be thoroughly equipped for every good work.
—2 Timothy 3:16–17

In Hosea 4:6, God says that His people are being destroyed. In this context, He does not say they are destroyed because of sin or because of the devil, but because of a lack of *knowledge*. Where there is a breakdown in communication, or any other problem in your relationships, there is often something more you need to learn about the other person's needs and your own creation design that can meet those needs. Where do we get the knowledge that we need? From the Word of God.

We have seen that the primary areas of need for women and men are love/respect, conversation/recreational companionship, and affection/sex. Numerous couples have had their marriages transformed by learning to understand their spouse's needs and seeking to fulfill them while offering unconditional love. If you will apply the principles we've shared each day, I believe they will make a significant positive difference in your relationships.

These principles are drawn from God's Word. We need continual training in God's principles. The Bible equips us to be the women and men that we were designed to be. I encourage you to be a person of the Word as you endeavor to understand God's purposes and design for humanity and seek to meet the needs of those with whom you are in relationship. May you be blessed as you are a blessing to others.

Thought for the Day

Numerous couples have had their marriages transformed by learning their spouse's needs and seeking to fulfill them while offering unconditional love.

Reading: Amos 1–3; Revelation 6

December 16

Principles of Gender Differences

Review these principles of gender differences and reflect on how you can apply them in your relationships with members of the opposite sex.

1. Men and women have perfectly complementary designs. They bring balance to one another's lives and are interdependent.
2. When men and women don't appreciate their differences, they experience conflict. When they value each other's purposes, they can have rewarding lives and relationships.
3. The primary needs of males are (1) respect, (2) recreational companionship, and (3) sex. The primary needs of females are (1) love, (2) conversation, and (3) affection.
4. A male is naturally a "logical thinker," while a female is naturally an "emotional feeler." A male generally expresses what he's *thinking*. A female usually expresses what she's *feeling*.
5. Men are often like filing cabinets: they make quick decisions and mentally file them away, or they create mental "to do" folders to review at a later time. Women are generally like computers: their minds keep working through problems until they are solved.
6. A man's job is an extension of his personality, while a woman's home is an extension of hers. A man's personality is fairly consistent, while a woman is continually changing.
7. Men are generally nomadic, while women often need security and roots.
8. When encountering something new, men tend to stand back and evaluate, while women are more ready to accept new experiences, and they participate in them more easily.

Heavenly Father,
Thank You for Your perfect design of males and females. We know Your Word says You have made us wondrously. Help us to accept the strengths and weaknesses in one another so that we can truly live in the harmony You intended for us as we seek to meet each other's needs. We want to see Your purposes accomplished through us as we serve You together. In Jesus' name, amen.

Reading: Amos 4–6; Revelation 7

Ten Keys to True Manhood

As we have seen, the foundation for the human family is the male. How the male perceives himself and how he lives affect all of his relationships and the quality of life of those around him. Starting tomorrow, I would like to share ten keys to becoming a real man that incorporate the themes, truths, and principles we've learned throughout these months—all of which come down to a stewardship of the lives and resources God has entrusted to us. When God gave man dominion over the earth, He was saying, "I am giving you stewardship over creation. Take care of it, so that it will always be a reflection of My character and purposes." To be a steward means to be given a trust over what belongs to someone else. A man is responsible for living out God's purposes in the world and enabling others to do so, also.

Men, you must realize that you are *born* a male, but you have to *become* a man. This means that someone could actually grow up to be just an old male, never living as a real man. We have learned that a male can be transformed into the man God purposed when He created the world. Becoming God's man is the only way a male can live a satisfying and meaningful life, because His purpose is the key to fulfillment.

Meditate on the keys presented over the next several days until the true meaning of what it is to be a man permeates your understanding, and God's presence and purpose overflow from your life to the world around you.

Thought for the Day

You are born a male, but you have to become a man.

Reading: Amos 7–9; Revelation 8

December 18

Keys to True Manhood: Loving and Reflecting God

You have made known to me the path of life; you will fill me with joy in your presence, with eternal pleasures at your right hand.
—Psalm 16:11

Key #1
A real man desires and loves God.

A real man seeks intimate communion with God by remaining continually in His presence. He loves to worship the One who created and redeemed him. A real man's spiritual priorities take precedence over his physical and temporal ones. In Luke 4:3, the devil tempted Jesus with a physical need: *"If you are the Son of God, tell this stone to become bread."* Jesus replied, in essence, "No, you don't understand. I have My priorities sorted out. I would rather be in God's presence than satisfy any temporal hunger." (See verse 4.) A real man is clear about what his priorities are.

Key #2
A real man seeks to restore God's image in himself.

A real man wants to be spiritually renewed so that the fullness of God's image and likeness is restored to his life. He seeks to return to the original plan that God intended when He first made man. This plan is that males and females would reflect the nature of God, who is Spirit, while living as physical beings on the earth. A real man is not deceived by or enamored of counterfeit images of manhood, such as the popular culture presents. A real man wants to be what he was created to be. He wants to be like his Father God.

Thought for the Day

A real man wants to be like his Father God.

Reading: Obadiah; Revelation 9

December 19

Keys to True Manhood: Developing Your Gifts and Talents

"My food," said Jesus, "is to do the will of him who sent me and to finish his work."
—John 4:34

I have brought you glory on earth by completing the work you gave me to do.
—John 17:4

Key #3

A real man aspires to work and to develop his gifts and talents.

Jesus was intent on doing His Father's work to completion. A real man aspires to do the work of God the Father while developing and using the gifts and talents God has given him. He isn't lazy; he has a vision for his life, and he is willing to work to fulfill it. In God's economy, a man who works and makes mistakes is better than a man who doesn't do anything.

A real man's motivation for work is to fulfill the purposes for which he was created. Jesus said, *"I tell you the truth, you are looking for me, not because you saw miraculous signs but because you ate the loaves and had your fill. Do not work for food that spoils, but for food that endures to eternal life, which the Son of Man will give you"* (John 6:26–27). In other words, there's a higher reason to work. Don't work just to pay bills. Don't work just to buy food. Understand the true nature of work. In the garden of Eden, there was no supervisor, no one to hand out paychecks. Work was given to Adam because it was a natural part of his being. Through work, he fulfilled his purpose as a man. God wants us to go to work to multiply His kingdom on earth.

Thought for the Day

A real man aspires to do the work of God the Father.

Reading: Jonah; Revelation 10

Keys to True Manhood: Honoring Your Marriage

Marriage should be honored by all, and the marriage bed kept pure, for God will judge the adulterer and all the sexually immoral.
—Hebrews 13:4

Key #4

A real man honors his marriage and family above personal interests.

Jesus' first miracle was at a wedding. (See John 2:1–11.) In this way, His ministry was introduced to the world as one that supports the family. Jesus is a family Man. His number one desire right now is to be married to His bride, the church. The books of Ephesians and Colossians say that the Holy Spirit is our seal of salvation. Like an engagement ring, the Spirit is our promise that we're going to be married to our Bridegroom, Jesus. The book of Revelation says that Jesus is waiting for His bride. After He returns to earth for us, we will be with Him at the Marriage Supper of the Lamb. We will be consummated with Christ.

Jesus loves His betrothed. He is a family Man, and He takes care of His bride. The Bible says that He gave His life for her. He cleanses her "*by the washing with water through the word*" (Ephesians. 5:26). A man is to love his wife "*just as Christ loved the church and gave himself up for her....Husbands ought to love their wives as their own bodies*" (vv. 25, 28). A real man protects and takes care of his wife and family, looking out for their needs before his own. A few real men who truly understood this truth and endeavored to live it out could set a standard for entire nations.

Thought for the Day

Jesus is a family Man, and He takes care of His bride; husbands need to do the same for their wives.

Reading: Micah 1–3; Revelation 11

Keys to True Manhood: Filling Your Life with the Word

I have hidden your word in my heart that I might not sin against you....I meditate on your precepts and consider your ways. I delight in your decrees; I will not neglect your word.

—Psalm 119:11, 15–16

Key #5

A real man endeavors to learn, live, and teach God's Word and principles.

In Genesis 2:15–17, God commanded the first man to keep His word, saying that if he disobeyed it, he would die. In this act, He established the principle that "*man does not live on bread alone, but on every word that comes from the mouth of God*" (Matthew 4:4).

A real man is a man of principles. He realizes that his spirit must be nourished by the Word of God or his spiritual health will decline. God's Word determines the precepts by which he lives. Because he is a responsible leader, he is also committed to teaching the Scriptures to his family.

A real man allows the Word to transform his life so that he can represent God's will on earth, thus spreading the garden of God's presence to a world living in the darkness of sin and separation from God.

> *Do everything without complaining or arguing, so that you may become blameless and pure, children of God without fault in a crooked and depraved generation, in which you shine like stars in the universe as you hold out the word of life.* (Philippians 2:14–16)

Thought for the Day

A real man allows the Word to transform his life so that he can represent God's will on earth.

Reading: Micah 4–5; Revelation 12

December 22

Keys to True Manhood: Living by Faith and Cultivating Others

Now faith is being sure of what we hope for and certain of what we do not see.
—Hebrews 11:1

Key #6

A real man demonstrates faith and inspires it in others.

When you return to God's original image for men, you become a person who helps people believe that anything is possible. You become like Jesus. He was the only One in history who said, "*Nothing is impossible with God*" (Luke 1:37). Jesus not only said it, but He also believed it. That's why the beggar, the prostitute, and the religious man all kept coming to Him. He made them believe nothing was impossible. A real man has a spirit of faith and inspires others.

Counterfeit men have no faith. But, even in the darkest hour, a real man believes there's a way out. He will tell you a thousand times, "Get up again; you can do it." A real man might be scared, but he won't worry, because he trusts in God to finish the work He began. The faith of a real man believes in what God said, not in what he sees.

Key #7

A real man is committed to cultivating others to be the best they can be.

A real man encourages others to reflect the image and creativity of God in all they are and do—spiritually, emotionally, psychologically, and physically. He prays for wisdom and guidance on how to cultivate his wife and children so they can mature in Christ and become all that God has created them to be. He encourages his family to develop their gifts and talents in any way he can. He delights in seeing these gifts unfold in their lives, just as God delights in seeing us use our abilities for His glory.

Thought for the Day

A real man helps people to believe that anything is possible.

Reading: Micah 6–7; Revelation 13

Keys to True Manhood: Treating Others as God Treats You

What does the Lord *require of you? To act justly and to love mercy and to walk humbly with your God.*
—Micah 6:8

Key #8

A real man loves compassion, mercy, and justice.

A real man exercises compassion, mercy, and justice. Through them, he shows true strength and brings the kingdom of God to others.

Compassion is passion that is aimed at setting people free. Jesus was compassionate. If people were hungry, He had compassion and fed them. If they were "*like sheep without a shepherd*" (Matthew 9:36), He had compassion and said, "I am the Good Shepherd; I'll lead you." (See John 10:11–15.) To show compassion means to apply one's strength to meet people's needs.

Mercy is not treating a person as he deserves when he has committed a wrong against you. God has extended mercy to us in salvation. "*But God demonstrates his own love for us in this: while we were still sinners, Christ died for us*" (Romans 5:8). As His representatives on earth, we are to show mercy, also. We are not to seek revenge against others, but to freely forgive them and do everything we can to lead them to Christ. "*We are therefore Christ's ambassadors, as though God were making his appeal through us. We implore you on Christ's behalf: Be reconciled to God*" (2 Corinthians 5:20).

Justice means doing what is right by others. God hates injustice. A real man reflects His nature and character by following His command to "*act justly and to love mercy and to walk humbly with your God.*"

Thought for the Day

Through compassion, mercy, and justice, a real man shows true strength and brings the kingdom of God to others.

Reading: Nahum; Revelation 14

Keys to True Manhood: Committing to God and His Kingdom

Your kingdom come, your will be done on earth as it is in heaven.
—Matthew 6:10

Key #9

A real man is faithful to the kingdom of God and His church.

In Matthew 6:33, Jesus reduced life to one thing: *"Seek first his kingdom and his righteousness, and all these things will be given to you as well."* He was saying, in effect, "You are talking about your mortgages, cars, clothing, food, drink, and everything else. Get your priorities straight."

A real man has a passion to see the kingdom of God established. Sinners make him sad. Broken lives depress him. People who don't know Christ concern him. A real man rejoices when people are delivered from the devil. Jesus sent out His disciples with the authority to cast out demons, heal the sick, and raise the dead. (See Luke 10:1–20.) When they came back, what did Jesus do? The Bible says He was *"full of joy"* (v. 21). Jesus was excited about men setting other men free. Real men have the spirit of the Great Commission in their lives: a love for souls and a passion for others to know Christ.

Key #10

A real man keeps himself in God.

Our final key is that a real man doesn't take God's presence in His life for granted. He guards his heart and actions so that he can stay close to God and continually reflect His character and ways. He puts the entire weight of his trust in the Lord because he knows that God is *"able to keep* [him] *from falling and to present* [him] *before his glorious presence without fault and with great joy"* (Jude 24).

Thought for the Day

A real man doesn't take God's presence in his life for granted.

Reading: Habakkuk; Revelation 15

December 25

Called to Peace

Glory to God in the highest, and on earth peace to men on whom his favor rests.
—Luke 2:14

Peace I leave with you; my peace I give you.
—John 14:27

From the night of His birth, throughout His earthly ministry, and up to the present, Jesus gives us peace. As redeemed men and women, we are called to peace with one another. What Paul wrote about the reconciliation that Christ brought applies to the male-female relationship: *"For he himself is our peace, who has made the two one and has destroyed the barrier, the dividing wall of hostility"* (Ephesians 2:14).

Jesus understood people thoroughly, and He also knew who He was. Understanding the nature of others—and of yourself—is crucial to maintaining right relationships and not falling prey to selfishness, pride, resentment, or bitterness, which sow seeds of conflict with others. Always remember that we have been called to peace.

Now that we have become aware of male/female motivations and our different approaches and communication styles, we should try not to react to one another in anger or frustration. Instead of a *reaction*, let's give one another a *response*—in love. To react is to take action against someone else before thinking. To respond is to act responsibly in your dealings with others because you are aware of their motivations and circumstances. A *reacting* person does what is irresponsible by becoming angry or resentful at another's behavior. But a *responding* person takes responsibility by seeking to understand the other person and by *"speaking the truth in love"* (Ephesians 4:15).

Thought for the Day

Instead of a reaction, give a response—in love.

Reading: Zephaniah; Revelation 16

December 26

LET THE PEACE OF CHRIST RULE

Therefore, as God's chosen people, holy and dearly loved, clothe yourselves with compassion, kindness, humility, gentleness and patience. Bear with each other and forgive whatever grievances you may have against one another. Forgive as the Lord forgave you. And over all these virtues put on love, which binds them all together in perfect unity. Let the peace of Christ rule in your hearts, since as members of one body you were called to peace.
—Colossians 3:12–15

Understanding that God designed females and males with different ways of thinking and communicating will go a long way toward helping us bear with one another in love. We are all in the process of learning to be like Christ, of learning how to become what God originally intended for us to be when He created males and females. While we're still in that learning curve, it is important for us to be patient, kind, and considerate with one another's failings.

> *Now the Lord is the Spirit, and where the Spirit of the Lord is, there is freedom. And we, who with unveiled faces all reflect the Lord's glory, are being transformed into his likeness with ever-increasing glory, which comes from the Lord, who is the Spirit.*
> (2 Corinthians 3:17–18)

As we continue to study God's Word and to follow His Spirit, who dwells within us and speaks to our hearts, we will be transformed daily to become more Christlike. As Christ's true followers, we will reflect His love and peace toward one another.

Thought for the Day

We are all in the process of learning to be like Christ.

Reading: Haggai; Revelation 17

December 27

Made for One Another

I am convinced that neither death nor life,...nor anything else in all creation, will be able to separate us from the love of God that is in Christ Jesus our Lord.
—Romans 8:38–39

Because of his great love for us, God, who is rich in mercy, made us alive with Christ.
—Ephesians 2:4–5

Our relationship with our heavenly Father is essential to all other relationships. A relationship of love was the primary purpose for which God created man. This is not an abstract concept. This means that the entire human race—including you and me—was created by God to be loved by Him. We must always remember this as we seek to apply His principles to our earthly relationships.

Some years ago, I was pondering the question of why, when humanity rejected God's ways, God didn't start over and make a new race of men. The reason is that God is not a two-timer. His love is pure and unconditional; it is not based on the actions of the receiver. Therefore, when we offer our lives to God, we should not do so believing that God merely feels sorry for us. We should go to God because, in response to such unconditional love, we can't love anyone else the way we love God.

God and humanity were made for one another. It doesn't matter whom else you love, you are never going to be satisfied until you love God. No matter how many relationships you have and how many gifts you buy for others, when it's all over, you will still be lonely. Why? It is because the Person whom you were made to love above all else—God—doesn't have the place in your life that He needs to have. You were made to love God. Your love was designed to be fulfilled in Him.

Thought for the Day

Your love was designed to be fulfilled in God.

Reading: Zechariah 1–4; Revelation 18

December 28

What Will Your Legacy Be?

A good man leaves an inheritance for his children's children.
—Proverbs 13:22

My prayer today is that parents and potential parents will take a look at their lives and ask themselves, *What can I leave my children?*

Do you want to leave them a house? Fine. However, that doesn't mean you will leave them a home. Do you want to leave them a car? Good. But that doesn't mean you will have taught them to be responsible enough to take care of it. Do you want to leave them some books? Wonderful. Yet that doesn't mean you're going to leave them with the interest to read them. Values are transmitted by example, not talk. Morals are transmitted by personification, not lectures.

Proverbs 17:6 says, *"Parents are the pride of their children."* I think the greatest thing parents could hear their child say is, "These are my mother and father. I'm proud of them. They are the best parents." Will your children be able to say of you, "The pride of my life are my parents"; "I want to be just like my father"; "I want to be just like my mother"?

When your children want to be like you, they want to be like God, whom you represent. Ephesians 5:1 says, *"Be imitators of God, therefore, as dearly loved children."* As you imitate your heavenly Father, your children will imitate you and reflect the character and life of their Creator. That is what the dominion assignment is all about.

Thought for the Day

What legacy will you leave your children?

Reading: Zechariah 5–8; Revelation 19

December 29

THE COMMUNITY OF GOD

We have seen that one of the greatest problems we face today is fatherlessness. The church has a corporate responsibility to father the fatherless. We are not in this alone. Together, we are a community of faith; we are God's family, in which every member supports and cares for every other. I believe that the church should form the most magnificent "adoption agency" in the twenty-first century. The way you change a nation is not by attacking the government but by fathering your own children and the fatherless. Godly fatherhood is the key to this generation and all to come.

Consider this thought: God's Son entered this world and had to be adopted by an earthly father—Joseph. Joseph could have rejected Mary, thinking that she had been unfaithful to him and had become pregnant by another man, but he didn't. He believed what God told him through the angel about Jesus' conception through the Holy Spirit. At great personal risk and sacrifice, Joseph stepped out responsibly and became the earthly father of Jesus, Savior of the world.

Fathers, be like the heavenly Father to your families, communities, and nations. If the male doesn't hold like an anchor, we lose the vision and destiny of the country and the resources of the community. Ask the Lord to fill up any empty spots in your life that your father couldn't fill. Forgive your father if he wasn't there for you, or if he was an alcoholic or an abusive father. Go to your heavenly Father and let Him make you a secure anchor, so you can help bring healing to the land, restoring individuals and families. Join with other members of God's family to meet these needs. Then, future generations will rise up and give glory to our Father.

Thought for the Day

Together, we are a community of faith; we are God's family, in which every member supports and cares for every other.

Reading: Zechariah 9–12; Revelation 20–21

December 30

Press On to Your High Calling!

We have been looking at God's ideal purposes for women and men, which we desire to move toward. However, we must keep in mind that entering into God's purposes will be a continual process of learning and transformation. We are starting where we are now—not at the place we should be, and not at the place at which we will arrive.

Paul told us, in regard to our spiritual growth, that we are to forget the things that are behind us and reach for what is ahead of us. We are to press on to the mark, which is the *"high calling of God in Christ Jesus"* (Philippians 3:14 KJV). When Jesus came to earth, He showed us the mark that we are to hit. So, whatever He says is what we're supposed to pursue. He showed us God's original plan so that we could have something to aim at. We should never accept what we currently have as the norm.

When you begin to understand and live in the purposes of God, some people may become very uncomfortable with you. When you tell them, "Look, I know what it is to be a man. I know what it is to be a woman. I went to the Manufacturer and got the right Manual," they may say, "Oh, no, that's an old manual; it's out of date." However, we cannot improve on the original.

When we—both women and men—gain an understanding of our uniqueness and purpose in God, we will be able to assist one another in properly understanding and fulfilling the lives God created us to live. What's more, when we mend the broken relationships between female and male, both of whom are created in the image of God, we will begin to see healing and new purpose for the individuals, communities, and nations of our world.

Thought for the Day

Jesus showed us God's original plan so that we could have something to aim at.

Reading: Zechariah 13–14; Revelation 22

December 31

A Final Word

See to it that you complete the work you have received in the Lord.
—Colossians 4:17

Brothers in Christ, communities and nations will be transformed when men return to God and His purposes for them. God is looking for those who will dedicate themselves to standing *"in the gap on behalf of the land"* (Ezekiel 22:30). He wants to bring His life-changing power to broken marriages, damaged families, shattered societies, and individual men, women, and children who need reconciliation with God and a restoration of His purposes for them. But He's waiting for men like you—real men who will commit themselves to fulfilling their dominion purpose of spreading God's presence throughout the whole world. I pray that people will be able to look at your life and say, "Now I know what a real man looks like," as they are transformed by God's presence in you.

Sisters in Christ, I wholeheartedly encourage you to pursue all of God's purposes for you. He created your spirit out of His being and out of His love. He designed you perfectly to fulfill your calling in Him. Accept the freedom He has given you in Christ. Know that you are esteemed by Him. Develop the creative ideas He has given you in your innermost being. Use the many gifts and talents He has placed within you. Be the blessing to yourself, your family, and your community that He created you to be. Yet most of all, discover that *"your life is now hidden with Christ in God"* (Colossians 3:3). Your place is with and in Him.

Thought for the Day

God wants to bring His life-changing power to broken marriages, damaged families, shattered societies, and individual men, women, and children who need reconciliation with God and a restoration of His purposes for them.

Reading: Malachi; Revelation 23–24

My Prayer for You

Heavenly Father,

You are our Designer and Creator. You knew exactly what You wanted when You thought of the male and the female. You had them in mind before You made them. You first concluded what You wanted, then created them and enabled them to function in exactly the way You had planned. You are the only One who knows how humanity is intended to successfully function. I pray that all those who read this daily devotional will commit to becoming the men and women You designed and created them to be. Let them experience lasting fulfillment in their relationship with You and in all their human relationships. Enable them to be complete in You so that they can be a blessing to themselves, their families, and the world. In the name of Jesus, Your beloved Son, amen.

About the Author

Dr. Myles Munroe is an international motivational speaker, best-selling author, educator, leadership mentor, and consultant for government and business. Traveling extensively throughout the world, Dr. Munroe addresses critical issues affecting the full range of human, social, and spiritual development. The central theme of his message is the maximization of individual potential, including the transformation of followers into leaders and leaders into agents of change.

Dr. Munroe is founder and president of Bahamas Faith Ministries International (BFMI), a multidimensional organization headquartered in Nassau, Bahamas. He is chief executive officer and chairman of the board of the International Third World Leaders Association and president of the International Leadership Training Institute.

Dr. Munroe is also the founder and executive producer of a number of radio and television programs aired worldwide. In addition, he is a frequent guest on other television and radio programs and international networks and is a contributing writer for various Bible editions, journals, magazines, and newsletters, such as *The Believer's Topical Bible, The African Cultural Heritage Topical Bible, Charisma Life Christian Magazine,* and *Ministries Today.* He is a popular author of more than forty books, including *The Fatherhood Principle, The Most Important Person on Earth, The Principles and Power of Vision, The Spirit of Leadership, Understanding the Purpose and Power of Men, Understanding the Purpose and Power of Prayer,* and *Understanding the Purpose and Power of Woman.*

Dr. Munroe has changed the lives of multitudes around the world with a powerful message that inspires, motivates, challenges, and empowers people to discover personal purpose, develop true potential, and manifest their unique leadership abilities. For over thirty years, he has trained tens of thousands of leaders in business, industry, education, government, and religion. He personally addresses over 500,000 people each year on personal and professional development. His appeal and message transcend age, race, culture, creed, and economic background.

Dr. Munroe has earned B.A. and M.A. degrees from Oral Roberts University and the University of Tulsa, and he has been awarded a number of honorary doctoral degrees. He has also served as an adjunct professor of the Graduate School of Theology at Oral Roberts University.

Dr. Munroe and his wife, Ruth, travel as a team and are involved in teaching seminars together. Both are leaders who minister with sensitive hearts and international vision. They are the proud parents of two college graduates, Charisa and Chairo (Myles, Jr.).

For Information on Religious Tourism
Email: ljohnson@bahamas.com

1.800.224.3681

www.worship.bahamas.com

The Most Important Person on Earth:
The Holy Spirit, Governor of the Kingdom

Dr. Myles Munroe

In *The Most Important Person on Earth*, Dr. Myles Munroe explains how the Holy Spirit is the Governor of God's kingdom on earth, much as royal governors administered the will of earthly kings in their territories. Under the guidance and enabling of the Holy Spirit, you will discover how to bring order to the chaos in your life, receive God's power to heal and deliver, fulfill your true purpose with joy, become a leader in your sphere of influence, and be part of God's government on earth. Enter into the fullness of God's Spirit as you embrace God's design for your life today.

ISBN: 978-0-88368-986-8 • Hardcover • 320 pages

www.whitakerhouse.com

Women of every culture and society are facing the dilemma of identity. To live successfully in today's world, women need a new awareness of who they are and new skills to meet life's challenges. Best-selling author Dr. Myles Munroe helps women to discover their God-given purpose and potential. Whether you are a woman or a man, married or single, this book will help you to understand *the woman as she was meant to be.*

Understanding the Purpose and Power of Woman
Dr. Myles Munroe
ISBN: 978-0-88368-671-3 • Trade • 208 pages

Understanding the Purpose and Power of Men
Dr. Myles Munroe
ISBN: 978-0-88368-725-3 • Trade • 224 pages

The male is in crisis. Today, the world is sending out conflicting signals about what it means to be a man. Many men are questioning who they are and what roles they fulfill in life—as males, as husbands, and as fathers. Best-selling author Dr. Myles Munroe examines cultural attitudes toward men and discusses the purpose God has given them. Discover the destiny and potential of *the man as he was meant to be.*

www.whitakerhouse.com

Daily Power & Prayer
365-Day Devotional
Dr. Myles Munroe

Are you struggling with prayer or unsure about God's plan for your life? Dr. Myles Munroe affirmatively proclaims that God desires a rich, personal relationship with every Christian and has a unique plan for their lives. During the course of a year, Dr. Munroe will encourage and teach you in the area of spiritual power and prayer, while also providing a Scripture reading to help you read through the entire Bible. Now you can unlock these spiritual truths and others on a daily basis. See for yourself how spending a few moments in God's presence can affect every area of your life.

ISBN: 978-0-88368-799-4 • Hardcover • 384 pages